THE PRACTICAL HANDBOOK OF BLACKSMITHING & METALWORKING

Other TAB books by the author:

No. 1179
$15.95

THE PRACTICAL HANDBOOK OF BLACKSMITHING & METALWORKING

BY PERCY W. BLANDFORD

TAB BOOKS Inc.

BLUE RIDGE SUMMIT, PA. 17214

FIRST EDITION

FIRST PRINTING—MAY 1980

Copyright © 1980 by TAB BOOKS Inc.

Printed in the United States of America

Library of Congress Cataloging in Publication Data

Blandford, Percy W.
  The practical handbook of blacksmithing & metalworking.

  Includes index.
  1. Blacksmithing.   2. Ironwork.   I. Title.
TT220.B43   682'.4   79-27909
ISBN 0-8306-1179-7
ISBN 0-8306-9947-3 pbk.

Cover photo courtesy of Ryobi America Corp.

Preface

One of the longest established crafts known to civilized man has held its place of importance through all the changes of thousands of years, when civilizations have come, grown and gone, while others have taken their place. The skills of the man who could work iron and steel were always needed and the blacksmith always held an important place among his fellow men. The methods have changed little. Very early smiths mastered the principles and these still hold good today. Improvements are in detail. A smith described in the Holy Bible would be able to comprehend what was happening in a twentieth century smith's shop, while a modern smith, provided only with the tools of two thousand years ago, would know what to do with them and be able to achieve creditable results.

After thousands of years with little change, a good deal of change has come to blacksmithing in the last 100 years or so, due to the Industrial Revolution. With the development of machinery, metalworking has beome something requiring equipment not suitable for a small shop. It was the introduction of the internal combustion engine that ousted the horse from its position of real importance and really marked the decline of the traditional smith as someone essential to the life of every community.

So where does that leave us? There are still blacksmiths able to earn a living, primarily from smithing, but most have to broaden their scope to embrace metalwork that was not previously considered their work. There are still apprentices to blacksmithing. There are still manufacturers of the necessary equipment, although a smith is in the fortunate position of being able to make most of his own tools. There is still a demand for wrought iron work that shows the mark of individuality and does not obviously come from a factory where hundreds of similar pieces have been made. Above all there is still a place for the man or woman determined to express themselves through craftsmanship.

Many people looking for a craft turn to wood, but not everyone wants to work wood or is capable of becoming a competent carpenter, wood turner or carver. Much work in metal requires a considerable investment in equipment, but blacksmithing as described in this book, need not be expensive. A small portable forge and an anvil of modest size (not necessarily new) are the essentials, then a few tools lead the way to making more tools. Much material can come from scrap sources. What other people throw away can be recycled by a smith into things of use or beauty or both.

Working on the anvil is a mixture of physical effort and artistic application. There is always a lot of satisfaction to be obtained from physical effort properly directed. There are few other occupations today where you can produce something aesthetically pleasing as the end product. If it does not come out right the first time, it can usually go back into the fire for another attempt.

Blacksmithing can be an adjunct to another craft. A mastery of hot iron allows the making of many things that can be used with other metal or wood constructions and the individually-made smith's metalwork will be a fitting companion to the individually-produced specimen of another branch of craftwork.

There is a feeling among those who know about crafts in general that blacksmithing has gone past the low it reached in the commercial and industrial world and there is now more scope for blacksmiths who can pursue the craft profitably or just as a hobby. They agree that this is an activity that should be more widely known and practiced. I hope this book will show the way to a great many potential blacksmiths, who will come to enjoy their work at the anvil and in doing so will carry on a great tradition.

Percy W. Blandford

Contents

SECTION 1
BLACKSMITHING

Blacksmithing Tradition

When Stone Age man first succeeded in separating metal from ore and made something from it, the first smith was born. The first metals were impure copper with traces of other metals and these have become known to us as bronze. Men of the Bronze Age made tools and weapons from this comparatively soft metal that must have been much more successful and convenient than their crude stone implements. But it was not until they discovered how to obtain iron from ore that tools and weapons of adequate hardness could be made. The Iron Age spanned a very long time and man learned to use heat in the fashioning of iron. The workers who did that were more truly smiths and they laid the foundation of smithing that has not changed in principle today.

The Stone Age was a very long time in man's existence. It was more than 10,000 years ago. The Bronze Age followed and this blended into the Iron Age. Both bronze and iron were melted and cast. The first evidence of smithing by hammering iron into shape is a dagger found in Egypt and dated 1350 BC, although it is believed to be the product of a Hittite craftsman. It is fairly certain that the Hittites invented tempering and forging, then they kept their ironwork techniques secret. The Hittite empire was overthrown about 1200 BC and a large number of migrants spread throughout what is now Europe associated with the devil in the minds of superstitious people. and the Middle East, taking their ironwork skills with them first to Greece and the Balkans. This early Iron Age was from about 800 BC to 500 BC. Then ironworking spread further west in Europe and to Britain during what is often called the Late Iron Age, but there are obviously no clearly defined boundaries of dates.

It was the use of iron with wood that made possible the cultivation and clearing of land, the general use of wheeled vehicles, together with a settled existence in villages. Iron also made better weapons for hunting and warfare. Amist all this the smith who could fashion iron into the things needed must have been an important member of every community.

By later Biblical times, the smith with an air-blown fire to heat his iron was working in ways not vastly different from those used today. A smith who might have seen Jesus Christ would recognize many tools and processes in a smith's shop today. Woodworkers and metalworkers worked close together and it is probable that Jesus, as a carpenter, would have been familar with the smith's trade.

The smith finds a place in classical mythology , not only in that of the Romans and Greeks, but in that of such people as the Aztecs and the Phoenicians. In Roman mythology Vulcan, who was the son of Jupiter, is credited with being the founder of smithing. According to the stories, he made the axle for the chariot of the sun and the gates of dawn. He forged the thunderbolts his father used. As in other mythology, this smith was ugly and misshapen and supposed to be possessed of evil. In Norse mythology, Loki gave power to Thor as a smith. Quetzalcoatl of the Aztecs brought skill in ironworking and other crafts to the people. A similar story goes with Tuba-Cain of the Phoenicians, yet all these skilled workers are treated as if they are evil or at least not of great esteem.

Somewhat similar has been the treatment in some countries of smiths in more recent times, possibly because they worked with fire in semi-darkness and these things were

Smiths were important in medieval times with the need for armor and weapons, but in some places they were almost outcasts. This did not apply everywhere and there are records of kings working with their favorite armorers. It must have made sense to take part in the production of something that had to be relied on to preserve life. An armorer was a very skilled smith. In a few countries smiths were honored. Some smiths were artists in metal and proof of this is seen in surviving gates and other ornamental wrought ironwork. The ordinary person might think of a smith as someone whose main attribute was brute strength. A smith certainly needs to be strong, but he may also direct that strength to produce items of practical or artistic value, or both.

You might have noticed that the name of the craft has been given as *smith* and not *blacksmith*. The family name *Smith* indicates how many people were once concerned with the craft of smithing. It was not until the Middle Ages and mostly not until the coming of the Industrial Revolution that there was a need to be more specific about what was meant by the name. The earlier smith did all kinds of metalworking, as it was needed. Later developments brought specialists in working lead and other metals. In particular, the worker in lead became known as a *whitesmith*, so the worker in iron became known as a *blacksmith*. That is the usual name today for anyone who uses heat and hammer to shape iron or steel.

To many people the name includes the craftsman responsible for the making and fitting of horsehoes. Strictly speaking, that craftsman is a *farrier,* although most craftsmen in the days of the great use of horse transport were also farriers. However, there was and there still is a distinction and not every farrier or blacksmith could do the other man's job. There were other specialist smiths. A chain smith forged links in a chain. A nail smith (often a woman) did nothing but make nails. Today a blacksmith, whether professional or amateur, can expect to do all kinds of smithing and may need a knowledge of horseshoeing as well.

In the days when most countries depended on a rural economy there was a blacksmith's shop wherever there was a cluster of dwellings. His customers were the farmers and workers who lived nearby. He probably farmed a piece of land himself. A comparable life was led by the village carpenter, who did all that was wanted in wood. Quite often they had adjoining shops and certain implements needed on the land or some piece of equipment to be used in a house would be a combined effort. Wagons and carts needed both of their skills. In later years the wheelwright became a specialist craftsman, leaving the carpenter to other woodworking. There are many places in Europe where it is still possible to see the stone base (probably an old millstone) on which the blacksmith and the wheelwright worked together to assemble a wheel and draw the parts together with its iron tire. The base might have survived where all other evidence has gone.

There would also have always been blacksmiths working in towns and some of them would have specialized in making gates and other wrought ironwork. There would have been armorers who made weapons as well as armor. Smiths were also employed on the great estates, attached to feudal castles and working with other craftsmen on ecclesiastical buildings and furnishings.

Like most other craftsmen, most blacksmiths were their own master and independent, depending on payment from customers. This would often have been in kind, as little money was circulated. Work might be done by barter for a share in the crop at harvest time or in return for some service rendered by the other man. These methods continued until the Industrial Revolution, not two centuries ago, when factory production began to take over from individual craftsmen. This affected blacksmiths in the same way as others who had enjoyed the independence of their craft. The need for individual smiths diminished, but many smiths were able to find places for their skills in industry. Many of them became factory workers.

The use of steam and other power brought in processes and techniques that would have been beyond the smith and his helpers with only their muscles for power. Gas and electric welding made possible the fabrication of parts that would have previously involved lengthy and laborious work at fire and anvil. Mass production had taken over and people were able to have products they could afford made to identical designs. They had no use for the one-off products that cost more from the smith or other craftsman.

Of course, horses were still being used in considerable numbers and there was still need of rural smiths—even if some of them used horseshoes that had at least been partly made in a factory. The use of working horses did not really decline rapidly until the end of World War I. By then, the internal combustion engine in vehicles and particularly tractors had shown it could take the place of horses. Those smiths who wanted to maintain their independence had to broaden their scope. Some learned to maintain motor vehicles or they became agricultural engineers, with blacksmithing being only part of their activities.

Blacksmithing as a craft is no longer in great demand for its practical purposes. Much of what a smith did for purely utilitarian purposes in the past might be done more effectively by other means. However, there is still the need for a one-off product which would be better made by smithing and there is still a place for the artist blacksmith, who can create wrought ironwork in a way that cannot be emulated by any other means. There is no longer a need for a blacksmith in every community, with his skill needed to maintain the everyday life of those around him, but there is still a place for the worker who treats blacksmithing as a means of using craft skill in the same way that others may hammer a copper bowl, make furniture or pottery, carve wood or weave a basket. Whether he does this for profit or just for the love of a craft, he will get a tremendous satisfaction out of forming iron into shape and carrying on what must be one of the oldest crafts.

DESIGN

Throughout most of history the majority of blacksmiths were mainly concerned with producing implements for use. Any design work involved was directed toward making the thing as suitable as possible for its intended purpose. Its appearance was of secondary importance. In some cases there was a need for the thing to be massive. Other things might have had to be light in weight. More care was needed for that sort of work and this might have resulted in an improved appearance, but most of the products of the general smith aimed at fitness for purpose. Anything made, whether in wood, metal or other material, that has been produced so as to best suit its purpose, will usually look better than something not as suitable.

Sword hilts and similar things were decorated with cuts and punchings. Other products of the blacksmith were often more substantial and obtained any artistic effect from their layout and proportions. The art of the blacksmith is more appropriate to large items than small ones and the artistic ability of individual blacksmiths can be seen in railings, gates, screens and ecclesiastical decorations. On a smaller scale were locks and hinges, where iron was wrought to shape and decorated with cuts and stamping.

There are still in existence in Europe elaborately scrolled hinges with rather rudimentary surface decoration made with punches. Twisting strip metal into scrolls is a feature of much early wrought ironwork.

Blacksmiths concerned with decorative ironwork were influenced by the Gothic style in architecture. In the 15th century tracery intended for stone was repeated in iron, sometimes more effectively. This continued into the 16th century, when much cast iron came into use. There was some sign of a decline in blacksmith's decorative work at first, but then the quality of blacksmith's products improved and much good wrought ironwork was made.

Up to this stage, there seemed to be no recognizable overall trend. Design was the concern of the individual. There are some surviving examples of excellent work, but some was not of a very good design standard. This could have been said about work in other materials. In particular, wood-workers used their own ideas in making furniture. They might have copied good ideas from each other, but designs were comparatively local. The printing press altered this. Chippendale and other great furniture designers and makers published pattern books and other furniture makers were able to produce chairs, tables and many other things to these designs.

DECORATIVE BLACKSMITHING

Almost the same thing happened to decorative blacksmithing. A Frenchman, named Jean Tijou, was called to England to work under architect Sir Christopher Wren on the ironwork for the royal palace at Hampton Court, alongside the River Thames to the west of London. He was an outstanding designer of ironwork and a very skilled blacksmith with techniques that were mostly new to English craftsmen. He was at work on the palace ironwork in 1690 and he remained in England to publish designs in 1693. There were used by blacksmiths all over the country. His shapes and styles, with applied leafwork, became embodied in most smith's work. Decorative ironwork of that time done by nearly all smiths showed his influence and this spread via immigrants to America. Much of his work was rather elaborate and flamboyant. This demonstrated skill, but English smiths modified his style to give a more restrained effect. However, Tijou can be credited with having raised wrought ironwork towards a more classical perfection, with an influence extending to today.

Iron And Steel

Almost all blacksmithing is done with iron and steel. None of the other common metals can be fashioned by hammering after heating in the same way. Iron is the base metal from which steel is derived.

Very little iron is found in the natural state. Early man might have found some metals in a form that he could use without special treatment. Meteorites could be pure iron and the lucky finder might have used one. However, meteorites were never very plentiful. Iron has to be obtained from ore by heat. Fortunately, iron occurs all over the world and much of this earth is supposed to be composed of iron. How the extraction of iron from ore was first discovered can only be surmised. A simple fire would not be enough. There would have to be forced draught to intensify the heat. Maybe the heat of a forest fire produced enough heat to show how iron could be obtained from ore.

In some places the best ore has been used, but with improved methods iron is obtained from inferior ore and there is no fear of iron production coming to a halt because of shortage of supplies. The world supply seems inexhaustible.

When primitive man in the dawn of the Iron Age discovered how superior iron was to the previous bronze and stone for his weapons, tools and implements, he must have tried many ways of building up sufficient heat to extract the desired iron from the ore he found by digging or dragging in swamps. The wind might have been directed through channels in the side of a hill to a pit containing the fire and ore. Where there was no suitable hill, a stone and earth tower might have been built to contain the fire and ore, with a draught hole for the prevailing wind to enter. Early fires would have been fueled by wood and later by charcoal or coal. Bellows were developed to produce the draught and remove the dependence on a fickle wind. At the end of the process, the fire was raked out and the iron brought out of the botton of the pit. Its quality was uncontrolled and luck decided what could be used for tools and what might have to be discarded or used in its cast form.

Iron produced in this way would have contained many impurities. Iron had to be reasonable pure to be suitable for smithing. An excess of impurities would have caused brittleness and other faults.

Metallurgy and the history of iron making does not have a place in a practical book, but a smith will find it useful to have some knowledge of the material he or she is working with his tools. Modern iron is produced from furnaces that have developed those primitive fires into great industries. What first comes from these blast furnaces is called pig iron. Pig iron got its name from the molten iron that is run into channels that look like a sow with her piglets beside her. This pig iron contains a great many impurities in small quantities. It may be about 95 per cent iron, with up to 4 per cent carbon and the remainder including such things as silicon, sulfur, phosphorus and manganese. The impurities have a considerable effect on the quality and characteristics of the iron.

CAST IRON

Cast iron is made from pig iron by remelting it and pouring it into molds. Its quality can be controlled by varying the contents and by cooling rapidly or slowly. It is possible to make ductile cast iron by a further process, but this is still unsuitable for smithing. Cast iron in its many forms is used extensively for machine parts, many domestic articles and anything where weight and bulk are wanted or acceptable. There can be no intention to alter the shape by heating and hammering. Ductile cast iron can be machined successfully and this is the material used for parts that are turned or otherwise formed with cutting tools. Some decorative work is done in cast iron and a smith may make wrought ironwork to link with something that has been cast as a head, stylized flower or classical decoration. Cast iron contains 2 percent to 4 percent carbon, whatever other elements are present in smaller quantities.

WROUGHT IRON

It has been wrought iron that has been favored by smiths throughout nearly all of ironwork history. This is produced by refining and rolling after further heating of the first pig iron, so as to reduce the carbon to a very small amount—not more than 0.3 percent—and to remove most of the impurities. The resulting iron that has been rolled to produce strips has a fibrous nature that makes it particularly suitable for shaping by hammering. It is the most tough, ductile and malleable form of iron. It also has a greater resistance to corrosion than most other types of iron. The first light rusting forms a protective film that reduces further corrosion.

Unfortunately, wrought iron is no longer readily available. Its place has been taken by mild steel. This is iron with a controlled small amount of carbon in it. For structural work, machining and general engineering, this is a superior material. It is not as satisfactory for blacksmithing. It was some time before mild steel usurped the place of wrought iron, but in the latter part of the 19th century it gradually took over so that today there is very little wrought iron produced and anyone engaged in blacksmithing has to use mild steel. Most of the usual work can be done, although mild steel is not as amenable to fine work and it is difficult to weld by the smith's method.

The amount of carbon in mild steel does not affect its hardness and there is no way that heat treatment can have any appreciable effect in hardening or softening it. If the proportion of carbon is increased, the characteristics of the steel are altered. If the carbon content is about 2 percent, this is high carbon or tool steel. Steel with this amount of carbon can be made harder by heating and quenching, in the processes of hardening and tempering described later. Another heat treatment removes the hardness. It is this steel from which tools are made by a blacksmith. It will make springs and was used for parts of armor.

The traditional blacksmith found that wrought iron and tool steel fulfilled all his needs. The modern smith has to use mild steel instead of wrought iron for much of his work. Although there are now many special steels available, it is still advisable to only use ordinary high carbon steel for tools. Some of the other steels—which have been alloyed with small quantities of other metals to give special qualities and are used for some industrially-produced tools—require special precise heat treatments with equipment the ordinary blacksmith would not have available.

ALLOY STEELS

Steel is often described as an alloy of iron and carbon, but this is not strictly correct as the word *alloy* applies to a mixture of two or more metals and carbon is not a metal. Some of the special steels are collectively called *alloy steels*, indicating that other metals have been added to the steel. With modern techniques the proportions of these metals can be closely controlled. Quite small amounts of some other metals can make considerable differences to the steel. Nickel, chromium, copper and tungsten are some metals added to steel in small quantities to impart special qualities.

24

With 18 percent chromium and 8 percent nickel added to steel, corrosion resistance is increased and *stainless steel* produced. This is a relative term, as no steel can be proof against all kinds of corrosion. The addition of silicon can produce resistance to acids. *High-speed steel* is produced for cutters that retain their strength and hardness when hot. High-speed steels vary, but they can be alloyed with one or more of the following: tungsten, chromium, molybdenum or vanadium. Cobalt added to steel improves its magnetic qualities. The range of special steels available today appears to be almost limitless. The smith obtaining steel to heat and hammer into tools and then harden and temper by heat treatment should stick to a straight high carbon steel, without any other metal alloyed to it.

Of course, iron, mild steel and tool steel can be bought as new stock in sheet form or in strips with round, square, rectangular, hexagonal and many other sections. For quantity production, this was the way to obtain material. But many oldtime blacksmiths had a stock of scrap material behind their forge and they would draw on this for iron or steel to make some items. It is possible to use the same iron or steel many times. A new part might be nothing like the old part it was made from. One attraction of blacksmithing is the ability to heat metal and use your skill with the hammer to form it into a new shape. It is also possible to weld pieces under the hammer to form them into a larger piece. In pioneer days, when new iron or steel was difficult to obtain, much small scrap iron was joined to make a larger item. The work might have been time-consuming, but if there was no other iron available, that was the only way.

A modern blacksmith might find it worthwhile to collect suitable discarded iron and steel parts for possible future use. Cast iron does not have much use to a blacksmith for making things, although a piece might be found to use as a special anvil or for some shaping purpose. Very old things made from strips, such as railings or gates, might be wrought iron and welcomed as the best material for much new shaping and welding. Even mild steel from these and other assemblies can provide the stock for new work.

Anything that has obviously been a tool has possibilities for reworking to make another tool, even if the original was worn out. A good source of high carbon steel is any sprung vehicle. Leaf springs are good high carbon steel suitable for making tools. Coil springs are the same steel and might not have quite as many uses, but they can be straightened and cut to make tools. Anything that has formed part of a solid structure is likely to be mild steel if it is not very old. If it is known to be very old, and particularly if it has been given much ornamental shaping to the ends, it is probably wrought iron.

The special alloy steels are mostly used in small pieces for machine tools. Larger tools, such as gardening tools, most carpenter's cutting tools and most knifelike large cutters, as well as the cutting parts of many farm implements, are likely to be straight high carbon steel that can be used again for making tools.

Sometimes among the scrap will be other metals that are unsuitable for smithing. When old and corroded they might appear similar to iron and steel. If they are rubbed with a file or abrasive paper, any difference should be apparent. Copper, brass, aluminum, lead and other *non-ferrous metals* are not useful for smithing, although they might have other metalworking possibilities. *Ferrous* and *ferric* are terms derived from the Latin *ferrum* meaning iron and are used when it is necessary to distinguish metals and alloys that might or might not contain iron.

Forge And Anvil

3

Blacksmithing is the shaping of hot iron and steel, usually by hammering. A means of heating and something to hammer on form the basis of the required equipment.

Early smiths might have heated iron in wood fires, but they soon found that the intensity of heat could be increased with an air blast. They would have also found that wood converted to charcoal produced a better fire for their purpose. In its simplest form, the air blast was produced by air blowing through a pipe. It might have been made by the wind blowing air through a hole into the base of the fire or by using a fan when there was no wind. Crude piston-type pumps were devised, usually in pairs, so a helper moving the pistons up and down in turn produced a fairly even blast. Bellows are of great antiquity. Wooden pieces with leather between and simple leather flap valves over holes were used to control the flow of air. Small single-acting bellows were used in pairs, so a reasonable steady airflow could be maintained, Some were small enough for one helper to work with his feet. Others had to be operated by two helpers.

BELLOWS

In the Middle Ages, someone devised the double-acting bellows. It had two parts, one of which was operated by hand or foot and the other took air from it and was weighted so it forced air out while the other part was filling (Fig. 3-1A). This sort of bellows continues to the present day and examples can be found in some surviving blacksmiths' shops as well as in museums. There is an advantage in having a larger air capacity. A comparatively slow movement of the operating handle or lever delivers an ample flow of air to the fire. This meant that bellows in some shops were of considerable size. They did not have to be directly connected to the forge, but could be joined by a pipe. They were usually close so that the smith or his helper could operate the bellows while tending the fire.

Portable forges were made with round, double-acting bellows under the forge pan and a foot pedal was used to operate it. Both hands were free to tend the fire and the iron in it.

FAN BLOWERS

With advances in engineering knowledge came the development of the fan blower (Fig. 3-20). For nearly all blacksmithing purposes, this has taken over from the wood and leather bellows. The fan uses centrifugal force to take air drawn in from near the center of its casing to throw it out to a tube directed at the fire (Fig. 31-B). The fan needs to rotate at high speed. For hand operation, the drive from the crank handle can be stepped up through internal gearing. Older types had external belting (Fig. 3-1C). The fan can also be driven electrically. Since an electric motor is most efficient at high speeds, this suits a fan blower, often with a direct drive. However, there is a need to control the blast so the fire can be dormant when there is no steel in it to be heated or when more or less heat is required. Hand control allows this. With an electric blower, there could be a rheostat to adjust the amount of blast electrically or there could be a damper in the air pipe. In both cases it is best to arrange for the air blast to turn off automatically when your hand or foot is removed from the control. Otherwise the fire could go on growing dangerously.

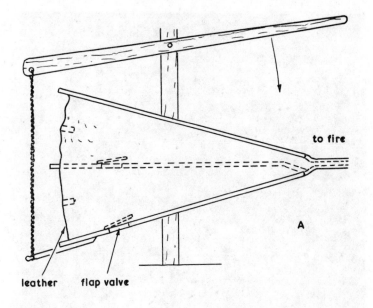

to fire

A

leather   flap valve

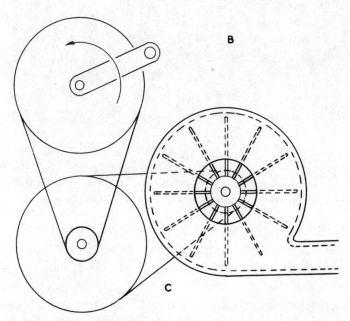

B

C

Fig. 3-1. Air blast to a force was traditionally provided by bellows: (A) bellows; (B) fan; (C) external belting.

Fig. 3-2. This hearth has a fan blower and a hood that can be lowered.

There might still be uses for charcoal fires, but most blacksmithing is done with a coke fire. At one time, coke could be obtained cheaply as a by-product from the making of coal gas. With the general use of natural gas, this supply has ceased in most areas. Instead, the smith has to use small coal, which is converted to coke in the first burning of the fire, as described later.

When forging, it is possible to heat steel with a torch. You can use a torch intended for welding or a torch that uses air mixed with butane or propane gas that is primarily intended for brazing. Both types of torch produce an intense heat in a restricted space. There are occasions when this is desirable, but a greater spread of heat is usually required to get work hot

Fig. 3-3. Starting a portable forge with a belt-driven fan blower.

over a sufficient expanse for normal smithing. A torch can be useful in the shop as an addition, but not an alternative, to the coal or coke forge.

There are gas forges in which many gas jets are used to provide a good spread of heat. They can be fixed or portable and have uses for horseshoeing and work with rods and strips of moderate size. For general smithing most workers prefer a coal-burning forge.

FORGES

A forge is a container for the fire, arranged at a convenient height and with an inlet for the air blast (Fig. 3-3). For indoor use, there is a hood and flue above the fire. Even for outdoor use, there is an advantage in partly enclosing the fire and providing a flue. The color of hot metal is best seen in a dim light. Consequently the forge is normally placed away from any natural light in the smithy, while shrouding an outside forge gives shade for viewing steel drawn from the fire.

A forge can be made of sheet steel or cast iron. Many were made of stone, brick or wood and some still are. The wood is not as vulnerable as might be expected. The hearth is formed, inside whatever supports it, with fire bricks and fireclay or other refractory (heat resisting) materials.

A traditional form of forge has a pan supported on legs with a square open form on three sides and the back taken up to support the hood (Fig. 3-4A).

TUE IRONS

The air pipe feeds into the fire through a *tuyere*, which is pronounced *tweer* and is of French origin. However, the English smith adapted this to *tue iron* (pronounced *twee iron*) and that seems the common term today. The two possible locations for the tue iron are at the back or in the bottom of the hearth. European forges and some used in America have the tue iron at the back. The cast iron nozzle or tue iron projects

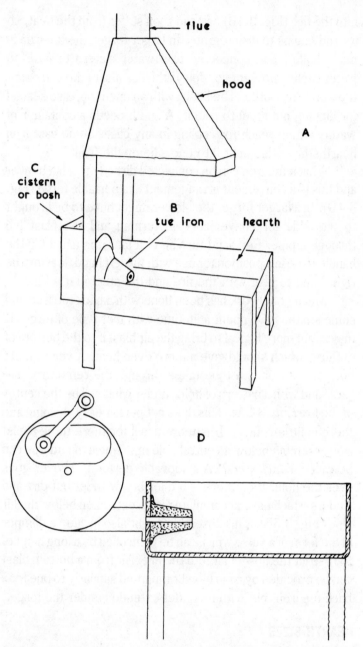

Fig. 3-4. The hearth has a hood (A) and a tue iron (B). The air blast enters through a water cistern (C). A small hearth might have a fan directly mounted on it (D).

into the fire (Fig. 3-4B) and can soon suffer from the heat, so its end begins to disintegrate. In larger forges the tue iron is made hollow and connected to a water cistern or *bosh* so water cooling prevents or delays the burning of the end of the tue iron (Fig. 3-4C). The bosh, with an open top, also served for dipping hot steel to cool it. A smith needs a container of water, within reach for cooling in any case. Some cast iron hearths have this built into one side or the front.

A back tue iron can be connected directly to a fan blower and this is a convenient arrangement in a portable forge (Fig. 3-4D). In a larger forge, the blower might have to be brought to one side for convenience in turning and the blast led through a pipe. For hand turning of a fan, it is usual for the handle to be in a position for use with the left hand, leaving the right hand to deal with the fire and the steel in it.

Much good work has been done with a back tue iron and some smiths have spent a lifetime with that type of forge. It may seem more logical to bring the air blast into the bottom of the fire, which should give a more even heat. A very simple bottom tue iron is a tube taken through the refractory material and with a pattern of holes under what will be the center of the fire (Fig. 3-5A). This does not permit easy cleaning and there is little control. It is more usual for there to be a cast iron assembly below a central hole in the hearth and this can be called a *duck's nest*. A removable perforated cover goes over the hole, then there is a door below to let out dirt and cinders which have accumulated in an extension below the air pipe (Fig. 3-5B). This assembly might also include a damper in the form of a valve which can be controlled by a long handle, to restrict the flow of air into the fire. Air from a bottom blast can be provided by a fan blower mounted similarly to one for a back tue iron, but with its outlet extended under the forge.

HEARTH SIZES

The size of a forge depends on its intended use. A large one can have a small fire, but there is a limit to the size of fire

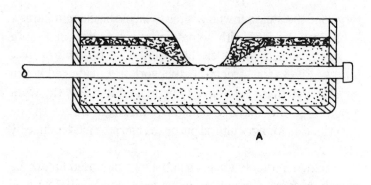

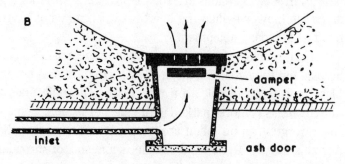

Fig. 3-5. The air blast can be taken into the bottom of the fire through a perforated pipe (A) or a more elaborate tuyere (B).

that can be made in a small one. However, space is usually important and a forge no bigger than absolutely necessary will have to be chosen. The height of the hearth top above the floor should not be more than about 30 inches and may even be better a little lower. However, the depth inside also has to be considered. A deep fire is an advantage for welding. The hearth can be up to one foot deep and have its edge higher than a shallow forge. Some forges have parts cut out at one or both sides to get long bars into a deep fire.

A general-purpose smith may use a hearth up to 6 × 4 feet to accomodate anything he might have to work. It was more usual to have a square forge. Something between 30 inches and 42 inches would accomodate most work. With its hood, this extended to 6 feet high and the addition of a blower extended the back. The sort of forge was needed for full time smithing. The steel worker who has only occasional use for a forge and the amateur who wishes to tackle blacksmithing as a hobby can manage with something much lighter and more compact. Smaller forges can be described as portable or rivet forges. Rivets for structural steelwork are made red hot in small forges that might have to be moved to follow the work around—so they have to be light. Other light forges can be described as for agricultural purposes and intended for use by farmers.

Earlier portable forges had bellows mounted below the hearth. Modern versions are square or round, with four legs and a fan blower behind the hearth—which may not have a hood as standard equipment.

Large portable forges have fire pans or hearths 24 inches across, but they could be made down to 18 inches. A bottom blast type is preferable to a rear blast. The difference in effectiveness is more marked in the smaller forges. Some of these forges can be taken apart for ease of transport. If a portable forge is to be used outside, some sort of shrouding and flue should be devised. If it is used inside with coal, there will have to be a hood and flue. If the hood is adjustable, it can be lowered to collect smoke and increase draught when starting with coal. As the fire flames and becomes clean, it can be raised.

ANVILS

If red hot iron or steel is to be hammered and the greatest effect is to be obtained with each blow, there has to be sufficient support under the iron to take the blows solidly—without bouncing or reacting. From the earliest days of the craft, an anvil made from a substantial piece of iron or steel has been used for the support (Fig. 3-6). Today there is a generally-accepted form for this, with some minor variations, but anvils have not always been like that. It would have been possible to use a large stone, but that must have soon given way to iron.

Some of the nearly square, flat-topped anvils were made without beaks. Some were given beaks at opposite sides.

Fig. 3-6. An anvil, tongs and a hammer are the main blacksmithing tools.

There might have been other rounded blocks of iron for shaping. The smith must have accumulated a variety of heavy blocks of iron of different shapes. Modern anvils bring these shapes into one piece.

All early anvils were iron, which suffered in use so the original faces became misshapened and damaged. Medieval smiths mastered the welding of steel to iron and produced anvils with fairly thick tops of steel. The steel was tempered to give a face that stood up to long use. In the middle of the nineteenth century, a method of welding molten steel to a cast iron anvil was devised. Modern anvils are formed almost entirely of steel, cast in one piece.

Traditional blacksmiths favor an anvil that rings like a bell when hit. Whether this sound signifies any special quality is debatable, but a ringing anvil is pleasant to use. Anvils are graded by their weights rather than by dimensions. The usual type for general smithing may weigh from 100 pounds to 200 pounds but for more delicate work they might be down to 50 pounds or less and for heavy work they may be up to 800 pounds. As a guide to main sizes, the dimensions offered by one manufacturer are shown in Table 3-1.

Table 3-1. Anvil Sizes.

Weight in pounds	length in inches	Width in inches
56	15	7
84	19	7
112	23	8
168	25	10
224	28	10

Most modern anvils conform to the London pattern. The main working surface is the face. At one end there is step down to a *table* and then the *beak* or *horn*. If a used anvil is bought, examine the state of the face and horn and check that the edges of the face form reasonably sharp and straight angles. However, a part of one edge might been deliberately rounded for special work. The table will have been used for cutting steel. It is softer than the face so as not to damage cutting tool edges and it might have been damaged by cuts. This is to be expected. Some damage to an old anvil can be corrected by filing or grinding, but this does not put back metal. That can only be done by welding. Building up an anvil by this method is not easily done satisfactorily.

A proper anvil is not something that can be made by an individual. Even traditional smiths working full-time at their craft and making just about all their other tools, had to buy anvils from specialized manufacturers with the necessary heavy equipment. This means that there is really no alternative to a proper anvil, except that some simple light work can be done on an iron block—possibly salvaged from discarded large machinery.

A piece of railroad track has a section something like an anvil. It is smaller than the anvil needed for general smith's work, but for light work—such as might be done with iron rods up to one-half inch across—there are possibilities. A piece of track might be used just as it is, but it could be burned to shape and completed with a beak and overhanging tail by grinding and filing. If it is made somewhat too long proportionately there will be a gain in bulk to stand up to hammering. The base could be drilled for screwing down or spikes could be used. If this little anvil is permanently mounted on a thick rectangular wood block, it could be used on a bench, in a vise or on the floor.

At the other end of the anvil the overhang is the *heel* or tail. This will normally contain two or more holes going right through. One hole is square and is the *hardie* hole. A hardie is one of the tools that fits into this hole, but there are others. One or more *punch* or *pritchel* holes are there to give clearance when a punch is driven through hot steel.

The anvil is shaped down to a fairly broad square base with cutouts to leave corner feet that will stand firmly and resist tipping, even when the anvil is not fixed down. The base is usually shaped so that the corners can be held with bent spikes. However, some small anvils are pierced for bolts.

An anvil has to be mounted at a convenient height for working. The height should be such that you can stand almost upright and hold a steel rod in one hand horizontally on the face. Standing beside the anvil puts the anvil face at about the height of your knuckle—an average of 24 inches from the floor. Of course, the anvil must be firmly in position and should not move in any way while being used.

There are cast iron and fabricated stands for anvils where the anvil base fits into a recess (Fig. 3-8A). However, these have never been popular. Most experienced blacksmiths prefer a wooden support. In an established permanent blacksmith's shop, the support is a section of hardwood tree trunk, set into the earth floor. The anvil rests on the flat top of this and is held in place with spikes made by the smith (Fig. 3-7).

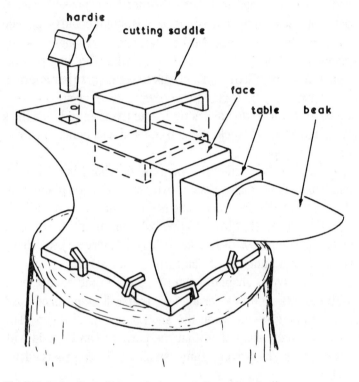

Fig. 3-7. An anvil can be mounted on a section of tree trunk.

For an anvil that is not set up permanently, it might be better to make what is in effect a substantial stool, giving it a slightly conical shape for steadiness and a recess in the top to hold the anvil (Fig. 3-8B). Use thick wood so that there is plenty of bulk that will take the shock of hammering almost as well as the section of a tree trunk. The form is very similar to that of a cast iron stand, but the iron stand is noisy and might cause rebounds of the anvil. Wooden supports do not add to the noise of hammering and they cushion the effect of heavy hammering. A leather strap can be nailed around a wooden support to provide loops into which tools can be positioned.

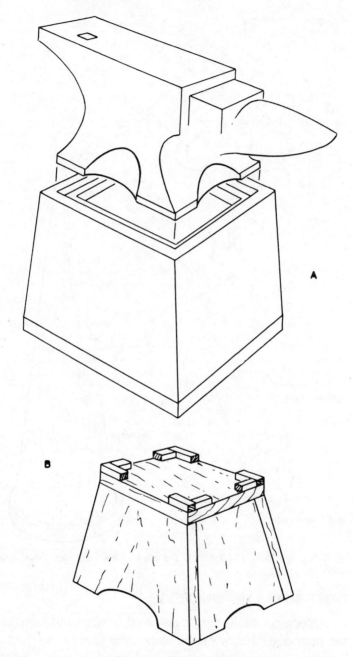

Fig. 3-8. An anvil stand (A) can be cast iron or built up from wood (B).

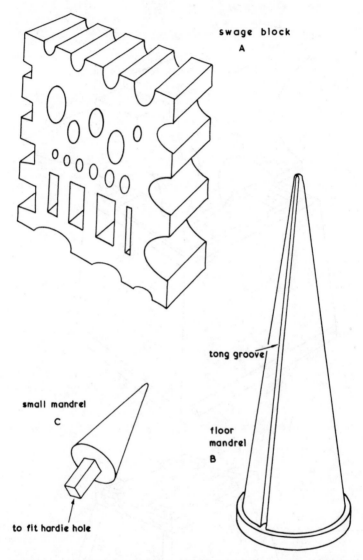

swage block
A

tong groove

small mandrel
C

floor
mandrel
B

to fit hardie hole

Fig. 3-9. Large tools, in addition to the anvil, include a swage block and mandrels.

SWAGE BLOCKS AND MANDRELS

Specialist smiths use anvils of other sizes and patterns and their peculiarities will be mentioned later in this book. However, there are two other anvil-like devices that most smiths use. One is a swage block and the other is a mandrel or cone.

A swage block is a basically rectangular block of iron or steel that has an assortment of hollows of different sizes and shapes around its edges and holes of many sizes and shapes through its body (Fig. 3-9A). Patterns vary and not all hollows

Fig. 3-10. A conical floor mandrel stands out among other equipment.

or holes are round. This is a bottom tool that can be moved around to get the desired shape upwards. There can be a cast iron stand or the swage block can be mounted on its own section of tree trunk or a made-up wooden stand. Sizes might be from 11 inches square by 5 inches thick, with a weight of about 100 pounds or up to 24 inches square by 7 inches thick, with a weight of about 700 pounds. The larger sizes need lifting tackle to turn them. A swage block is not essential for all blacksmithing, but it is convenient to have one when curves have to be made to exact sizes or many parts have to be made to match. Individual swages (see Chapter 4) that mount in the hardie hole of the anvil, will do for similar work in smaller curves.

A smith's cone or mandrel (Fig. 3-10) is a round cast iron cone with a truly round section and an even tape (Fig. 3-9B). It is used to make rings truly circular. Some mandrels have a long groove into which the tip of the tongs can fit when putting a ring in place. The size of a mandrel varies according to needs, but in a general blacksmith's shop it might stand up to a 4 feet high and weigh over 100 pounds. For smaller rings, there could be a mandrel with a square projection to fit in the hardie hole of the anvil or be gripped by a vise (Fig. 3-9C). Some large mandrels have their tips formed by one of these pieces that can be lifted off to use elsewhere.

FIRE TOOLS

The fire is tended by tools which the smith makes and remakes as they wear out. For pushing coal and coke into place, there is a poker (Fig. 3-11A) with a straight or bent end. It is given a blunt point and the other end is shaped to form a handle and possibly an eye for hanging. A rake (Fig. 3-11B) has similar uses, but it is used for pulling fuel instead of pushing it. The simplest and most common form has a flat-tened end bent at right angles to the shaft. Another sort has two or three prongs bent downwards. For light work all of these tools could be made from three-eighths inch or one-half inch round rod and with an overall length enough to keep the hand away from the heat. That depends on the size of the hearth, but 24 inches to 30 inches should be satisfactory.

A slice supplements the poker and rake when hot fuel has to be lifted and moved around the metal being heated. It is

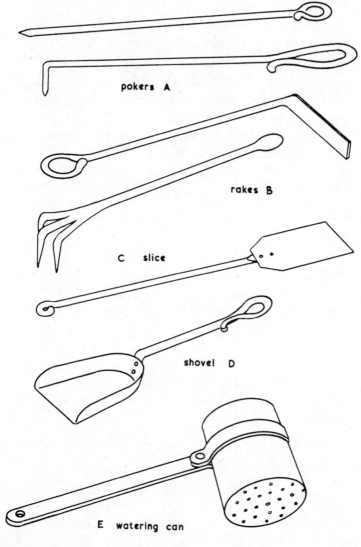

pokers A

rakes B

C slice

shovel D

E watering can

Fig. 3-11. The fire is managed with a few tools made by the smith.

a simple piece of flat plate rivetted to a handle (Fig. 3-11C) and about the same length as the other tools.

Reserve coke or coal can be kept in a bin or bucket near the forge and a shovel (Fig. 3-12D) used to transfer it to the hearth. This could be a domestic type of shovel, although the smith might prefer to fashion his own of more substantial steel.

The fire has to be kept within bounds and sometimes it is necessary to keep one part cool while another is hot. Water is sprinkled for cooling, using a watering can (Fig. 3-11E). This is just a can with an open top and a number of holes punched in its bottom. A handle can be fashioned by rivetting on a bar. However, a handle that wraps around will be stronger. If a bolt is used to tighten it, the handle can be put around another can when the first has worn out.

Smith's Tools

4

Nearly all of a blacksmith's work is done with hand tools. Often one tool is supported on the anvil and another held over it by hand. For heavier work, there have to be power tools that apply greater force, but for most things the smith has to make the only power come from his or his helper's muscles.

Most of the tools a smith requires can be bought, but a smith can also make most of them. However, you cannot make tools without tools and anyone starting blacksmithing will need to buy the first tools. Replacements and others of different sizes or for special purposes can be made in the shop or smithy.

Tools might take a long time to wear out and it is possible to reforge or grind old tools to make them servicable again. If used tools are available and they appear to be in poor condition, they should be examined so the possibility of putting them back into working order can be assessed. Even if a tool has been worn away to the point of appearing useless, it might be possible to weld on more steel so it can be used again.

HAMMERS

By far the most commonly used tool is a hammer. There is very little that a smith does that does not call for a hammer blow, either directly onto the metal or against a tool over it. Many of the early smith's hammers were made by blacksmiths. It is still possible for a smith to make a hammer once some skill has been gained, but the first hammers will have to be bought.

An engineer's ball peen hammer (Fig. 4-1A) is a good general-purpose choice. This has a steel head with a flat or slightly domed face at one side and an approximately hemispherical face at the other side. The handle should be ash or hickory. A similar hammer with the head and shaft in one piece of steel, as is found in some engineer's hammers, would transfer too much shock to the hand during the frequent hammering a smith does.

The hammer should be as heavy as can be controlled. Sizes are by weight and usually up to 3 pounds. Anyone using a hammer all day can control a heavier one than could be used by an occasional smith. A weight of 2 pounds will be easier to use.

Other lighter and heavier hammers can be added to stock. There is much less use for the face opposite the flat one, but a ball peen is useful for rivetting. Other shapes with occasional uses are the cross peen (Fig. 4-1B) and the straight peen (Fig. 4-1C). These are shown in the form a smith might forge them himself, but it is possible to buy them in a general form similar to the ball peen hammer.

These hammers are used in one hand, usually by the smith working alone and controlling the work with the other hand. When heavier blows are needed, a helper also uses a hammer. This is usually the heavier, two-handed sledge hammer (Fig. 4-1D). The sledge might be double-faced, as shown, or could have ball, straight or cross peens. The handle is usually hickory.

As with the single-handed hammers, there is an advantage in weight in a sledge hammer. But this has to be limited by what the user can control. Sledge hammer weights start at 4 pounds and may go up to 14 pounds. For amateur or occasional use, 7 pounds is a reasonable choice.

The security of the joint between the head and the

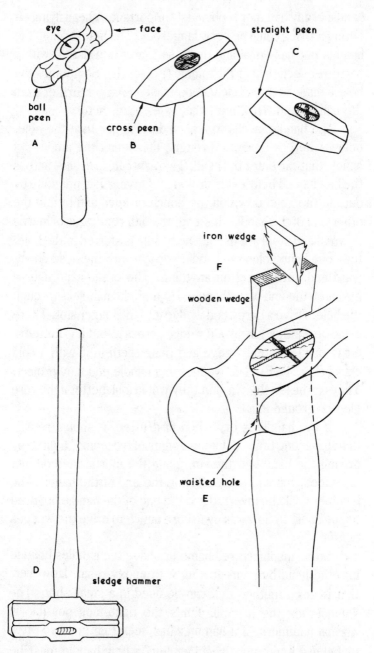

Fig. 4-1. A smith uses a variety of hammers that must be securely attached to their handles.

handle of any hammer is obviously important. A head flying off during a swing could be very dangerous. The hole through the head is normally oval and made so that it is waisted, with a narrower section near the middle (Fig. 4-1E). Sometimes the hole is made with a single taper so that it is larger further from the handle end. However, this is less satisfactory.

The handle swells to a shoulder, bigger than the hole, below where it is to go through. This limits the amount of handle that can enter the head. Two saw cuts are made across the handle end before it is driven in. Driving in is not done by putting the head down on the bench or anvil and hitting the other end of the handle. Instead, the different rates of inertia of wood and steel are used. The handle is started in the hole, then one hand holds the handle vertical with the head downward and not resting on anything. The other hand uses a mallet on the end of the handle. Hit until the handle is through the hole. Drive a hardwood wedge into the longer slot. There could be another hardwood wedge across it, but it is better to forge or file a steel wedge and raise teeth in it with a cold chisel (Fig. 4-1F). The wedges and handle end may project. They can be left this way but they would look better if they are filed or ground level.

If the handle is dry when first fitted, it should remain tight for a long time. If it shows signs of loosening, tighten by driving the handle further in, using the inertia method just described. Instead of a mallet on the end of the handle, the hammer could be inverted and the end of the handle bounced on the anvil. Follow this by using a punch to drive the wedges tighter.

Some manufactured hammers have the handles bonded into the head by impregnating with epoxy resin. However, that is not a method that can be used in a small shop. The shoulder on the hammer limits the tightening possible in normal hammers. If a hammer has been tightened so often that there is no more shoulder left, a new handle must be fitted.

HARDIES AND SETS

There are some occasions when a smith cuts steel with a hacksaw the same way as other metalworkers. A hacksaw of reasonable size and some spare blades should be included in a blacksmith's tool kit. Most cutting is done with a blow on a cutting edge, either completely through or partway through and then snapped off. If the tool is used over the metal, it is called a set (sate). If it is used underneath it is a hardie. The cutting edges and the effect might be the same, but it is the direction of cut that determines the name.

Hot metal can be cut with a more acutely angled cutting edge than cold metal. A cold set (Fig. 4-2A) might look like a hammer, but it is a handled tool for hitting with a hammer and is not intended to be swung. The head has a cutting edge at one end and a flat top to be hit. The wooden handle is usually round and held in place with a single wedge. The hot set (Fig. 4-2B) has a finer cutting edge and is usually a more slender tool.

The comparable tools used below are the hardies which give their name to the square hole in the anvil. They are made to fit easily into the hole. As with the sets, a hot hardie (Fig. 4-2C) is usually taller and more slender than the cold hardie (Fig. 4-2D).

Some sets are grooved around instead of made with holes through. The handle is then made from thin round rod wrapped around and with its ends welded together, as shown for the top swage (Fig. 4-3A). Either method is satisfactory. Sets and hardies are sold by weight and can be as much as 4 pounds.

Some smiths use flexible wood rods that are cut from woodland undergrowth, wrapped around in the same way as iron rod and bound in place. This does not transfer as much shock to the hand, but renewal has to be frequent if the tools are often used.

A cold chisel (Fig. 4-2E) works like a set, but has no handle. It is common to other forms of metalworking and a smith would use it to make lighter cuts. It can be made from round or octagonal high-carbon steel and the width of the cutting edge can be up to 1 inch.

There are many shaped cutters for special purposes. A farrier uses shaped ones when making horseshoes. A round cut-off (Fig. 4-2F) is typical.

A hardie and set can be matched for a slicing cut. The set is made with an angle at one side (Fig. 4-2G). The hardie can be straight across or hollowed (Fig. 4-2H), with its angle at one side.

SWAGES AND FULLERS

Most swages are rounding tools and are in pairs (Fig. 4-3A). They can also be made for squares and other sections. The bottom swage fits in the hardie hole. The top swage is handled and has to be located over it. Its top is shaped for hammering. Since the work and the top swage have to be held by the smith, he needs a helper for hammering. For single-handed work, the top and bottom swages can be combined with a spring handle (Fig. 4-3B). This is satisfactory for light work. But for heavier sections, the two parts and a helper are better.

The curves, or other sections, of swages have to match the intended final shape so that each pair of swages is for one size only. This means that there have to be several pairs, although it is possible to get bottom swages with several grooves to reduce the total number of bottom parts needed. Although swage sizes are controlled by the diameters they are intended to round, they may be sold by weight.

Fullers are also matched pairs, but their curves are the other way (Fig. 4-3C). The top fuller is hit by a hammer over the bottom fuller, which is fitted in the hardie hole. The effect is to pinch and hollow the metal held hot between them. There are fullers with different curves, but there is not such a need for a range of sizes as there is with swages.

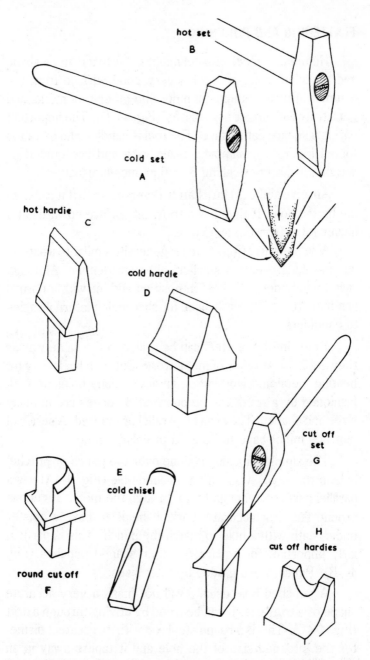

Fig. 4-2. Cutting tools for hot and cold metal can be held to cut downward or mounted on the anvil to cut upward.

FLATTENING AND PUNCHING

Hamming a piece of steel might get it to a general shape and a skilled smith can get a very good surface from the hammer. But to remove hammer and other tool marks and get a truly flat surface use a flatter (Fig. 4-3D). The important part is a square flat surface. The tool is handled and has a top for hitting with a hammer. Sizes vary and are graded by weight. A flatter weighing 5 or 6 pounds is usual.

An anvil stake is like a flatter reversed so that it can fit in the hardie hole. It then has a truly flat surface upwards at a higher level than the anvil face.

A set hammer (Fig. 4-3E) is generally similar to a flatter, but the square end is smaller, although deeper. Although called a hammer, it is held in position and hit with a normal hammer. It is particularly used for sharpening internal angles to shoulders.

Holes in iron or steel can be drilled in the same way as they are in most types of metal work. But with his facility for heating metal and working on an anvil, many holes in work fashioned by a smith can be punched. Punches are in many sizes and shapes. They can be parallel or tapered. A series of punches might have to be used to enlarge a hole.

The simple punching is done over the punch or pritchel hole in the anvil. A punch for a round hole (Fig. 4-4A) has a parallel part long enough to go through the metal. Its end is ground flat. For accurate work, it helps to have a bolster underneath with a hole to match the punch. This is particularly important for square or other shaped punches (Fig. 4-4B). Punches are graded by their sizes.

A punched hole usually will not finish a very accurate shape or a true size. It can be trued by driving through a drift (Fig. 4-4C). This is a round steel rod with its greatest diameter the intended size of the hole and it tapers away in an elongated barrel shape. If it is hammered through the punched hole in hot metal, it will bring it to size and shape.

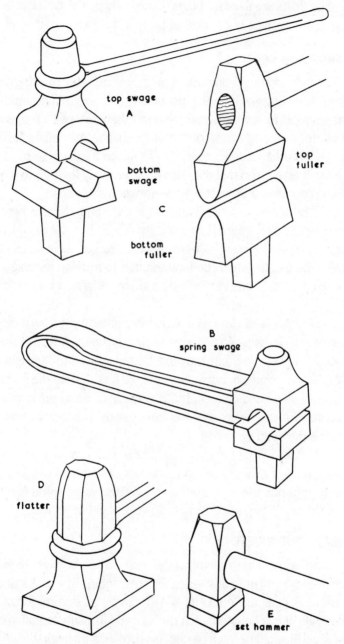

top swage
A

bottom
swage

top
fuller

C

bottom
fuller

B
spring swage

D

flatter

E
set hammer

Fig. 4-3. Some tools are used in pairs to squeeze or shape and others give flatter surfaces than can be obtained with a hammer.

Similar drifts are used for holes of other shapes. A drift can be used to alter the size of a hole or taper it, as in a hammer head.

BENDS AND SCROLLS

In decorative ironwork, much bending and twisting is done by pulling and levering instead of hammering. The smith makes tools to suit particular jobs, but there are two-pronged tools for levering strips of metal to shape. A bending fork (Fig. 4-4D) has a square neck to fit in the hardie hole or be held in a vise. Strip metal is then progressively levered to the required curve a little at a time between the pegs.

Where it is more convenient for the iron to be fixed and the pegs moved, there is a bending wrench (Fig. 4-4E) which can also be called a scroll wrench if making scrolls is its main use. The handle has to be long enough to provide leverage, although a short one can be extended by slipping a tube over it.

Both tools can be made with different size gaps between the pegs. The gaps do not have to match the thickness of the metal being curved, but they are better related to the tightness of the curves being made. A scroll fork serves the same purpose as a bending fork, but it is made like a letter H with different spaces between the opposite ends. It is held in a vise with either end upwards.

If many scrolls have to match, as in a decorative iron gate or a length of railings, the smith makes a scroll iron which is a pattern to pull the iron around and get the same spiral scroll each time. It has a leg turned down to hold in a vise.

HEADS AND RIVETS

In some smith's work, the ends of rods have to be enlarged to form heads, such as are required for bolts and rivets. A heading tool (Fig. 4-4F) can be in several forms. Basically it is a hole to match the size rod in a substantial iron or steel block. The hot iron end then projects through the hole so it can be hammered to shape.

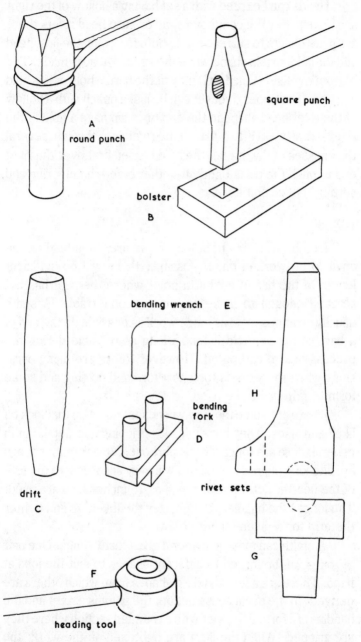

Fig. 4-4. Holes in hot metal can be punched. Other tools are used to bend bars or form heads on rods.

57

Heads can be trued with a set having a hollow of the right shape in it. For the common round or snap head rivets there are pairs of sets to suit each size, both for truing the first head and for holding it in shape while the second head is made. The bottom rivet set (Fig. 4-4G) may fit the hardie hole or it is held in a vise. The upper rivet set can be just a punch with a hollow of the rivet head shape in the end or it can have a hole of the rivet size as well (Fig. 4-4H). If the rivet goes through several thicknesses of thin metal, the hole is used first over the rivet end to push the parts tightly together before hammering and setting the second head.

TONGS

Iron or steel has to be put in the fire, then held on the anvil to be worked on. If possible, there will be sufficient length of the bar to hold at a point where the heat has not reached enough to make gripping uncomfortable. A smith usually arranges to do as much work as possible on the end of a bar, so he can hold it for as long as possible during the process before cutting off. However, there are many occasions when the work is too short for hand holding and some form of grip has to be used.

There are some modern wrenches (Fig. 4-5) that lock on like hand vises. They have uses for gripping hot metal, but in general there are tongs for this purpose. A blacksmith's tongs are like long pliers. The length will vary according to the size of the hearth, but tongs as much as 18 inches long are used. The longer the handles, the greater the leverage and tighter the grip for a given length of jaw.

A smith can make and alter a great many tongs. One pair of tongs can be forged to different shapes to suit the jobs at hand. There are a few standard shapes from which others are derived. In the usual construction, the pivot is a rivet and the handles are forged to taper with a rounded section where they are gripped. When the jaws are tightened on the work, the ends of the handles should not meet. In most cases, they will

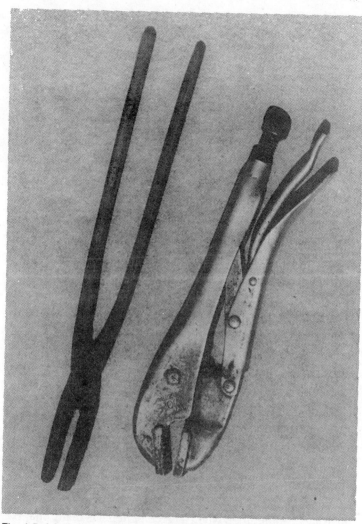

Fig. 4-5. A lock-on wrench is an alternative to traditional tongs.

be splayed outwards slightly. To lock the tongs on to the work, a sliding ring or coupler can be drawn towards the spreading ends of the handles to tighten the tongs (Fig. 4-7A).

General-purpose tongs have flat jaws. If they close completely they are closed-mouth tongs (Fig. 4-6A). They should close completely at the tips while being slightly open towards the rivet. This ensures they will hold thin material securely. If the jaws will not close completely, they are open-mouthed tongs (Fig. 4-6B). The amount of openness depends on the thickness of iron to be gripped. A smith needs open-mouthed tongs to suit one-quarter inch, one-half inch, three-quarter inch and other thicknesses, although each will suit sizes slightly thinner or thicker.

To hold a shaped rod end-on the jaws have to be hollowed and many sizes of hollow-bit tongs are needed (Fig. 4-6C). If the hollow is rounded (Fig. 4-6D), only round rod can be held securely. Square hollows (Fig. 4-6E) will grip round or square stock.

Hollow-bit tongs only suit parallel rods. If there is an enlarged end, as when a head has been forged on a rod, bolt tongs (Fig. 4-6F) are forged to suit.

If much rivetting has to be done and the comparatively small rivets have to be heated in the fire, lifted out and put into their holes quickly so as not to lose heat, rivet tongs have to be used. They have their ends shaped to match the diameter of the rivet (Fig. 4-6G) so that it aligns as it is gripped and can be quickly positioned.

For general pick-up work, where the small items have to be taken from the fire and put in a vise or transferred to other tongs, there are pick-up tongs (Fig. 4-6H) with more springy and open ends. They are not intended for holding work being hammered.

The best grip comes from having the work in line with the tongs. Sometimes when a piece of metal is being shaped, the end does not allow this and it has to be gripped crosswise. Holding a long piece of steel across the jsws can be rather insecure and it is better to have tongs that allow it to be alongside instead of across the line of the tongs. These are bent-bit or side tongs (Fig. 4-7 A&B). The bent or extended side part can be in various forms, depending on the section of metal to be held. Another type, also called side bit tongs, has the ends of the jaws bent over (Fig. 4-7C).

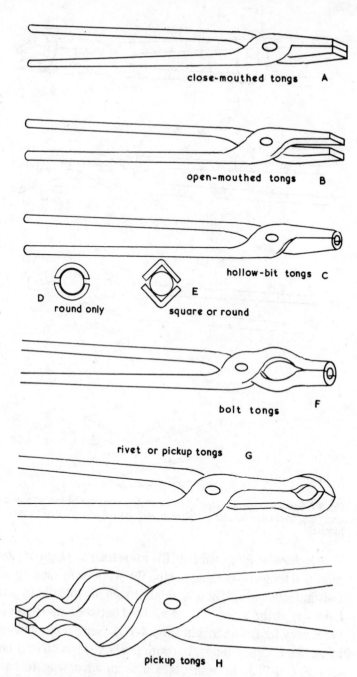

Fig. 4-6. Tongs have their jaws shaped to suit many purposes.

61

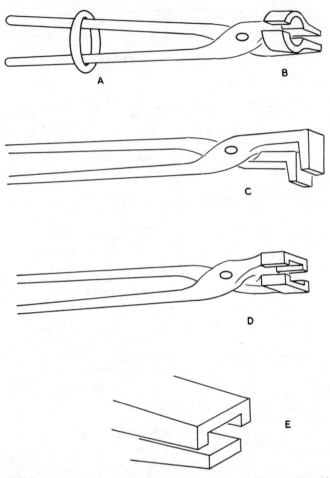

Fig. 4-7. Special tongs hold steel at an angle. Any tongs can be locked on with a ring: (A,B) bent-bit or side tongs; (C) side bit tongs; (D) box tongs; (E) semi-box tongs.

Hollow bit tongs will hold the iron straight. Open or close mouthed tongs do nothing to stop the work from slipping and twisting sideways. There are box tongs in which both jaws have lips at the sides. The work held between them cannot twist very far from straight (Fig. 4-7D). Semi-box tongs are made like ordinary tongs, but with the boxed lips on only one jaw (Fig. 4-7E). In both cases it is an advantage to have several tongs with different widths of boxing.

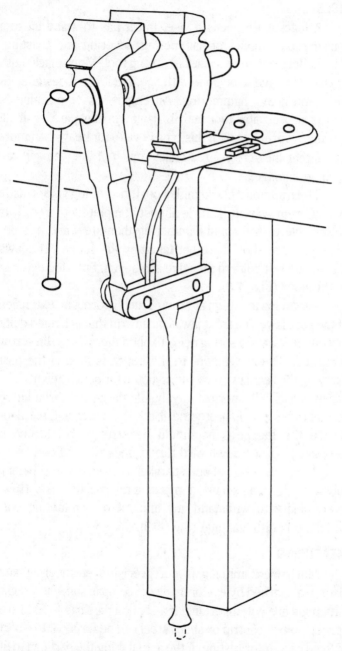

Fig. 4-8. A smith's leg vise is supported by the floor as well as the bench.

VISES

A blacksmith needs a vise, but it has to stand up to a considerable amount of hammering, levering and twisting. The modern engineer's vise is a strong tool. Much blacksmith work might have to be done with one, but it is not designed to withstand heavy hammering. An engineer's or machinist's vise is a precision tool and its jaws remain parallel at all settings. A problem with this type of vise, for heavy hammering, is that the screw thread takes much of the load and can become damaged.

The traditional blacksmith's post, box or leg vise is made in a different way. It is made almost completely of iron. It is better able to withstand hammering than steel and it is designed so that shocks are not taken by the screw. The jaws can be steel. It bolts to the edge of a bench, but a leg extends to the floor (Fig. 4-8).

Variations in design are few. The leg forms an extension of the rear jaw. The front jaw is on an arm that is hinged quite low on the leg and a spring helps to open the jaws as the screw is turned. The attachment to the bench is around the part carrying the rear jaw. It can be adjusted for bench height. The screw works in the normal way, but it is large and shrouded so the threaded part is protected. Both the bench and the floor where the leg pegs in should be strong—reinforced if necessary—since downward thrust goes to the floor.

A leg vise does not open parallel and a very wide opening might not have as secure a grip as a machinist's vise. However, ability to withstand any amount of hammering outweighs this disadvantage (Fig. 4-9).

MEASURING

Much blacksmithing is not precision engineering and sizes are checked by eye or by direct comparison when slight variations are not important. If a shaped part has to fit into a space, a piece of strip or sheet steel can be forged into a sort of fixed caliper for testing, if the actual thing the part has to fit is unavailable.

Fig. 4-9. A securely mounted leg vise complements the anvil.

Large calipers can be made by the smith, usually with an extending handle to keep the grip away from the heat. One caliper can serve two sizes (Fig. 4-10A). Joints are tight rivets.

For checking right angles a large L-shaped piece is used (Fig. 4-10B). It could have a handle and a large one could have a diagonal brace. Construction is from strip iron that is rivetted or welded.

A *traveler* is a wheel on a handle (Fig. 4-10C). There is a mark or hole near the circumference. This was used for measuring by counting the number of rotations as the wheel was rolled along or around the work. It was particularly associated with making a steel tire for a wooden wagon wheel, with the traveller run around the wheel and then along the strip of steel to make the tire, but it was used for other measuring as well. It is interesting as a curio of the past, but not much use today.

Ordinary engineer's rules are made of steel and tempered. If one is used on red hot steel, enough heat might be transferred to draw the temper of the rule. This will make it soft and easily bent. This can be avoided by measuring and marking along the edge of a piece of cold steel and using this to check dimensions of the hot steel. However, there are many occasions when the rule has to be brought to the steel being forged. Brass rules have been made for use by smiths, but they might be difficult to obtain today. The heat has little effect on brass, but the rule is not as durable as a steel one under normal circumstances.

CLOTHING

For anything but the lightest smithing, a smith should wear a strong apron that covers from his waist to below his knees. The best material is leather since this resists wear and knocks and is good protection against burning. A professional style apron might be made of 7 to 8 ounces of chrome-tanned leather, with a strong waist band and buckle. Joints can be glued and sewn, with rivets at stress points.

For general smithing, the apron can be in one piece, wrapping around at least halfway past each leg. For horseshoeing the farrier usually prefers his apron divided down the front so that there are overlapping halves or chaps that hang inside as well as across the fronts of the legs.

A good leather apron might be expensive, but it should be regarded as one of the essential tools if much smithing is to

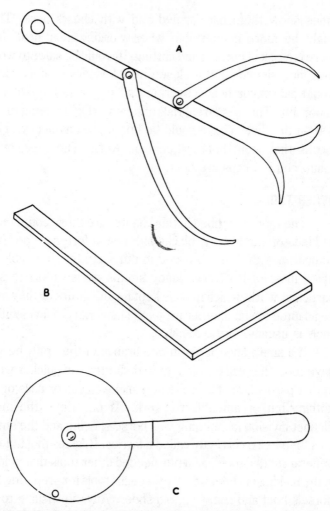

Fig. 4-10. Handled calipers (A) can be used to measure hot metal. A try square (B) is flat. A traveler (C) is run along metal to measure it.

be done. An occasional or amateur smith might want to use a canvas apron. This should not be a light one, such as would be suitable for general wood or metal working shop use, but should be a piece of quite stout canvas that will provide protection against hot metal.

Other clothing should be close-fitting. Avoid any clothing that hangs or is loose. Pictures of traditional smiths sometimes show them bare-armed and with chests bare. This might be more comfortable when working near heat, but there is a risk of burning and cutting. It would be safer to work with long sleeves and a closed neck. Modern safety ideas would also favor head covering and goggles. Footwear is important. There is a real risk of heavy weights being dropped on the feet. These could be hot as well as heavy. This means that stout boots should be worn. The types with reinforced toe caps are best.

OTHER TOOLS

The tools described in this chapter are those common to all kinds of smithing. A blacksmith is in a fortunate position compared with those engaged in other crafts. He is able to make most of his tools. Many smiths devise tools to suit particular work, which may be kept for the future or they may be adapted to suit another project. The variety of any smith's tools is usually very extensive.

If a smith specializes in one branch of the craft, he will have tools that will enable him to do better and quicker work in that particular sphere. He may make chains or nails or do nothing but ornamental ironwork. At one time, the most distinct division in smithing was horse shoeing and the smith was then more correctly called a farrier. Besides most of the general smiths' tools, a farrier needed other tools that helped in the making of shoes and a few special tools for preparing the horse's hoof and removing old shoes. Anyone wishing to do the same type of work today will need most of these tools. It is probable that ready-made shoes will be used and the work of adapting them to a hoof will be slight.

Specialist tools are described later in the book, where their uses show their special values. Although new or used special tools can be bought, in most cases the smith has to make his own. Being able to do this is one of the satisfying aspects of the craft.

Basic Techniques

5

The first requirement is, of course, to light a fire. How this is done and how the fire is tended is more important than might be expected. The quality and type of fire can affect the iron or steel being heated. Therefore, it may or may not be easily forged in the manner expected. Although the actual hearth might be fairly large, the actual fire is usually quite small, except when something more massive than is normally being worked has to be heated.

At one time charcoal was used. It could still be used but coke (breeze) is more satisfactory. If small coke is obtainable, that is probably the best choice for a smith's fire. But it is more likely that coal will have to be accepted. Coke is made by heating coal, so the aim is to convert the coal to coke from around the outside. Quite small bituminous coal is preferred. The size of the coal should be comparable to peas. If larger coal is broken up, avoid including much of the inevitable dust. It is possible to use almost any available coal. A little experience with available material should allow a satisfactory fire to be made.

If charcoal is used, spread some around the hearth, with a hollow above a bottom tue iron or in front of a rear one. Use paper or wood shavings and a small amount of kindling wood to start a fire there. As the wood begins to burn, put charcoal over it and work the bellows or fan. Adjust the amount of blast to make the wood flame through the charcoal and ignite it. Feed on more charcoal and adjust the fire to the size you want. Maintain a blast to build up the heat when iron is put in the fire.

With coal, have a reasonable amount in the hearth, but make a hollow where the blast comes so shavings and some kindling wood can be placed there. With some coal, it helps to wet it thoroughly with the watering can. This encourages it to stick together in a mass and more easily form coke. A smith might refer to unburned coal as "green" coal.

Light the wood and start the blast. Push the coal towards it so that it starts to burn. With a new fire there will be some smoke. Encourage the coal to flame by regulating the blast and this will consume much of the smoke. Rake more coal around the fire. Wet the surrounding coal. Near the center of the fire coke will form. Test for coke with the poker. It should be bonding together near the middle of the fire. With the wood burned away, you should have a coke fire burning and more damped coal around the outside ready to feed. Wetting stops the fire from spreading more than is needed. For most smithing with iron or steel of moderate size, the whole expanse of fire should rarely exceed 6 inches across.

While the fire is burning coal and before much coke has formed, keep the blast going, if only at idling speed, otherwise there is a risk of a blowback, this could damage the bellows or be disconcerting with an explosive sound in the fan. Once the fire is basically coke, it does not matter if the blast is stopped.

Once coke has formed, the fire should burn with little or no smoke. In a well-managed fire, the burning coke is surrounded by damped coal, which turns into coke as the coke inside is burned away. Coal might have to be raked in and it is probable that some smoke will be made. An experienced smith keeps his fire going with a minimum of smoke. If coke is brought, the smoke problem does not arise, but the fire has to be managed in a generally similar way.

Unfortunately, there are products of combustion that you do not want if the fire is to remain "clean", as it must be, particularly for welding and some other processes. There are impurities in the coal. Some might come from the steel, while other unwanted matter comes from the act of burning. When the fire is shut down, coke from the center should be kept for use when starting again. This allows you to start with the minimum amount of smoke since you do not want to have to start the new firing by converting coal to coke.

Besides forming coke, there will be some ash formed. This is the residue from burning and not useable. With an ash pan below the tue iron of a bottom blast forge you may be able to vibrate or open it and allow ash to drop out, but even then and in any case with a back tue iron, you may have to scrape and shovel ash away. As well as ash, there will be some clinker, which is hard and glassy and formed from sulfur and other impurities. In a burning fire, clinker will be seen as black dead spots in an otherwise bright fire. Clinker is heavy and will drop to the bottom of the fire, but in a bad case it could bond itself into quite a large irregular hard mass, that has to be lifted out with the poker or pick-up tongs. Clinker spoils a fire for welding. It should certainly be removed when a fire is shut down, but during a long working period it will have to be looked for and removed from the burning fire. Hot clinker can bond to the surface of hot iron or steel and affect its final appearance or prevent welding.

The desirable fire for most heating is a *reducing fire*. This is a compact bed of coke surrounded by coal that is well-banked around. The heat is then reflected inwards and consumes all the oxygen. At the other extreme is a shallow, board and fairly open fire with its center hollow. It has excess oxygen and can be called an *oxidizing fire*. It is difficult to heat the metal evenly in this fire and considerable scale can form on it. It could not be welded. The more common fire is a neutral one between these extremes and is satisfactory for general work.

Iron is heated in the heart of the fire, not on top of it and not thrust too low in it. There should be a good bed of burning coke below the iron and more raked over it. The iron should not be too close to the blast from the tue iron because the air oxidizes the metal. A steady blast of air should be maintained to keep the fire hot. Some experimenting will show how long to keep the metal in the fire to get the desired heat. Thin strips will heat quicker than thick ones and tapered pieces have to be manipulated so that the thin part does not get excessively hot and "burn" while the thicker part is still absorbing heat. It is worthwhile experimenting with pieces of scrap iron to check heating characteristics before attempting actual forging to shape on the anvil.

CUTTING

For practice in basic methods, it is convenient to use round iron or mild steel rod between one-quarter inch and three-eighths inch in diameter. This is easier to handle in strips about 18 inches to 24 inches long, rather than in shorter pieces requiring tongs. Pieces could be cut to length with a hacksaw while held in a vise, but a smith prefers to cut on the anvil.

It should be possible to cut the cold metal with a cold hardie or set. If only the more acutely sharpened hot hardie or set is available, the same method can be used with the steel heated to redness. With the hardie mounted on the anvil, hold the strip over it at the place to be cut and give a smart tap with a hammer (Fig. 5-1A). Turn the strip over and do the same to the other side to make two facing notches (Fig. 5-1B). Do not hit so hard that the cut goes completely through, with the risk of the hammer face meeting the hardie and damaging it. With a little practice, the notches can be taken to almost meet, then the rod is broken off in the hands or pushed into the pritchel hole and levered apart.

If a set is used, work on the table (Fig. 5-1C) and not on the face of the anvil where an inadvertent cut completely through or angling the tool might make the cutting edge meet the hardened face and become damaged. Cut from both sides and break off in the same way as using a hardie. Normally, a hardie is preferred as the use of a set means calling in an assistant to wield the hammer.

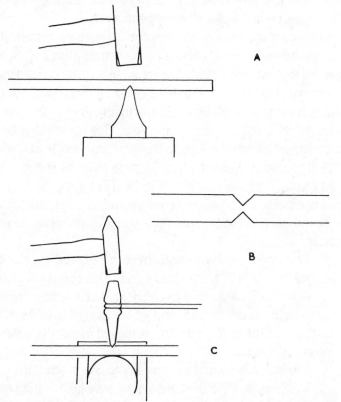

Fig. 5-1. A hardie cuts metal hammered on it (A,B). A set cuts downward (C).

BENDING

Much work under the hammer is bending. This is done by hitting in a way so that the blow does not pinch the steel between the hammer and the anvil, but the force comes to one side of the point of support, and so avoids marking by compression. If the strip is put across the beak for bending, the hit should come off center (Fig. 5-2A).

Have the rod heated to redness. Aim to get the same degree of heat for the length to be bent. How bright you get it depends on the particular mild steel, but it should be satisfactory if it glows red without being so brilliant that it is more golden. If it is bright and sparkling, you have heated it too much and the end might have been burned, leaving it semi-disintegrated and unsuitable for good work.

If you want to form an even curve, work progressively across the beak, hit off center and alter the hitting points by moving the rod (Fig. 5-2B). As you get used to it, you can use the curve of the beak and hammer toward it (Fig. 5-2C) to get the right shape. Avoid heavy blows tightly against the anvil. This would pinch and flatten the rod. This hammering to a curve might have to be repeated as you progress toward the shape you want. Reheat when the strip loses its redness. If you continue hammering after the steel has gone black, you will not make much progress and you might mark the metal with the heavier hammering while you are still trying to get results.

Sometimes a curve is made over the edge of the face of the anvil (Fig. 5-2D). Many smiths grind a curve on part of the edge of the face so bending can be done there without marking the inside of the curved strip with a sharp angle. As with curving over the beak, the strip is moved across to make a long curve.

Another way to make a curve is to use a scroll iron or fork, which might fit in the hardie hole or be held in the vise. Curving is done by levering the strip back a little at a time from its end (Fig. 5-2E). This is more appropriate to shaping a flat strip to produce decorative twists and curls. Simple shaping of round rod is generally better done by hammering on the anvil.

A common need is to put an eye on the end of a rod. It might not always be round, but a simple ring handle shows the

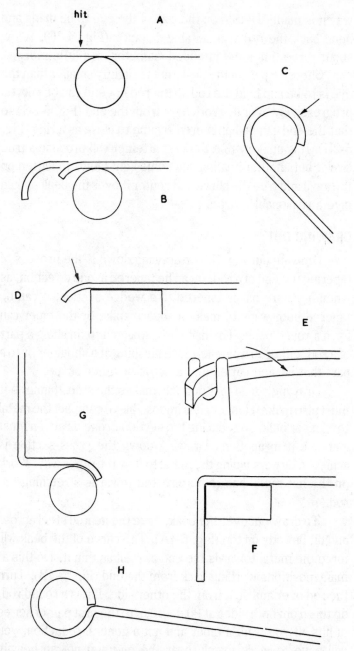

Fig. 5-2. Bending is done by hitting (A,B,C,D,F,G,H) to one side of the support or by pulling between jaws (E).

way it is made. Decide on the size of the eye to be made and bend back the rod at a suitable distance (Fig. 5-2F). Allow about three times the intended diameter or a little more.

Choose a part of the beak that is slightly smaller than the eye is to be and hold the rod so the red hot end can be curved progressively over it. Work back from the end (Fig. 5-2G) so that the end can be hammered around to close as a ring (Fig. 5-2H). It is unlikely that the first attempt will produce a true circle, but another heating and some light blows to flatten on the anvil and true the curve and center it over the beak should give a reasonable shape.

DRAWING OUT

Drawing out Fig. 5-3 or drawing down is the process of tapering the end of a rod. It can be tapered in one direction, as when a square bar is tapered to a wedge section, it can be tapered both ways to make a square spike or the taper can form a round point. The name is also given to finishing a part of a rod, either to a parallel piece finishing at a shoulder or to a part that is then curled into a scroll or other shape.

Drawing out a taper not only makes the steel thinner—it must also make it longer. It is impossible to compact the metal to a lesser bulk, so reducing the section in one direction must increase it in another. Drawing down the cross-section is achieved by persuading the metal to flow the other way. Work on the hot metal has to be directed towards stretching the rod.

To draw out over the beak, have the heated steel across and hit directly on top (Fig. 5-4A). The curve of the beak will force the metal towards the end as well as thin it. Do this at many positions working back from the end (Fig. 5-4B). Turn the rod over and do it from the other side. If it is a round rod, do this from both sides at 90 degrees to the first pair of series of hits. If you want a taper and not a general reduction, you will have to work mainly near the end and not so heavily further back. At this stage the aim is to produce a taper. If the

Fig. 5-3. Drawing out a bar on the face of the anvil. Note the balanced stance and the hand holding the tongs.

rod goes out of shape, it can be straightened on the anvil face. Reheat as necessary.

Although drawing out across the beak gets quick tapering, slight tapering, as it would be with thin rod can be done on the anvil face. Hammer so as to spread the steel in length (Fig. 5-4C). Rotate the rod between hits so as to reduce both ways. Even if the rod is round, it is easier to get a good taper by working it square. If it has to go to a point, a square taper is worked (Fig. 5-4D) and the final hammering is on the angles (Fig. 5-4E). This converts the section to octagonal. More hammering on the anvil face can be directed at taking off those angles and getting the taper straight.

Most of the work in tapering should be done at a bright red heat. Be careful not to let the thinned end get too hot. Final straightening is better done at a dull red heat. During work, scale will form on the metal. It will come away during hammering and should be swept off the anvil. At a dull red heat, it does not form. Truing as a final step is better done at this heat. It would not be hot enough for drawing out.

An alternative to drawing down across the beak is to use the edge of the face. The bar is drawn across the edge and hammered so as to pinch against it. This produces a series of notches that force metal towards the end, stretching and thinning the shape (Fig. 5-4F). The first series of hits will curve the rod, but turn it over and do the same the other side to get that side stretched with notches. Do it again at 90 degrees to the first series and the opposite side to straighten the rod. Move to the flat of the face and straighten the tapered parts by direct hits. Twisting as you hammer can be described as *tumbling* the cord.

Fullers are used for drawing out large-sectioned bars. The effect is similar to that of the beak or the edge of the face in stretching the metal towards the end and thinning it. Heavier blows are possible for greater and quicker effect.

If the end of a bar has to be reduced in thickness without increasing in width, the top fuller can be hit into the hot steel at the end of the reduction (Fig. 5-5A). More dents are made along the part to be reduced (Fig. 5-5B) with the bar turned on edge intermediately so that there can be hammer blows on the sides to bring the bar back to width. When working alone, a bottom fuller can be used to get a similar effect. The bar will have to be returned to the anvil face occasionally for

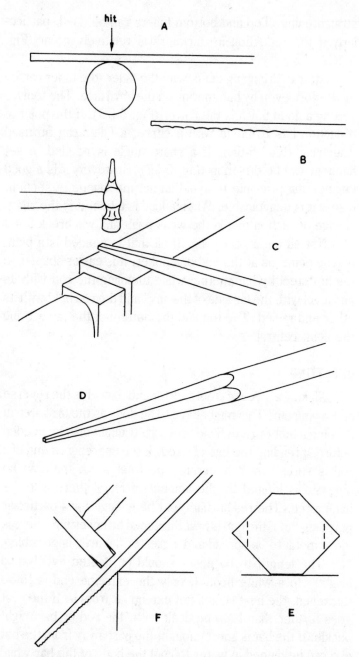

Fig. 5-4. Hitting (A) over a support compresses the metal (B,C) and is used for drawing out (D,E,F).

straightening. Top and bottom fullers can be used, particularly if the reduction in thickness is relatively great (Fig. 5-5C).

After overlapping dents with the fuller, the taper can be made more even by hammering on the anvil face. The tool for getting a good finish is the flatter (Fig. 5-5D). If the point of reduction has to blend with a curve, a fuller can be used diagonally (Fig. 5-5E). If a sharp angle is needed, a set hammer can be driven in (Fig. 5-5F). However, it is a good engineering principle to avoid an abrupt change of section, unless it is unavoidable. When a load is taken, it is the sharp change of section that is the weak point and will break first.

Not all tapers are long. If all that is needed is a blunt obtuse point, as at the end of a poker, it is easier shaped on the hot steel by hammering while tumbling the rod with its end level with the far side of the anvil and the rod held with its other end raised. The top and the bottom of the taper bring the point central.

UPSETTING

Making a piece of steel shorter and thicker is the reverse of drawing out. This might have to be done as the first step in forming a bolt or rivet head on a rod. It might also be needed before spreading the end of a rod. If the unprepared end of a rod is spread by hammering, the total width that can be obtained is limited by the amount of metal there is to be hammered. The result might not be enough for a particular purpose, but if the end is first thickened by upsetting, there is more metal to be spread and a greater flat area is possible.

The length to be upset should be heated evenly and brightly to a white heat. If only the extreme end is to be thickened, the heat should not extend far from it. If the heat goes further than is to be dealt with, the rod or bar might buckle. If the bar is short enough, the part away from the hot end can be dipped in water to cool the body of the bar while leaving the heat at the end. If a long bar gets heated too far,

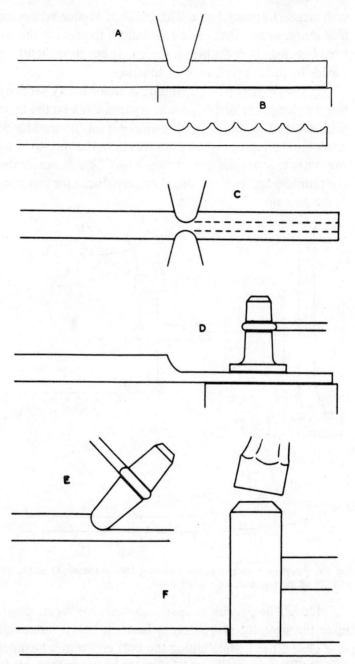

Fig. 5-5. Fullers draw out (A,B,C) and the surface can then be flattened (D,E,F).

water might be poured on it. The end should be flat across and filed if necessary, Otherwise it is difficult to prevent the bar from bending. It might help if the end is bevelled slightly all round, by filing, grinding or hammering.

A simple example of upsetting is with a heavy section a few feet long. The smith has a heavy iron block on the floor. With the end heated he then bounces it on the iron block, using his strength as well as the weight of the rod, to cause the end to shorten and spread (Fig. 5-6A). This demonstrates the principle and explains the alternative name for upsetting of *jumping up*.

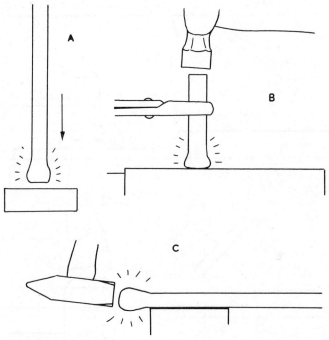

Fig. 5-6. Upsetting is the process of thickening white hot steel: (A) spread the end; (B) hit the cold end; (C) rotate the rod.

It might be possible to upset a shorter piece by jumping it up on the anvil. It will probably be better to hold it with tongs or a gloved hand while hitting the cold end with a hammer (Fig. 5-6B). There will probably have to be several reheats to

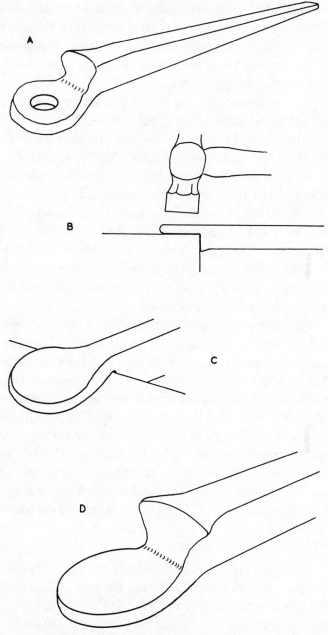

Fig. 5-7. Upsetting provides extra metal for a shaped end: (A) holdfast; (B) hammer; (C) spread the metal; (D) broaden the shoulder.

get a worthwhile amount of upsetting. Almost certainly, there will be some bending above the part being upset. Even after cooling almost up to that point has been arranged. Watch what is happening and straighten on the anvil face as necessary, before bends develop too far.

In most cases upsetting is best started by jumping up, Once spreading and shortening has started, the process can be continued with backing-up blows from the hammer. This is particularly appropriate when a good spread is needed on the end, as when forming a head. Have the end at a good heat. Hold it so that it projects over the edge of the face of the anvil, with your holding hand braced against your thigh ready to resist the shock of hammering. Hit the end strongly while rotating the rod between blows so as to get an even effect (Fig. 5-6C). This stance gives you a better view of how the upsetting is developing. But it is better as a follow-on step than as a first move in upsetting.

Although upsetting is often needed as the first step in forming a head, its application in giving an increased amount of metal for spreading is seen in making a holdfast for driving into a wall to hold a wooden post (Fig. 5-7A). The upset end is then shouldered by hammering over the edge of the anvil face (Fig. 5-7B). Spread it in the same positions (Fig. 5-7C) to give a good area of sufficient thickness to take a stout screw. A set hammer squares the shoulder so that it can be hit into the wall with a hammer. If some of the upsetting continues into this part, the shoulder will be broadened to give a better area for hammering (Fig. 5-7D). The other end is tapered to a point by drawing out.

TWISTING

Putting a twist in a rod is simpler than it might appear. It looks best in square sectioned bars, but they could be anything else angular. A twist in rounded rod would not be apparent, although an elliptical section has possibilities. A part of a round rod can be filed square (Fig. 5-8A) to allow a decorative twist along part of a rod handle (Fig. 5-8B).

To make a twist, heat the length that is to be twisted. Then grip close to one end of the intended twist in a vise and turn its other end. This could be done with an adjustable wrench or pipe grip, but it is better if you are able to twist with both hands. Use a piece of metal with a square hole near its center (Fig. 5-8C) if the work is square. This could be a screwing tap wrench or a square hole could be punched in a length of flat strip metal. If it is a handle made of round rod with a filed square, a bar could be put through the eye end.

To get an even helical twist, the part to be twisted must be heated evenly. If the heat is greater at any part, the twist

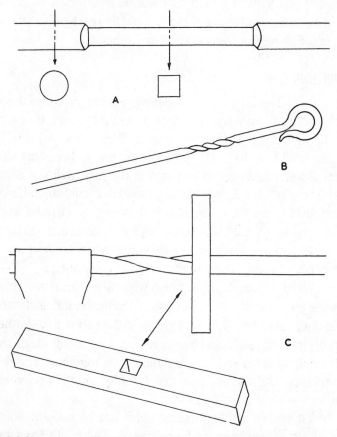

Fig. 5-8. Hot square sectioned rod (A) can be given a decorative twist (B). A hole (C) is useful for twisting.

will be tighter there. A long twist is more difficult to keep even than a short one, but providing the heat is the same for the length to be twisted, the result should be satisfactory. With most smithing, it is possible to reheat and correct work that is not as it should be. If a twist is unsatisfactory, there is usually nothing that can be done to put it right. This means that if a twist is to be put into a part that has smithing work to be done elsewhere on it, it might be best to tackle the twisting first.

There can be more than one twist put in a long bar by heating and holding at different points. It is also possible to put in a reversed twist next to the first one. One twist is completed and a short length that will be left untwisted comes between that and the next twist. Hold this part with a wrench while making the second twist the other way.

WELDING

A blacksmith's weld is a different thing from that made electrically or with oxy-acetylene. In a smith's weld, the parts to be joined are brought to near melting point and quickly hammered together. The principle is simple, but some skill and practice are needed to perform the task well and accurately every time. Iron is easier to weld than mild steel. If iron is available, that should be used for learning. Since most work will have to be done in mild steel, skill in welding that will have to be acquired. It is easier to weld square or rectangular stock than round rods, which tend to roll on each other.

Wrought iron has a very high welding temperature which melts away scale. It is possible to prepare the ends and hammer them together with no special treatment. All other forms of iron and steel require flux, which will clean the meeting surfaces and enable them to run together. The flux combines with the scale so that it melts and then prevents further scaling or oxidization.

There are welding fluxes which can be bought. Some smiths use clean fine sand for mild steel. This might be all that is needed, but another variation used is a mixture of about four parts sand to one part borax. For welding tool steel to itself or to iron or mild steel, it might be better to get the appropriate commercially-made flux.

Flux is not the complete answer to welding problems. Its plentiful use does not spell success, in fact too much is a bad thing. It could attract oxygen into the weld. There should only be enough of it to be forced out by the first hammering. Otherwise it will form a barrier to prevent the molten surfaces from uniting. A few iron filings can be included in the flux, They help to carry away the flux during the first hammering and they will burn and collect oxides away from the parts being joined.

Avoidance of oxides at the meeting surfaces is important. This goes back to the heating in the fire. Make a reducing fire, with a good depth burning below where the steel is to be placed and cover this with more fuel. Do not use too much blast, since that would cause oxidization. Keep a steady draught that will build up the center of the fire to a white heat that is so bright as to be difficult to look into.

Ends to be joined have to be prepared by scarfing. They are upset and hammered to thick tapered ends (Fig. 5-9A) with the surfaces that are to meet given round shapes (Fig. 5-9B). This is so that their centers meet and force out flux and scales. If the meeting centers flow together during the first hammer blows, the weld should be satisfactory.

Heat the ends that have been prepared by scarfing. When they have reached an orange heat, pull them from the fire and sprinkle flux on them. Return the ends to the fire, Make sure they are in the center where the greatest heat will be. As the heat increases and the steel glows light yellow, turn the faces downward. Continue to heat steadily. A few sparks coming from the fire will indicate that welding heat has been reached. By then the fire and the ends of the bars will be so bright as to be difficult to look at. Do not stare into the fire too much or you might not be able to see well enough when you turn to work on the anvil.

Have the anvil face clean and a hammer re dy. Your assistant holds one piece with its scarf upwards and you position the other over it and hammer the parts together immediately. It is the first few blows that are critical and one problem is getting them in before the heat is lost. The cold anvil face will take heat away and this can be reduced by bringing the parts together at a slight angle (Fig. 5-9C). The first blow brings the joint on to the anvil, but it also makes the weld. It helps to lightly tap each piece against the side of the anvil to remove any loose scales as you bring it into place.

Hammering has to be done systematically. The first few blows are at the center, then toward the ends of the scarfs, to close the thin parts (Fig. 5-9D). More blows come at the edges and the work can be turned on its side to get the width of the weld the same as the bars. It might be necessary to reheat, if the weld is not fully closed all round before it cools too much. A wire brush should be used to remove scale and dirt from the metal before returning it to the fire. Sprinkle on more flux and put the joint in the fire. Bring it to welding heat again and quickly hammer the parts that still need treatment.

There is no time to stop and examine the work while considering what to do. As soon as you take anything from the fire that is to be welded you must start hammering. When you have made the weld, continue lightly hammering all over it until it cools almost to blackness. Welding enlarges the grain in steel. Light hammering refines it to a more normal size, with a gain in strength.

HEAT TREATMENTS

All that a smith does can be described as heat treatment, but the name is specifically applied to what is done by heat to tools and other things made from high carbon steel. Iron and mild steel are little affected by heating and cooling, but high carbon steel can be made harder or softer by the way it is heated and cooled. There are special alloy steels for particular purposes, but many of them need controlled heat treatments

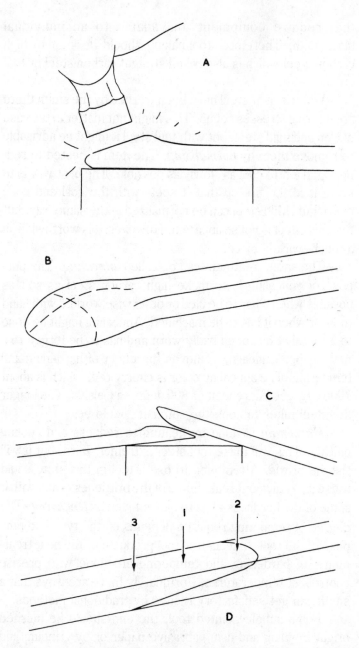

Fig. 5-9. Parts are welded after shaping and raising to white heat: (A) thick tapered end; (B) round shapes; (C) parts brought together at a slight angle; (D) the first blows (1) are at the center and more blows are made at the edges (2,3).

that require equipment unavailable to an individual blacksmith. Therefore, toolmaking should be kept to high carbon steel which is also called straight carbon steel or tool steel.

When iron or steel have been worked by the smith there are internal stresses set up. This might not matter in the case of iron and mild steel, but with tool steel it might be advisable to remove them by *normalizing*. The item is heated to redness and left to cool as slowly as possible. The best way is to leave it in the fire so that it cools with the coal and coke overnight. Mild steel can be normalized in the same way, but the final effect is not so apparent. However, it is worthwhile in a much-worked piece.

The same treatment can be called *annealing*. The purpose of annealing is to make high carbon steel as soft as possible when it has to be filed or otherwise worked with hand tools or when it has to be machined. Annealing might be done to a tool that has been badly worn and has to be forged to a new shape. Annealing removes the effect of hardening and tempering. The annealing color is cherry red, which is about 1000 degrees Fahrenheit or 800 degrees Celsius. The longer the steel takes to cool, the softer it should be.

Hardening is done by heating to redness and cooling quickly. This will make tool steel extremely hard, but it will also be brittle. Attempting to use a tool in this state could cause it to crack or break. Some of the brittleness - and with it some of the hardness - has to be removed by *tempering*. The degree of tempering required depends on the type and purpose of the tool. In industrial tool production, the heat treatments of hardening and tempering are done with precise controls of temperatures. Fortunately there are ways that a smith can get satisfactory results by traditional methods.

For a simple pointed tool, the end should be finished bright by filing and using abrasive paper or by grinding and polishing. Then it is heated for a short distance to a full red heat. It will not take long to reach this heat and it is probably best held vertically in the fire with tongs and examined frequently. When the end is hot enough, lower the tool vertically into a container of water (Fig. 5-10A). Move it about after immersing so as to cool as quickly as possible.

The brightened end will discolor, but the preliminary polishing will help in later stages as well as in getting a good finish on the completed tool.

For tools that are broader than pointed ones, it is important to cool them all over rapidly and as close to the same time as possible. Otherwise there is a risk of cracking or distorting. Thin items such as knife blades are more prone to this trouble. For something that has to be given an all-over hardness, turn it about in the fire to heat evenly and try to get the same degree of heat everywhere. Quench the tool as soon as the correct heat has been reached. Steel might suffer if heating is prolonged excessively.

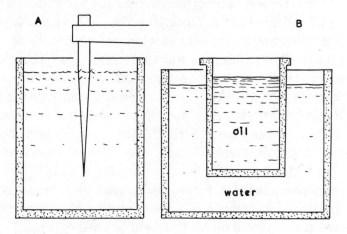

Fig. 5-10. Steel can be quenched in water (A) or oil (B).

Quenching by dipping the hot steel in the bosh or water tank that is used for all other cooling is generally satisfactory. However, there are other quenching baths that have advantages. Cold water can give maximum hardness, but it could induce surface cracks. Tepid water (60F) might be better.

Hardness might not be quite as great, but the risk of cracking is reduced.

Brine makes a good cooling bath that conducts heat away quickly. This should be a saturated solution of common salt—as much as the water will dissolve. Sal ammoniac can be used, but ordinary salt is more readily available.

Oil is also used for quenching. Obviously it must not be an oil that will burst into a flame when red hot steel is put into it, but many oils have possibilities. Quenching oils can be bought, but olive oil is a clean one suitable for small tools. Crankcase oil can be used, but is obviously more messy. Water and brine (Fig. 5-10B) can be palced in almost any container, but with oil it is advisable to keep it within bounds by suspending the container of oil in another of water. This way spilled oil is trapped by the water, which will also quench any flame.

Another way of using oil as a quenching bath is to float it on a container of water. This can be mineral oil, vegetable oil or even grease. As the hot tool is lowered through the oil, it gathers a layer of this surface film and takes it through into the water. This is claimed to produce a tougher steel with freedom from cracks. Whatever a quenching bath is used, it should be deep enough for the tool to be fully immersed and moved about in enough liquid to carry away the heat. For small hand tools there should be at least two gallons of liquid.

Tempering is the process of heating again to a lower temperature and quenching again. Although it is the temperature that is important, there is a very useful guide to temperature in the colored oxides that form on polished steel. The colors play no part in the treatment of steel. They are just indicators. The oxides can be cleaned off, but removing the wrong color does not put right the mistake! If a mistake is made in tempering, it is necessary to reharden the tool and temper again.

Heating for tempering is probably better done with a propane torch than with a fire. To use a smith's fire, an iron pan filled with sand can be put on the fire and the tool rested on that. This method is better than a torch, with a torch, tempering has to be the same all over a long cutting edge, such as a knife. For pointed tools or end cutting tools, like chisels, a torch gives better control.

If a piece of tool steel has been worked smooth before hardening, it can be rubbed bright again fairly easily with abrasive paper. An alternative popular with smiths is a flat piece of sandstone. The essential thing is that the steel should be clean and bright enough to show oxides for some way back from the end or cutting edge.

If the colors of the oxides are observed as heat is applied slowly, the first color is pale straw, which deepens to an orange and then brown, continuing to a reddish brown before deepening into purple and blue, before going on with further heat to become red hot. The temperatures these oxides represent go from about 430 F (220C) at the straw color to 500 F (260 C) for the deep brown and 580 F (300 C) for blue. The tempering colors for edge cutting tools come around the middle of the range.

The higher the temperature for tempering, the softer the tool steel becomes (Table 5-1). When the desired temperature is reached, the tool is plunged into any of the cooling baths suggested for hardening. The oxide color will still be visible after cooling.

The steps in hardening and tempering are best observed by dealing with a simple pointed tool, such as a scriber. This is drawn out to a point. When doing this, or making anything from high carbon steel, do not be tempted to cool the tool in water while forging as this will harden it and make it brittle. Having forged the point to your satisfaction, anneal it by leaving it to cool for several hours in a dying fire or in the coal at the edge of the fire if that is still in use.

The body of the tool can be left black. A few inches back from the point, file it smooth and round. Then brighten it by pulling abrasive paper around it (Fig. 5-11A). Harden the

Table 5-1. Heat Treatment.

Oxide color	Temperature F	C	Tools
	400	205	
	410	210	
Yellow	420	216	Engravers, scrapers, razors,
Pale straw	430	220	burnishers
	440	227	Stone drills, reamers
Straw or orange	450	232	Saws for metalcutting
	460	238	
Deep straw	470	243	Scribers, knives, punches
Brown	480	250	
	490	255	Dies
	500	260	Knives, plane irons, taps
	510	263	Chisels, twist drills
Bronze	520	270	Surgical instruments
Light purple	530	275	Hammers
	540	281	Axes, center punches
Purple	550	285	Cold chisels, stone-working tools
	560	293	
Blue	570	300	Screwdrivers
	580	306	
Dark blue	590	310	Wood saws, springs
	600	317	Large saws
	610	322	Springs
	620	327	
Greenish blue	630	332	

point in the fire or by using a propane torch. Heat to redness followed by quenching. Use the abrasive paper or a piece of sandstone to brighten the point again. Be careful not to treat it roughly as the brittle steel could snap off.

Use the torch to heat about 2 inches back from the point. In quite a short time, the oxide colors will begin to appear and spread out from the place you are heating. They will continue to spread, showing how the heat travels towards the point, even after the torch flame has been removed. Watch their travel. If they stop, apply the flame again. The greater the spread of the colored oxides the better it will be for the tool. The straw color will reach the end and deepen there into orange, which will get darker and begin to change to brown. At that stage, quickly quench the tool. The oxides will still be there. All of the darker orange part will be correct for a scriber. This is likely to extend for about one-half inch and all of that will be available for sharpening before the tool needs rehardening and tempering. If more heat had been used, the colors would have moved quicker and closer. Only a shorter part near the point would have been at the correct temper for a scriber.

There is another way of hardening and tempering an end-cutting tool that only requires one heating. The tool starts with a bright surface and its tip is heated to redness for hardening. When it is quenched, only the point is lowered into the liquid so that there is still a hot part above the surface (Fig. 5-11B). The point that has been under the surface is then dried and quickly rubbed bright with a piece of sandstone. There is still plenty of heat in the body of the tool and this travels towards the point. As before, watch the oxide colors and the tool is quenched completely when the correct color reaches the point.

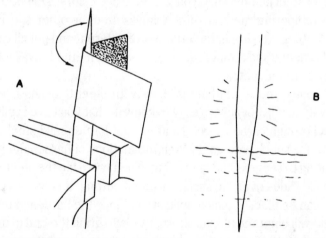

Fig. 5-11. Polish a point (A) for tempering and partially quench (B) for hardening and tempering with one heat.

For a steel tool that needs an overall equal tempering an iron tray filled with sand and placed over the fire can be used, It might be necessary to pick up the tool frequently with tongs to see the colors. The colors do not move from one part to another. You have to act quickly since the sequence of colors appear all over and you have to catch and quench at the color you want. It helps to prevent the cold tongs from affecting the temper at the point of grip if they are allowed to heat at the same time and place as the tool being worked on.

An alternative to the tray of sand is a fairly thick iron plate, that is larger than the tool to be tempered. This is heated almost to redness on the fire, then pulled to the side of the fire and the tool to be tempered placed on it. Heat will transfer from the iron to the tool laid on it and the colors can be observed in the same way as with sand. However, this method suits a thin steel piece, like a knife blade, but a more bulky item heats better if it is partly buried in the hot sand.

Colored oxides are not exclusive to tool steel. They will appear on polished iron or mild steel which is heated. They do not indicate any change in its characteristics, as they do with tool steel. Do not be misled into thinking that you have a piece of tool steel just because you get the oxide colors. Do not try this tempering method with stainless steel or other special alloy steels. Their characteristics are different and not all can be hardened and tempered, even by special methods available only in the industry.

Since much smithing is done with steel that has been salvaged, it is not always easy to know if what you have is mild steel or high carbon steel. Heat will not harden mild steel so the sure check is to go through the motions of hardening, by heating to redness and quenching. Then try to file the steel. If the file slides over the surface without cutting, it is tool steel. If it can be filed, you have mild steel. Since the hardened tool steel will blunt the file, an alternative is to grind the end fo the file across so that it makes a cutter and try to scrape the steel. If it will not produce a scratch on the heat-treated steel, you are dealing with tool steel (high carbon steel). It should easily make a mark on iron or mild steel after that has been heated and quenched.

CASE HARDENING

The difference between mild steel and tool or high carbon steel is the amount of carbon alloyed with the iron. This difference affects the characteristics of the steel. Untreated high carbon steel is harder than mild steel and it can be hardened and tempered to adjust its relative hardness to further degrees. If more carbon can be added to mild steel, it should be possible to convert it to high carbon steel. Unfortunately there is no way this can be done throughout the steel by the blacksmith. However, there is a way of giving mild steel a thin outer layer of high carbon steel.

The process is called case hardening or carburizing. The conversion of the outer layer can only be about one-thirty-second of an inch and at the best is unlikely to reach one-eighth of an inch. The effect of case hardening is to provide a wear-resistant surface that can be hardened and tempered. The whole thing will benefit from the toughness of the mild steel core with the hardness of the skin. This property is worth having if the skin is subject to considerable wear. For instance, a much-used screw on a machine might suffer from the frequent use of a wrench on its head, but if the head is case hardened the risk of damage from the wrench is reduced.

Case hardening is done by heating the mild steel in contact with something of high carbon content. The amount of heat and the length it is applied affects the degree of penetration. Some carbonizing agents are charred bone, wood, charcoal, charred leather and parings of hoofs and horns. There are also some commercial case-hardening preparations. Carbonates of barium, calcium and sodium can be added to the mixture in small quantities. They help the process of getting carbon to penetrate.

As the articles to be case-hardened and the carburizing materials have to be heated together for a long time, they have to be put in a container that can be heated as well without damage or disintegration. A steel box with a lid could be used or a piece of iron pipe might have its ends sealed with fireclay. Allow spaces for the pieces being treated to be separated and be sure each has an ample supply of carburizing material around it.

The carburizing agents should be in an even granulated form, not a mixture of solids and dust. Charcoal from hardwood can be the main agent. A mixture consisting of about 50 percent this and the rest made up of approximately equal quantities of the three carbonates should be satisfactory. Charred bone is even more effective. Do not use uncharred bone, which may build up pressure as it burns. A larger proportion of charred bone can be used than charcoal.

Sealing is best done with fireclay cement intended for fire brick. It is possible to put the steel and the carburizing material in a cloth and encase this thickly with fireclay. However, a steel container presents less risk of failure during a long heating.

Heating should be taken at least to the stage where a steel container glows cherry red. Maintaining this temperature for six hours might only achieve a penetration of one-thirty-second of an inch. Raising the temperature shortens the time, but even at a bright orange heat there would have to be about three hours for the same result. Obviously, if there is a fire for central heating or some other purpose burning continuously, its use would be better than keeping the forge fire going for a long time.

Another way to case-harden uses a commercially available powder. One type has to be sprinkled on the red hot steel or the hot steel rolled in it. Reheating then causes carbon penetration. The process has to be repeated several times. The result is a very thin layer of high carbon steel, but it might be sufficient as wear protection.

Another method case-hardening use cyanides. They are poisonous and their fumes are dangerous. They are not materials to be used in a blacksmith's shop.

When mild steel has been case-hardened by any method, it should be treated in the same way as high carbon steel. After case hardening, it should be allowed to anneal by cooling very slowly. If it is to be hardened it can be quenched in water or oil. The hardened surface might chip or crack during heavy use, so it is common practice to reduce some of the hardness and brittleness of tempering. Of course, any heat treatment only affects the skin, while the core is not affected any differently from when the whole thing was completely mild steel.

Advanced Processes

6

For a great many things that can be made by a smith, you will find the work to be combinations of the basic techniques described in Chapter 5. It is useful practice for anyone new to blacksmithing to examine something that has been made at the forge by someone else and try to break it down into the sequence of operations that made up the whole. Try to visualize the steps and how they relate to the final shape. In nearly all cases, each step or nearly all of them, will be found to be quite basic and comparatively simple, despite the apparent complication of the final article.

The saying "strike while the iron is hot" obviously comes from the smithy and it is very pertinent to the blacksmith's work. It is no use taking the iron from the fire and wondering what to do with it or to have to search for the tools needed. Iron does not hold its working heat for long. You must know in advance what you intend to do and have everything ready to do it. In that way, you can get the maximum amount of progress out of each heating of the metal. The difference between an expert blacksmith and a beginner is often shown in the way the experienced smith completes his work with far fewer returns to heating in the fire. He will also get more for his actions. He knows from experience what the effect of an action will be on the iron and he works in a way that gets the best results. He might also be stronger. It is not essential to have powerful arm muscles, but if you have them, you can wield a hammer with greater force and get more effect for each stroke. Of course, strength in the correct muscles comes with practice and special exercises are not really necessary.

A newcomer to blacksmithing should learn to appreciate the ways of steel and how to get the effect he wants by making simple things that involve the basic techniques. Then he can tackle more advanced work that combines these operations and the further processes described in this chapter. An important skill is the ability to make a weld with certainty, particularly some of the variations described later. Much work can be done without including welding, but the range of designs possible gets much larger if you are able to weld as required.

Much blacksmithing is pure utility. Other work is primarily decorative and artistic. Even with the utility items, there is beauty in good design. If an object is made so that it is fit for its purpose, it can be a very satisfying thing to the user as well as to the maker. If much utility ironwork of the past is examined, you can usually find some little decorative touch that was not essential to the functioning of the article. There might be twists and curls that do not make the item work any better, but they make it look more attractive. When the wheelwright and blacksmith worked together to make wagons, the ironwork was purposeful and much of it showed the artistic inclinations of the particular smith.

Decorations might have been at least equal to the functional needs of some ironwork. Examples can be seen in old churches, where grills and partitions show considerable skill, both practically as well as artistically. Gates and railings are other examples that are worth examining for the detailed artistic work that was lovingly done. Even a blacksmith with little artistic knowledge can produce attractive decorative work if he uses examples found in drawings and photographs. A smith who is also an artist might use his own ideas. Iron and steel are not the easiest materials to work with, but they offer a challenge. Many smiths in the past faced up to the challenge and worked the materials into beautiful forms. There is no reason why modern smiths should not produce work equally as good. Some guidance on decorative work is given later in the book. Before that sort of smithing can be tackled there has to be a mastery of a great many relatively simple steps.

HEADING

Upsetting has been described previously. In some work, the thickening of the end is all that is required or it might be a preliminary to spreading the end, as described in Chapter 5. But more often, upsetting is a preliminary to forming a head on the rod. This might be a knob to prevent the rod from sliding through another part. It might be a head for riveting or it could be a bolt head. In a small size, it could be the head for a nail. The methods of working are generally similar, whatever the size.

A heading tool is needed. One example is shown (Fig. 4-4F). This is particularly suitable for nails since the raised top gives space to work around the head. A simpler tool is a piece of steel with a tapered hole to suit the rod. One piece of steel could have a number of holes of different sizes to suit more than one size of rod.

If the heading tool is made, its thickness should be enough to resist buckling under heavy hammering. Providing this is taken care of, it need not be much thicker than about half the diameter of the rod it is to hold. Too great a thickness increases the difficulty of punching it and making it accurately. For smaller sizes, it is satisfactory to drill the hole if power drilling facilities are available. Make the hole slightly smaller than the finished size to allow for tapering.

It is customary to punch the hole. Use a flat-ended punch or a smaller diameter than the rod over the pritchel hole in the anvil (Fig. 6-1A). Have the steel cherry red. It might help to put the steel on the anvil face and drive the punch a short distance from each side before putting it over the pritchel hole to drive through. If the steel distorts, it can be hammered reasonably flat. Finishing is done after the next stage.

Use a tapered punch with its small end less than the size of the rod and the larger part of the taper greater than the rod size. It could have a handle, although a tapered steel punch to hold in the gloved hand is easier to control for small sizes. Reheat the steel and drive in the tapered punch until the smaller size of the hole matches the rod (Fig. 6-1B). Test with the rod to see if it will slide through easily. After heating, its diameter will increase slightly. Flatten the steel.

The amount of upsetting has to be arranged so that there is sufficient thickened steel to form the head. You cannot make a head of a certain size if the volume of metal to do it with is not sufficient. At the same time try to keep the thickening as near the end as possible. It will have to taper, but keep the bulk as great as possible confined to where you want it by cooling with water the part that has to remain parallel. The first upsetting will produce a tapered swelling (Fig. 6-1C). After probably three heatings and jumping up and backing up with a hammer, the enlarged part will be almost bulbous (Fig. 6-1D).

To make the head, place the heading tool or plate over the pritchel hole, if that is large enough, or over the hardie hole, with the smaller side of the hold uppermost. If your intention is to make a knob end to the rod, have your hammer ready on the anvil. Heat the end to cherry red and quickly drop the rod into the tapered hold. Make sure enough projects to make the knob. If too much projects, the rod can probably be driven down so the tapered hole cuts and compresses the rod. Hammer around the end as well as on its top (Fig. 6-1E). Hitting downward will spread the steel, but the hits around the edge will force the metal downward as well as form the head into shape. The head formed might not need to

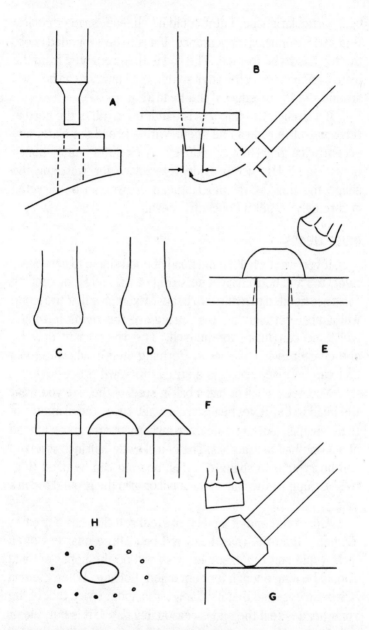

Fig. 6-1. A header tool can be punched and used to support an upset end for forming a head: (A) punch the hole; (B) match the size of the hole; (C) a tapered swelling; (D) enlarge the part; (E) hammer the end and top; (F) form the head as you prefer; (G) invert the road; (H) center punch dots as a reference for shaping.

be a particular shape, but it could be cheese, snap or conical (Fig. 6-1F) for a neat appearance. If it is to be a rounded knob, the top has to be formed. The rod is then removed from the plate and inverted in the anvil so that the hammer can be used around the lower edge of the head (Fig. 6-1G).

If a circular heading tool is used, the truth of the head in relation to the rod can be seen. With a broad flat plate, any eccentricity might not be noticed. A circle of center punch dots (Fig. 6-1H) will provide references for watching the shape the head is taking. Hammer blows can be directed accordingly to get a concentric result.

RIVET HEADS

If you want a half-round head of good shape to serve as a rivet, top and bottom rivet sets (Fig. 4-4G and H) or cupping tools are needed to make two heads. Examples that the smith will almost certainly soon be using are the rivets in tongs, which he can make for himself. The rivets may only be one-quarter inch in diameter. Forming their heads with tools that can be made easily is a straightforward process.

You need a ball or half a ball in steel of the size you want the head to be. Rivet heads are usually twice the diameter of their shanks, so a one-quarter inch rivet may have a head about one-half inch across. The end of a one-half inch steel rod can be ground to shape or a ball bearing can be used (Fig. 6-2A). Support the ball on the anvil or grip the ground rod in a vise.

Upset the end of a piece of steel rod that has a greater diameter than the rivet head will be. Three-quarters of an inch would suit the example. This will be the upper set and should be long enough for convenient holding. When the end has been upset so that its diameter is about twice that of the rivet head, see if the end is reasonably flat. If it is not, file or grind it flat. Heat the end again and drive it on to the rounded rod or the ball (Fig. 6-2B). There might have to be more than one heat to allow you to drive it on far enough. If a manufactured rivet head is examined, it will usually be found to be slightly less than a complete hemisphere. There is no need to make the hollow that far, although you must allow for a little levelling of the bottom to make it ready for use.

The bottom rivet set could be a similar piece to hold in the vise, but it would be better if given a slight shoulder (Fig. 6-2C). It could be shouldered more so that it would fit in the hardie hole. In both cases, the shouldering is an application of the technique described in Chapter 5 that uses fuller, flatter and set hammer.

Following the method for forming a knob on a rod, the upset end of the rivet is positioned through the heading plate and the first shaping is done by hammering. Be careful to stop the head from spreading too much. It is better to leave a little excess height so that when the cupping tool is driven on it pushes down and does the last spreading (Fig. 6-2D). You have to estimate the exact amount of metal required for a head. If there is too little you might finish with a flat top to the round head or a part that does not take a good curve. If there is too much metal, you will get a full round head, but there will be a rim at the bottom. If the first attempt with the cupping tool is unsatisfactory, you can go back to hammering and try again.

When you assemble the tongs or something else with the rivet, start with it too long. There will not be an upset end to work on, so estimate how much you should stand up to make the second head (Fig. 6-2E). You cannot reheat the end once you have started shaping, so know exactly what you will do and have everything ready. Support the lower head in its set and hammer around the projecting end quickly to start spreading (Fig. 6-2F). Then put the cupping tool over while there is still plenty of heat in the end and drive it down (Fig. 6-2G). Make sure the hammering gets the edges of the head close to the surface. Driving directly downward might cause the rivet to bend in the hole slightly, instead of becoming shaped above the surface.

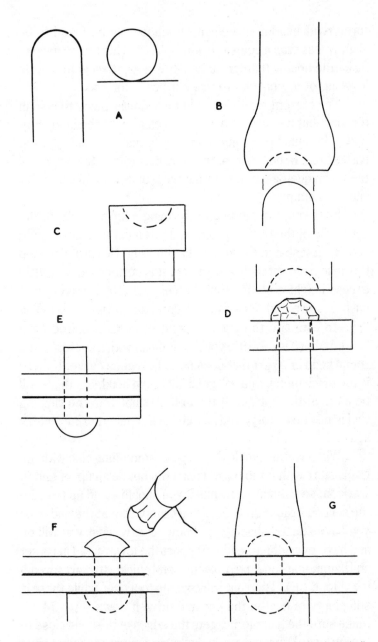

Fig. 6-2. A rivet set holds and shapes a rivet head: (A) use a steel rod or a ball bearing; (B) drive the end onto the rod or ball; (C) give the bottom rivet set a shoulder; (D) drive on the cupping tool; (E) make the second head; (F) hammer to start spreading; (G) drive the end down.

108

REDUCED RIVETS

The method of heading just described starts with a rod and makes the head larger. For some things, there is the alternative of starting with rod of the head diameter and reducing the part for the neck of the rivet. This would not be satisfactory for a long rod, but where the rivet or other part is quite short, this is a method sometimes preferable. For satisfactory work, there must be a pair of swages of the size the rivet is to be.

For a one-quarter inch rivet with a one-half inch head, start with a one-half inch rod long enough to hold. Reduce the end for slightly more than the final intended length by hammering while the rod is rotated. Check constantly that the work is remaining central. Use a set hammer to sharpen the shoulder (Fig. 6-3A) and turn the rod between blows. In this way, bring the reduced part almost to size. Check with

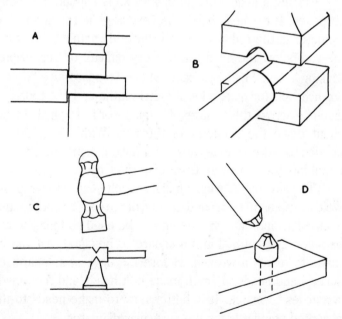

Fig. 6-3. Instead of upsetting, a rod can be reduced to make a bolt or rivet. (A) sharpen the shoulder; (B) true the shape; (C) cut the head; (D) use the heading plate.

calipers. Put the steel between the pair of swages and true the shape (Fig. 6-3B). If the shoulder under the head is untrue, pass the reduced end into the heading plate while it is red hot and hammer downward with light blows.

Use the hardie to cut around and above what will be the head (Fig. 6-3C) until there is only a small amount left to snap off. This could be done in the heading plate (Fig. 6-3D). From that point on, forming the head is the same as in the earlier example.

There should be no difficulty in tapping a rivet or other rod out of the heading tool. The tool or plate should not be allowed to get too hot since that would soften it and might cause the hole to be damaged. Dip the plate in water whenever necessary. If this is done with a finished rivet in place, it will usually fall out.

BOLT HEADS

Making a head from an upset end is suitable for many purposes. If the head has to be very large in relation to the diameter of the rod, upsetting sufficiently without distorting the rod below the head can be very difficult or impossible. Making a bolt head is a case where standard size to fit a wrench calls for quite a lot of metal on the end of a rod. The distance across the corners of a square or hexagonal head is about twice the diameter of the rod. With the thickness needed to make a parallel head of sufficient depth, much more metal has to be built up than for a rivet head.

The alternative way of making a bolt head is to wrap and weld a strip of metal around the end of the rod. Of course, this is circular, and enough steel has to be used so that you can hammer the material into a square or hexagon that can be made to match a wrench. Before the days of standardized screws and heads, a smith made bolt heads and then made wrenches to match. It is better now to make heads to the accepted standards for the particular diameter.

Strip steel, of the correct width for the depth of the bolt head and of enough thickness to allow for the build-up needed,

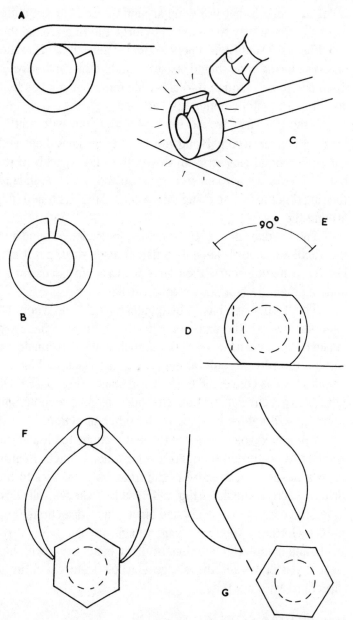

Fig. 6-4. A bolt head can be made by welding a strip around a rod: (A) forge the ring around the rod; (B) estimate the gap; (C) hammer around the strip and over the ends; (D) the opposite side is flattened; (E) convert to square in stages; (F) set calipers; (G) obtain the correct size.

is cut to a length that will wrap around the rod but not quite meet. The best way to do this is to forge the ring around the rod (Fig. 6-4A) until it is almost a circle. Then saw and file the end. The facing ends should be fairly flat, but the gap between them has to be estimated to allow for them being stretched and drawn together under the hammer (Fig. 6-4B).

Wrap the strip around the end of the rod, with a little welding flux between. Bring the head to welding heat and hammer around the strip and over the ends quickly (Fig. 6-4C). The effect is to stretch the strip and weld the ends of the ring together. In so doing, this will weld the tightened ring around the rod.

The head, at this stage, should be reasonably round and the shoulder under it should be flat. If necessary, put it in a heading plate or a hole of the right size in a scrap piece of steel and hammer the head down to get it flat.

The head shape has to be obtained freehand. When the hammer is used, the side opposite that hit is also flattened against the anvil (Fig. 6-4D). A square head is made by turning the rod through 90 degrees at intervals so that the circular head is converted to square in stages (Fig. 6-4E). Do not try to get the flats on opposite sides in one direction right down to size before working in the other direction.

For a hexagon, there are three directions to hit and the rod has to be turned 60 degrees at a time. It might help to draw a hexagon of the size required and set calipers to the distance across the flats (Fig. 6-4F) so that checks will show when the correct size is obtained in all three directions (Fig. 6-4G). Getting a regular hexagon might involve several re-heats and hammering sessions. Follow hammering with hits over a flatter to get the surfaces true. Then check in all directions with a wrench.

MAKING NAILS

At one time, all nails were made by smiths—one at a time. Specialist smiths did nothing else and had tools to speed production and allow the maximum convenience. But even then output was quite slow and nails comparatively valuable. Old woodwork was burned so the nails could be salvaged.

There probably will be no need now to make individual nails, except for use in reproduction work when the appearance of a typically handmade head would lend authenticity.

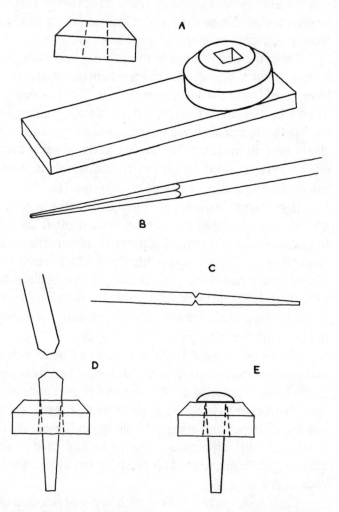

Fig. 6-5. A nail head is made on a rod with a square heading tool: (A) a square tapered punch; (B) draw out a square taper; (C) nick the steel at opposite sides; (D) place the rod in the heading tool; (E) hammer into the head shape.

Nearly all handmade nails were tapered and square. A farrier might still use tapered nails to match the tapered pritchel holes in a horseshoe. For nailmaking, a heading tool with a square hole might have to be made. This is similar to that for round rod, except that the hole should be made with a square punch, followed by a tapered square punch or drift (Fig. 6-5A). Since most nails are comparatively small, the heading tool should be extended at one side to act as a handle when positioning over the pritchel hole.

Taper the end of a rod to the size nail you want, with a little extra for the head. The rod need not be square, but the taper should be drawn out square (Fig. 6-5B). The size has to suit the heading tool. The tapered part should go through for the length the nail shaft will be, but should stop with enough above to form the head. Try the nail in the heading tool and mark where it should be cut off. Nick the steel at opposite sides with the hardie at this point (Fig. 6-5C).

Heat the rod in the fire and put the nail in the heading tool so that the unwanted rod can be broken off (Fig. 6-5D). Immediately use the remaining part to hammer into the head shape (Fig. 6-5E). A round heading tool with a raised center allows easier hammering, particularly if the head is to be patterned. It should be possible to break off and make a head in one heating. If a small nail has to be reheated, it should be held carefully or it might be lost in the fire.

There are several traditional forms of handmade nails and some examples are shown (Fig. 6-6). There is not much scope for decoration of the visible parts of the heads of small nails, but larger nails can be given various patterns. Doors of castles, churches and other old buildings in Europe are often decorated with large nails with ornamental heads. Similar ideas might be applied to bolt heads or the knobs that keep rods in place.

Clout nails today are those with larger heads than usual. The name comes from the hits or clouts that the smith gave nail heads to decorate them. A common arrangement is three

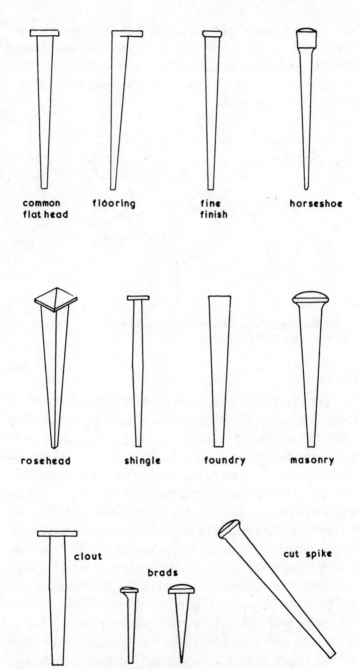

common flat head   flooring   fine finish   horseshoe

rosehead   shingle   foundry   masonry

clout   brads   cut spike

Fig.6-6. Handmade nails differ mainly in the shapes of their heads.

115

or four clouts around a broad head (Fig. 6-7A), possibly with another flat at the center (Fig. 6-7B) to take the driving blows. A variation was a pattern of rounded dents made with a ball peen hammer (Fig. 6-7C). Any of these nails can be described as rose heads.

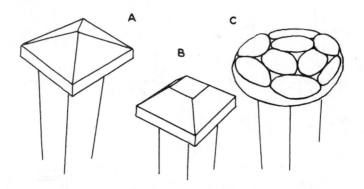

Fig. 6-7. Nail heads can be patterned to provide decoration: (A) broad head; (B) flat center; (C) rounded with dents.

WELDS

The method of joining two bars by welding, described in Chapter 5, covers the basic method of making a blacksmith's weld. Other welding situations require similar treatments adapted to the particular circumstances. It is always necessary to get just the right heat in a clean fire, the surfaces have to be prepared the right shape, there has to be freedom from scale and flux has to be used. A beginner should master a weld between two bars so that he appreciates what is involved and can get a satisfactory result. However, the weld between two separate pieces brings the need for a helper. A weld between two parts of the same piece of iron or steel allows holding with one hand and hitting with the other. It is also easier to keep the joining surfaces in the correct relation to each other.

An example is a welded eye. For something like a poker handle, where there is no appreciable load on the eye, it is sufficient to merely bend the rod around without any firm joint being made between the end and the main part of the rod. However, if the eye is to come under strain, the end should be welded. This happens in making a lifting hook for the end of a chain. When properly welded, both sides of the eye should be of equal strength. Although it is possible to weld the end of a circular eye, it is easier and better for resisting a load if the sides of the eye meet at an acute angle (Fig. 6-8A).

Prepare the end by upsetting it and giving it a scarfed shape with a rounded surface as would be needed for an end-to-end weld (Fig. 6-8B). The round section of the main part of the shaft where the weld will be made is already of a suitable shape.

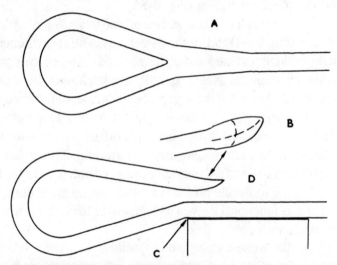

Fig. 6-8. An eye can be welded on the end of a bar: (A) sides of the eye meet at an acute angle; (B) scarfed shape; (C) bend the rod back over the edge of an anvil.

Allow enough length to go round the loop and bend the rod back over the edge of the face of the anvil (Fig. 6-8C). Form the eye so that the part to be welded comes in the right place (Fig. 6-8D) and the loop has taken the correct shape— although there can be final correction after welding.

Bring the steel to welding heat and position the joint on the edge of the face of the anvil with the end upwards. Hit first at the center of the weld, then at the thin edge and finally at the thicker part of the joint. Turn the rod about so more blows can come around the edges and shape the welded parts into a whole. There should be a neat taper from the eye into the rod. This hammering will probably distort the eye, so a further heat might be needed to allow the curve to be trued over the beak and flattened the other way on the face.

A development of the welded eye is a two-pronged poker. This can be of use at the forge or at the domestic hearth. The handled end could be another welded loop or it could be made into a more decorative shape. The two prongs are shaped and pointed so that one can be used for pushing and the other for pulling (Fig. 6-9A).

Make a welded loop of sufficient size to allow for cutting through (Fig. 6-9B) and for the longer part to be straightened. Bend the long part back out of the way and draw out the point on the short piece. Next, curve it to a hook over the beak (Fig. 6-9C). Draw out the long piece and shape that. Although a straight end might be functional, a curve will look better. This curve could be carried back in a double sweep into the main shaft. Although long tapers look graceful, if the poker is to get much use and if the will becomes red hot, it is better to avoid going to needle points. The ends will be more durable and just as functional if given long tapers to thick ends, which are made into obtuse points.

Similar welds can be used to make forks. A welded eye can be cut at its head and the two sides straightened and pointed. Alternatively, one piece with its prepared end can be held against the other and welded. In both cases the prongs have to be shaped and pointed. Such a small fork can be used for toasting bread in front of the fire or dealing with meat at a barbecue (Fig. 6-9D). A larger one could be used to throw bales of hay.

Faggot Weld

Another weld in one piece of rod is a faggot weld. It is used as an alternative to upsetting in order to thicken an end.

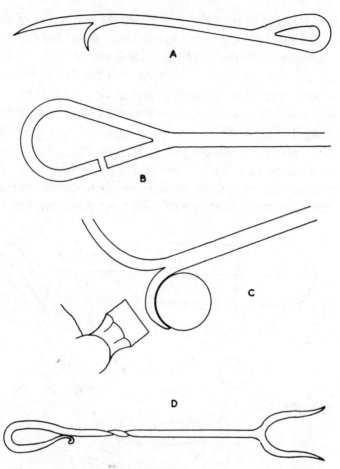

Fig. 6-9. Cut a welded eye (A,B,C) to make a hooked poker or fork (D).

It would be better than upsetting for a place where thickening has to be taken for a greater length than could be conveniently upset. Although the method puts the thickening to one side, this can be forged to bring it central after the weld has been made.

If the rod to be faggot welded is round, there is no need for much preparation of the end and it is folded back and welded (Fig. 6-10A). If the cross-section is flat, the surfaces that will meet in the fold should be given a curved cross-section (Fig. 6-10B) by grinding, filing or hammering.

It might be possible to fold back the end and weld all in one heating, but it is easier in two steps. Bend and fold back the amount to be dealt with. Sprinkle flux in the joint and along the edges as the piece is returned to the fire to bring to welding heat. Tap off any dirt and quickly position the end with the fold upwards on the face of the anvil and hammer along it (Fig. 6-10C). Turn it on edge and true the sides. Concentrate on making a good weld at this stage. Any shaping can be done with a further heating. For a very large thickening in relation to the bar section, it is possible to fold the end over again and make another weld with the further overlap.

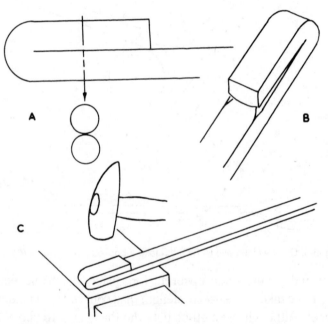

Fig. 6-10. A faggot weld (A) thickens a bar which has been doubled back (B,C).

Angular Welds

If bars have to be joined other than end-to-end, their preparation is mainly an adaption of scarfs to that method. For a right-angled corner, the ends are forged so that the scarfs project on to the other piece (Fig. 6-11A). Get the meeting surfaces slightly domed, so that the first hit at the center drives out scale, impurities and flux. This means quickly positioning the parts and hitting over the corner, to be quickly followed by hits at the thin edges on top and the work turned over for hits on the thin edges at the other side. The right-angle will have to be observed by eye as the parts are brought together, but slight correction is possible after a further heating.

Another variation comes with a T-joint. The piece that is to have its end against the other can be upset and the scarf formed in the usual way. The body of the other part cannot be upset, but it can be thinned to match the other piece (Fig. 6-11B). Make sure that when the parts come together their centers meet for the first welding hit to be effective. Start welding with the end piece on top, but quickly turn over after a few blows to hammer the other side.

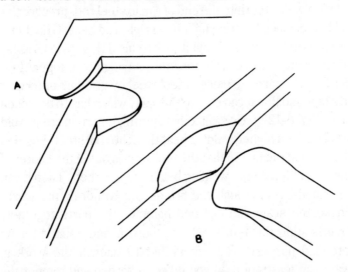

Fig. 6-11. Corners (A) and T-joints (B) in flat frames need special welds.

Many older tools can be found with bodies made of iron and only the cutting edges made of high-carbon steel. This was done for economy since iron was plentiful and steel was not. It was also done to take advantage of the toughness of iron, which is better able to stand up to heavy use. Iron was also easier to work. As iron is now almost unobtainable and it does not possess the characteristics of older iron in any case, there is less urge to weld cutting edges to it. Tools are now more often than not made completely of high-carbon steel. Toughness of the body is taken care of by tempering the edge to cut, while the rest of the tool is made softer.

If tool steel is to be welded to mild steel, it is not arranged as a direct lap, as can be done between two meeting pieces of mild steel. Instead, the tool steel is held between two parts of the mild steel in readiness for welding. Traditional axes and hatchets had their heads made by wrapping iron to form the main part and putting the steel for the cutting edge between the ends of the wrap (Fig. 6-12A). For an end-cutting tool, the steel went into a split end of the iron (Fig. 6-12B).

To weld steel into the end of a mild steel rod, prepare the mild steel piece by bringing it to a bright red heat. Grip it end upwards in the vise and split it with a chisel (Fig. 6-12C) as far as the joint is to be. Hammer the outsides to a taper (Fig. 6-12D). Prepare the piece of tool steel by grinding or forging to a taper so that it can go into the split, which has to be closed on it (Fig. 6-12E). Use a flux that suits high-carbon steel. Mild steel needs a higher welding heat than the tool steel. Position the work in the fire so that the tool steel is out of the center of the fire, at least until welding heat is approached. Then it can be pulled back through the fire as you withdraw the work. Shake the scale and dirt and hammer the parts together. Overheating the tool steel may burn it and spoil it for its intended purpose. Remember not to quench the work in water, at least not until you do so to harden and temper the tool. Forge or grind the tool shape so the outline blends the two steels together.

CHAIN MAKING

Chains have been made by blacksmiths for a very long time. They were needed in agriculture for traces and for use

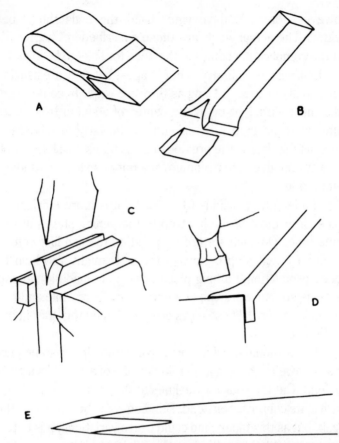

Fig. 6-12. Axes and other cutting tools can be made by welding high carbon steel into iron or mild steel: (A) the cutting edge is between the ends of the wrap; (B) split end of the iron; (C) split with a chisel; (D) hammer; (E) grind or forge to a taper.

with implements. They were also needed at sea for anchoring. Castle drawbridges and many other articles of war and defense were operated by chains. Chains for various purposes vary between quite delicate pieces to those with links each of considerable size and weight. For practice, it is easier to work with links of moderate size, possibly made from three-eighths inch rod and of 6 inch to 8 inch circumference.

For some simple decorative purposes, chain links can merely be bent so that the ends meet and are not welded.

However, for all load-carrying chains the ends should be welded. The actual welds are those described in Chapter 5, but the complication comes in the need for links to be joined.

Links can be round or other shapes, but they are usually oval and about twice as long as they are wide. In some large links the weld might be in the center of a sidem It is more common to arrange it at an end, particularly in moderate sizes, as that keeps the previous link as far as possible out of the way and gives the maximum amount of space for welding hammering.

If a length of chain is to be made, it is more efficient to make all or most of the links up to the joining stages at the same time. Do each step of preparation to each link before moving to next step on any of them. It might also help to speed production if a long piece of chain is made in several sections so that work can be done on one part while another part is in the fire. These parts are then linked together in the final stages.

Links should be of uniform size, although for some purposes there might be a larger link or one of a special shape at the end. Cut the rods for the links to the same lengths. Bend each at its center for one end. Bending could be done over the beak, but as this tapers and could cause variations, it is better to use a rod held in the vise (Fig. 6-13A).

Prepare the two ends by hammering them to the usual scarf shapes (Fig. 6-13B) while they are straight. Do not taper excessively thin or the link might finish thinner at the weld and you might have difficulty in completing the weld as the edges lose heat rapidly. Complete the shaping of the link around the rod in the vise. If this is not the first link, hook the previous one in while there is still space (Fig. 6-13C).

Holding is best done with tongs locked on at the end of a link furthest from the weld and arranged so that a previous link is kept away from the heat and cannot slip around when the chain is brought to the anvil. The work is comparatively light and will quickly heat, but the same considerations have

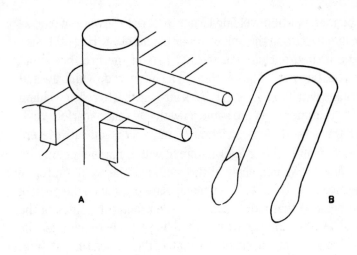

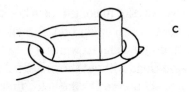

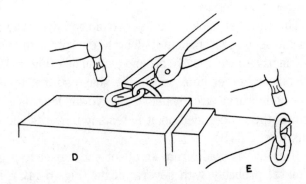

Fig. 6-13. Chain links have their ends prepared and welded: (A) hold the rod in a vise; (B) hammer to shape; (C) hook; (D) hammer on top of the face; (E) match the opposite end.

to be met as when welding larger material. Beware of oxidizing due to putting the link too near the air blast. Have the part to be heated enclosed in the hot part of the fire, but avoid overheating earlier links. Heat to a cherry red, withdraw and sprinkle with flux. Then put back into the fire to reach welding heat. Hammering is the same as with any other scarfed weld, but there is some restriction of movement due to the enclosed shape. Use a light hammer with a narrow peen. Get the first blows in quickly at the center of the weld, on top of the face (Fig. 6-13D). Then manipulate the link on the point of the beak so that blows can be made around the sides of the weld. At the same heat, it should be possible to hammer the welded end into a shape to match the opposite end (Fig. 6-13E).

CHAIN HOOK

There are two ways of making a chain hook. The eye can be welded or made from an upset end. A hook is normally of stouter section than the chain to which it is attached since it has to take the same load without the benefit of a closed loop. If made of the same section rod as the links, there is a risk that it might begin to straighten under a strain that would not affect the links. If all the loads likely to be taken are much less that this, the hook could be made of rod nearer the size of the links and given a welded eye.

The simplest hook is made of round rod that maintains the same section throughout its length, except for the point. This can have a welded eye around a chain link (Fig. 6-14A). In this or any other hook, make the shape so that the load comes in the curve directly below the eye and there is a good length of the open-ended point extending upwards and outwards (Fig. 6-14B).

If an eye is made from an upset end, upset to a good thickness, probably with several heats (Fig. 6-14C), until there is enough metal built up for a thicker part to be hammered (Fig. 6-14D). Such a hook is best made with the

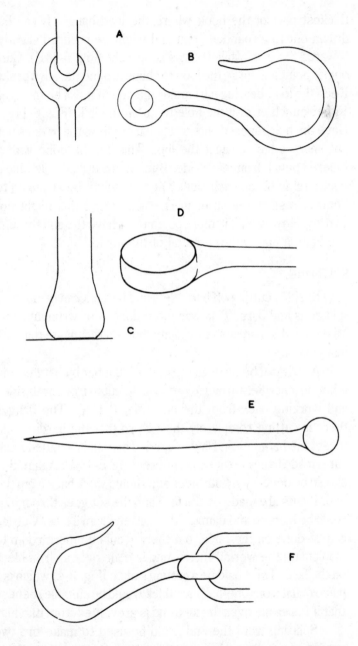

Fig. 6-14. Hooks have welded eyes (A) and are shaped for a direct pull (B): (C) upset to a good thickness; (D) hammer the thicker part; (E) draw out to a point; (F) punch or drill a hole to link.

thickest part of the hook where the load hangs. It can be drawn out to a rounded point and might be reduced slightly towards the eye, while the rod is straight (Fig. 6-14E). Curl out its point and forge the loop to shape around the anvil beak. Keep the load-bearing part under the end that will be the eye. Either punch or drill the hole to go on the link (Fig. 6-14F). Have the hole tapered outward to each side so that it does not put sharp edges against the link. This can be done with a tapered punch from each side. But if it is a drilled hole, use a countersink bit on each side. The hole might be arranged to come across the hook or in line with it and this might not matter. However, it is more common to have the link through the hole in line with the metal of the hook.

SPLITTING

Besides cutting off bars, sets and hardies can be used to split rods and bars. This was often done with wrought iron. Mild steel does not split as readily, but is a technique that has many uses.

A split can be made in the end of a flat bar by hammering it hot on a hardie, turning over so as to cut in from both sides and working back from the end (Fig. 6-15A). The danger there is cutting completely through so that the hardie edge meets the hammer and is damaged. The risk is avoided if the cut is made from above with a hot set (Fig. 6-15B). Again, this should be done from both sides and should work back from the end. If cuts are made on the face and the set goes through, it could be blunted and damage the hardened anvil face. Cutting can be done on the table, but there would be more room to manipulate the work if the cutting is done over an iron block on the face. This could be a cutting saddle (Fig. 3-4) which is a piece of flat iron (one-half inch thick would be suitable) bent so that it fits easily over the face and is prevented from moving.

Splitting from the end could be used to make the two prongs of a fork, instead of welding two rods together. After the parts have been split, they are forged separately to

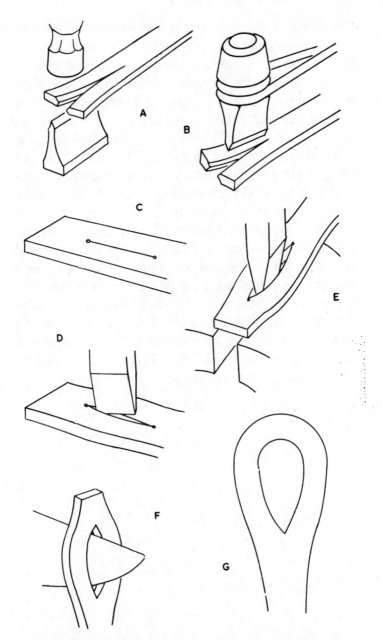

Fig. 6-15. Bar can be split (A) and the cut part (B) forged to shape: (C) the split is marked by small punched holes; (D) tilt the set into each hole; (E) drive to force the gap wider; (F) shape over the anvil beak; (G) forge to a curve.

remove the marks of cutting and produce round tapered prongs. A two-pronged poker could have its parts made by splitting, instead of being produced from a welded eye.

Another use of splitting is in forming a long eye in the body of a bar. In this case, the limits of the split are marked by two small punched holes (Fig. 6-15C). Use a hot set along a line between the holes. Tilt the set into each hole first (Fig. 6-15D) and then use it flat on the steel. Do this at both sides until the split goes right through. There might have to be several reheats of a large piece. Cool the set between heats.

When the set has broken through, the steel can be put over the partly-open vise so that the set or a steel wedge can be driven further to force the gap wider (Fig. 6-15E). What is done after that depends on the purpose of the split, but it often has to finish elliptical and this can be shaped over the anvil beak (Fig. 6-15F). The punched holes should stop the split from going further than intended. Their appearance in the finished hole might be acceptable, but it is possible to forge the whole end to a curve (Fig. 6-15G) so that the original form is not apparent.

Handles

7

Much interesting blacksmithing can be done making handles on the end of square or round rods. For most purposes, the rods do not have to be very large section. The work can be done with light equipment, mostly single-handed and without the need for great physical effort. Handles on the ends of domestic hearth tools, garden tools and a multiplicity of other implements can be tackled by a beginner.

Most handles are made on the ends of round rods, usually three-eighths of an inch or one-half inch in diameter. Some might be thicker or thinner, but they have to be related to the capacity of the hand. If the handle is on thin rod it might have to be made sufficiently bulky to provide a secure grip. If the rod is already thick, the handle might finish a little thicker or might be merely a knob or other stop on the end to prevent the hand sliding off. The handle will also have to be related to the use of the implement. If it is for picking up with a grasp, it must be long enough and shaped to be a reasonable fit in the palm of the hand. If it is a tool that has to be thrust, the end of the handle must be shaped so the palm can push efficiently and comfortably. Many handled tools have to hang when they are out of use, so the handle might be looped or have a hole through it. Quite often, the handle will not be heavily loaded and almost any shape would suit its use. In that case, decoration might be more important than the utilitarian shape.

Some of the handles take on a special interest if they are made from square, octagonal or other sectioned rod. The complete handle can be formed in the same way round rod is use, and most of the designs intended for round material will look and handle satisfactorily in other sections. Another way of using angular-sectioned rod is to forge all or part of the handle to round section.

Forging handles or anything else gives the blacksmith a chance to express his artistic intentions. There is a great satisfaction to be had from working red hot steel into a shape that pleases you. However, the results you get may not always be as satisfying as you expected. There are just a few artistic rules that might help you. Observe them and you have made a start. After that you are on your own.

Curved lines are generally more acceptable than straight ones. Some tools and other things you make will have to have straight parts. But sometimes a long sweeping curve would do just as well. The poker (Fig. 6-9) is an example of a double curve that looks better than just a straight rod. Even when the main part of the shaft has to be straight, there can be curves in the handle. It might be off-center or asymmetrical to give a more interesting shape than a uniformly symmetrical shape. Much depends on the intended use. A simple symmetrical loop handle might be more suitable for the purpose if all you are making is a tool for use in the garden. Squares look better if tilted to form diamonds (Fig. 7-1A) and are improved if made longer one way (Fig. 7-1B). A simple symmetrical square is not as artistically acceptable as a rectangle. Even that is not as good as a shape with curves in it.

The preference for a curve over a straight line may come in tapering. If a long taper is drawn out to make a scrolled handle, it could take a straight taper (Fig. 7-1C), but it would

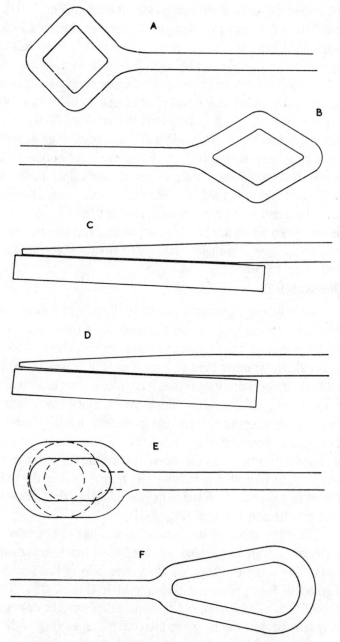

Fig. 7-1. Handles can be made into a number of shapes: (A) diamond; (B) drawn out diamond; (C) straight taper; (D) curved taper; (E) ellipse; (F) oval.

look better if it had a slight curve along the taper (Fig. 7-1D). Usually a hollow along the length of the taper does not look right, but it can come towards the end if that is to be rolled back or otherwise shaped tightly.

Circles are not as pleasing as ellipses or ovals. Circles are sometimes necessary, but if an ellipse would serve the purpose as well, it will usually look better (Fig. 7-1E). Because of the need to blend into a shaft, an oval (egg shape) might look even better (Fig. 7-1F) as the basic outline of a handle. Bear in mind the use of the tool. An ellipse makes a comfortable thing to hold in your palm of your hand. If there has to be a thrust, a pronounced oval with a thick knob end is better. Even when the handle is for lifting, the ellipse might look better if given a slight tendency to an oval shape with its thicker part toward the end.

LOOP HANDLES

Some examples of variations on the basic loop handle will show how appearance can be changed while the handle remains functional. The ordinary loop is a circle centrally placed on the shaft, whether bent to butt against it or welded (Fig. 7-2A). It can be made longer than it is wide, so that it becomes an ellipse (Fig. 7-2B). This should give a more comfortable grip, but might not be regarded as having much artistic merit. If the shape is converted to an oval (Fig. 7-2C) there is no loss of function and most people would regard the appearance as better. A further step is to bring the narrow end of the oval almost to a point, which is a help in welding, so that shape is both artistic and practical (Fig. 7-2D).

All of these shapes are symmetrical. They can be moved partly or entirely to the side without loss of function in many tools. The shaft can then go along one side of the handle, instead of being directed centrally at it (Fig. 7-2E). The almost conical oval need not have its sides straight or regularly curved, but can be given attractive shapes (Fig. 7-2F).

Much shaping of looped handles has to be done with a hammer over the beak of the anvil. Be careful to do most of

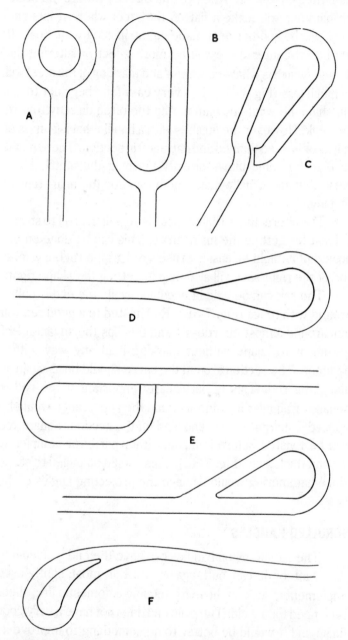

Fig. 7-2. Handles can be formed to suit special purposes or for decoration: (A) loop; (B) ellipse; (C) oval; (D) oval brought almost to a point; (E) a shaft along one side of the handle; (F) almost conical oval.

the hitting off-center. When you hit directly toward the beak, the hammer will make a flat on the steel where it hits and there will be another dent made on the inside by the beak. If you hit off-center there will be more effect on altering the shape—which is what you want—and marking of the steel will be much less (Fig. 7-3A). It is very easy for a beginner to get the shape he wants by hammering too often directly toward the beak. However, he finishes with a handle that is a mass of marks or is even thinned and flattened in section. There might have to be some blows directly pinching the metal. Keep these few and usually make them taps for the final steps in shaping.

The alternative to hammering is to pull the rod to shape, at least for getting the main curve. This can be done on the beak, but it might be easier to use a rod gripped in the vise. A rod of the right size will also help in getting the shape right.

The rod can be held in one hand while the end is pulled around with tongs (Fig. 7-3B). Rod heated to a good red will pull around almost effortlessly and this has the advantage of getting it to shape without marking it in any way with a hammer. The section around the curve should be as clean as along the rod. This is particularly important if the rod is square or angular in some way and the appearance would be spoiled if sharpness was knocked off the section. Square rod can be twisted before bending, either partly or completely around the handle (Fig. 7-3C). This should be pulled to shape since hammering would damage the projecting angles of the twist.

SCROLLED HANDLES

The variations on handles can have the end welded into the shaft or it can butt against it. For most lightly-used implements, such as those for tending a domestic fire, there is no need for a weld. The plain end does not have a very good finish and it would be better to do something to improve its appearance. One way is to taper the rod and provide a small

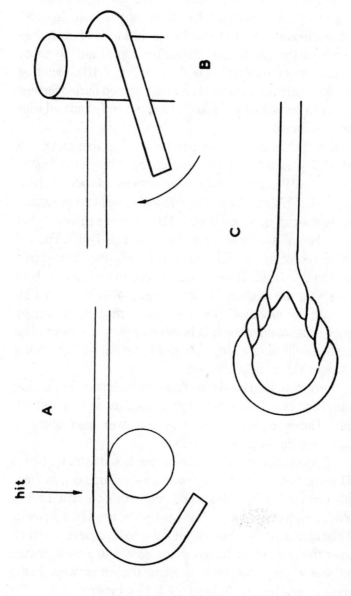

hit →

A

B

C

Fig. 7-3. A more advanced handle includes twists: (A) hit off center; (B) pull the end; (C) square rod can be twisted.

scroll or pigtail on the end (Fig. 7-4A).

This has to be done before shaping the handle. Draw out the end for the amount needed to make the pigtail and far enough to come almost to the crown of the loop. In most handles it looks better to keep the full thickness of the rod up one side of the handle and across the top. Taper to about one-quarter of the thickness of the rod (Fig. 7-4B). Tapering to a point could result in the end being burned during further work and a point does not usually look as good as an end with some thickness.

Heat the end for a short distance. The thin metal will heat quickly, so be careful of overheating. Bring it to a yellow heat and hold it over the edge of the anvil face so you can hit it (Fig. 7-4C). Hit mostly at the end and it will curl inwards.

As the curl develops (Fig. 7-4D), continue to hit on what is now the end so that more metal curls (Fig. 7-4E). You will have to reheat as you make progress since the thinned part will soon lose heat. The curl might have to be trued by light hits against the edge of the anvil (Fig. 7-4F), but do not hit heavily in this direction. Best progress is made in shaping by using a light hammer and light blows on yellow-hot metal. The end should finish as a fairly tight helix, but not so close that it no longer shows light through.

Forge the loop handle to shape by hammering or pulling around and close it so the scroll is outward and against the shaft. The scroll end is effective whatever basic shape is chosen for the loop (Fig. 7-4G).

If decorative ironwork is examined, some of the twists and twirls in gates and other examples will be seen to finish with pigtails, as just described, but others might have a broadened, flattened end. This can also be used on a poker or similar handle. It does not matter if the rod is square or round. Taper the end, but instead of going almost to a point, flatten and spread one way while thinning the other way. For a handle, it is advisable to keep the flat part narrow unless the twist will come outside the grip. This will roll narrow (Fig.

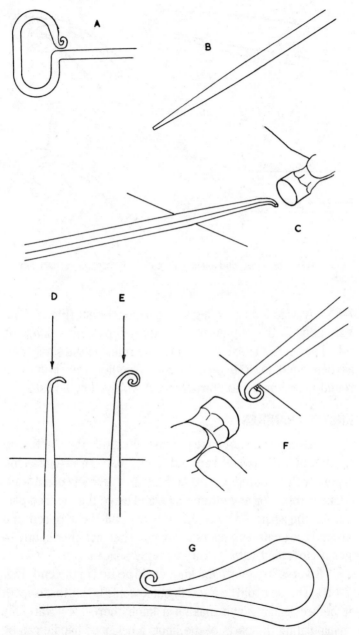

Fig. 7-4. A drawn out end can be turned into a scroll to decorate a handle: (A) small scroll; (B) taper; (C) heat and hit the edge; (D,E,F) continue to curl; (G) forge the loop handle.

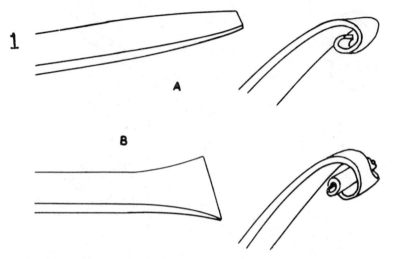

Fig. 7-5. By flattening (A) and altering the outline (B), different scrolls can be made.

7-5A). A widened end will give a different effect (Fig. 7-1B). Variations in the outline of the flattened part give different rolled patterns. These ends can all be rolled in the same way as described for the pointed rod. Another way is to use round-nosed pliers to start the curl with yellow-hot steel.

KNOTTED HANDLES

The end does not have to finish alongside the shaft. One treatment has it twisted around (Fig. 7-6A). Draw out a long taper for the twisted part, then form an eye in the usual way. Make it round or any other shape and leave the tapered part across the shaft. With another heat, pull the tapered end around the shaft with pliers or tongs. Then hammer lightly to get it close and with its turns evenly spaced.

An ordinary overhand knot could be tied in the end (Fig. 7-6B). The tip could be a scroll, but it would be better to upset it before shaping and making a knob there . By carefully manipulating the parts of the knot, a balanced handle can be formed. To get it to center more naturally, a figure-eight knot is more symmetrical. Turn an eye in the rod (Fig. 7-6C) with enough end left to complete the knot. Then pull the end through the eye after going around the shaft to the other side (Fig. 7-6D). The rod could finish with an upset knob or be tapered and made into a small eye (Fig. 7-6E).

UPSET HANDLE

If thickening the handle would produce a handle large enough to grip, the rod can be upset for a sufficient length and this part shaped to provide a grip. Alternatively, thicker material can be used and the shaft swaged down from it. A piece of one-half inch or seven-sixteenth of an inch rod could be upset enough to make a handle with the greatest diameter about three-fourths of an inch.

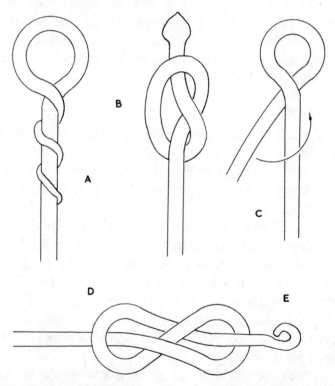

Fig. 7-6. Twists and knots make different handles: (A) twist around; (B) a tied overhand knot; (C) an eye in the knot; (D) pull the end through; (E) upset knob with small eye.

Make the handle before forging any other part of the rod. Heat the end and upset it first by spreading the extreme part (Fig. 7-7A). Wpen this has spread, heat further back so more of the rod gets bigger (Fig. 7-7B). Do this in stages until the length of the handle is built up. From this point on, heat to red and forge the handle to the shape required. It could be round, but it looks attractive and gives a firmer grip if there are flats on it. Most are simply arranged by forming an octagonal section.

Forge to the general outline first, usually with a mainly oval side view with a knob at the end (Fig. 7-7C). The knob can be separated by using narrow fullers to lightly tap in the groove while the work is rotated between blows. Upsetting will have provided the taper towards the shaft. When the shape is satisfactory in a round section, use the hammer lightly with the poker over the face of the anvil. First hammer flats in a square pattern, then hammer the corners to make an octagon (Fig. 7-7D).

CAGE HANDLE

A handle that looks like a spiral cage has the advantage of remaining cool as well as being an attractive decoration (Fig. 7-8A). Since making it involves welding, the work would be easier in iron than in steel. The handle and shaft are separate parts welded together.

The handle itself is made of six pieces of identical rods. Three-sixteenth of an inch diameter would be suitable. They could be 5 inches long. Pieces about 1 inch long are put between their ends so that they can be tied together with iron wire in a regular hexagonal section (Fig. 7-8B). Weld each end in turn while holding the other end with hollow-bit tongs. Remove the binding wire. The ends will be slightly smaller, due to hammering (Fig. 7-8C).

Upset one end of the handle enough to allow a welding scarf to be made. Do the same with the rod that is to be the shaft and weld the handle to it. Roll collars from three-fourth

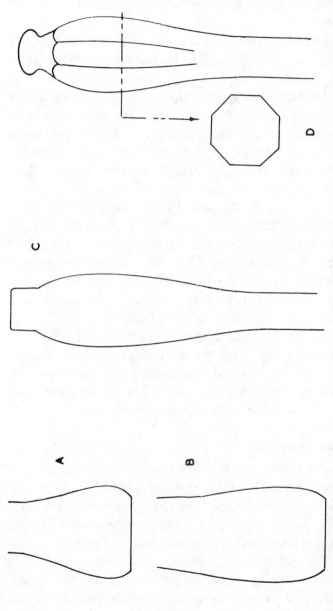

Fig. 7-7. An upset end and can be forged into an octagonal handle: (A) heat and spread the extreme part; (B) heat and enlarge; (C) forge to the general outline; (D) make an octagon.

inch by three-sixteenth inch strip and fit them over the ends of the handle (Fig. 7-8D). Weld them on. That completes the welding and further steps are aimed at forging the handle to shape.

The collar looks best if formed into a knob. Heat the end to bright red and shape this be hammering around the edges of the collar while rolling it on the anvil (Fig. 7-8E).

The twist is made mainly in the upper half of the length of the rods. Heat evenly from the end knob to within about 1 inch of the lower collar. When ready, quickly grip the shaft in the vise and use tongs or a pipe wrench on the knob to twist the handle (Fig. 7-8F). Give enough twists to make a close screw-like shape with the rods tightly touching.

Heat again for the same length. Quickly put the shaft back in the vise and use the wrench the other way on the knob to unwind partially, while at the same time tapping with a hammer on the knob (Fig. 7-8G). This will open the cage and spread the parts. It is unlikely that they will form a perfect shape first time, but after a further heating pliers can be used to get all the rods into a balanced form.

The bottom collar could be left as it is or decorated by filing grooves around it. An interesting variation is to introduce a ball into the cage by forcing two rods apart to let it in, then bring them back to the pattern. The ball should be larger than any gaps, but loose enough to move about.

ADDED HANDLES

The handle does not have to be one with the shaft and need not be steel. If it is a tool that will get hot, there is an advantage in the insulation from heat provided by a wooden handle. Brass, copper and plastics can be used to provide color and brightness in contrast to the dull plain steel.

For a wooden handle, the end of the shaft can be finished as a spike or tang, usually square, even if the rod is round. Teeth could be raised by cutting into the spike with a cold chisel (Fig. 7-9A) to give the maximum grip. The best handle

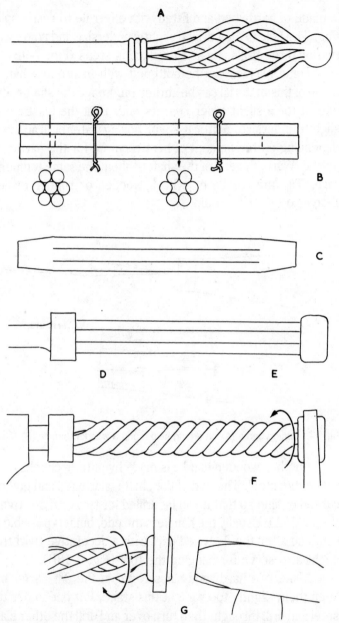

Fig. 7-8. A cage handle is built up from rods and welded to a shaft: (A) spiral cage; (B) rods wired together; (C) ends are hammered slightly smaller; (D) fit roll collars over the ends of the handle; (E) form the top collar into a knob; (F) twist the handle; (G) place in a vise and unwind slightly while tapping with a hammer.

is made of hardwood and fitted with a ferrule to resist splitting. The hole is then drilled slightly undersize and made with
two or three drills, so as to reduce in steps (Fig. 7-9B).

Some plastics can be softened with heat and a handle
made of this material can be shrunk on. Leave the shaft round
except for a slight taper near its end. Drill the plastic only
slightly undersize. Soften it—with boiling water or in an oven,
depending on the amount of heat required for the particular
plastic. Warm the end of the shaft to about the same temperature. Tap the handle on with a wooden or rubber mallet.
Leave to set and shrink.

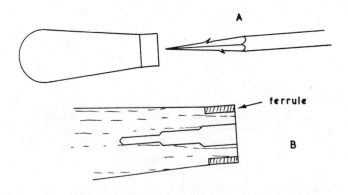

Fig. 7-9. Cutting barbs (A) on a tang help it grip a wooden handle (B).

Another wooden handle is made by putting cheeks each
side of the steel. The end of the shaft is flattened and given a
curved outline so that it can be drilled for two or more rivets
(Fig. 7-10A). Usually the handle is the end, but it is possible to
continue after the flattened part with a decorative twirl that
might also serve for hanging the tool (Fig. 7-10B).

Make two hardwood slabs to fit on the flat parts, but
keep them slightly too wide at this stage. Put one under the
steel and drill through, then turn over and drill the other slab.
The rivets could be brass or copper and with countersunk
heads. They need not be prepared rivets, but they can be rod,
hammered on alternate sides until they fill the hollows in the

wood (Fig. 7-10C). When the wooden sides are secure, file the wood and the edges of the flattened steel to give an elliptical cross-section and a neatly rounded handle (Fig. 7-10D). Remove file marks with abrasive paper and finish the wood with varnish.

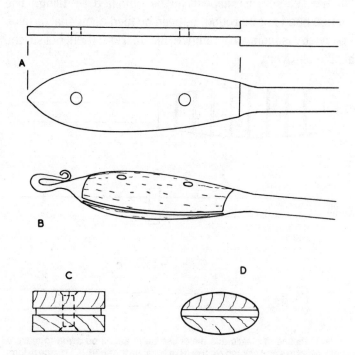

Fig. 7-10. A flattened part can have wooden cheeks to make a handle: (A) shaft end; (B) decorative twirl; (C) rod can be used to fill hollows; (D) file to get a rounded handle.

Another form of handle has discs of many sorts of material threaded on the shaft. Brass washers can be used to alternate with colored plastics (Fig. 7-11A).

A collar can be welded around the shaft to mark the limit of the handle (Fig. 7-11B). Another way of limiting the discs is to swage down the shaft slightly so as to provide a shoulder (Fig. 7-11C). At the other end, cut a thread to take a nut that will be shaped to match the other parts of the handle (Fig. 7-11D).

Build up the length of the handle with metal plastic. Tighten the nut at the end, lightly rivetting the end of the shaft to prevent the nut from loosening. What is done to the handle depends on the facilities available. If the job can be mounted in a lathe, it can be turned to an elliptical or other outline. Otherwise, similar shapes can be obtained by filing. The section need not be round, but can be filed octagonal or oval. Follow by sanding to remove file marks, then polish the handle all over.

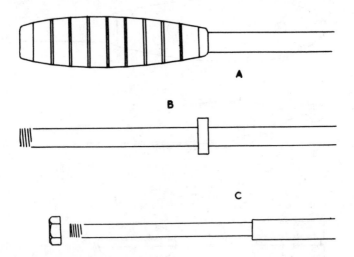

Fig. 7-11. Pieces of plastic and metal can be threaded on a rod to make a handle: (A) brass and colored plastic; (B) a collar on the shaft; (C) swage to form a shoulder.

A similar idea can be used with a wood or plastic rod handle that is drilled through the middle. It could be turned before or after fitting or it might be carved to make a head. In that case, the nut should be sunk below the surface of the wood.

Handles of other metals can be turned or cast and then attached to their shafts, usually by screwing. A brass or bronze handle on a steel shaft looks attractive. There should be enough screwed length to make a firm joint and keep the handle and shaft in line. On a three-eighth inch shaft, the

148

threaded part should be at least three-fourths of an inch. In the other part, make the hole deeper than that to give clearance for the screwing tap and to allow all of the thread on the rod to disappear when the handle is fitted. This also ensures a tight joint (Fig. 7-12). If the handle is turned, the hole can be drilled in the lathe to make sure it is in line. If it is a cast patterned handle, have the flat end center-punched where the hole is to come. Make sure the flat end is level when the handle is held in a vise under a drill press.

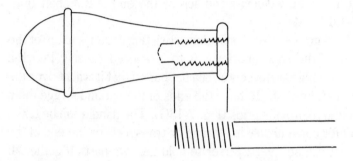

Fig. 7-12. Screwing is a good way to attach a handle made from another metal.

CROSS HANDLES

If a handle is required to provide leverage to twist the shaft with much force it has to be across the line from the shaft. A simple traditional way of arranging this is to forge the end of the shaft into a long flattened point (Fig. 7-13A) which can be driven into a hole in a wooden cross handle. The point could go completely through, so a small washer would allow it to be rivetted (Fig. 7-13B). The twisting action puts a splitting action on the shaft in the wood. With suitable hardwood of sufficient size, the handle should survive this.

A better arrangement encloses the wood in the iron so that there is no tendency to split. This necessitates making an eye at the end of the shaft so that the wood can be pushed through. If there is much load anticipated, the eye should be welded.

149

It is difficult to weld a full circle and it is better to make an oval eye first and bring it to round after welding. Flatten enough of the end to make the eye (Fig. 7-13C). Prepare its extremity for welding. Bend the eye and position the end on the shaft. Prepare it with flux and weld it (Fig. 7-13D). Having made a good joint, forge the eye round on the anvil beak or a mandrel so that a round piece of wood can pass through (Fig. 7-13E).

An iron rod or tube could be put through the eye instead of the wooden rod. A more permanent T- haped handle might be made be welding a rod across the end of the shaft (Fig. 7-13F).

Another way of providing a twisting action is to upset the end of the shaft and forge it to a tapered square. Punch a square hole at the center of a flat bar so that it will fit over the end of the shaft. Reduce the ends of the bar and swage them round to provide grips (Fig. 7-13G). The handle can be taken off for convenience in storage or transport, or the end of the shaft can be ivetted over to hold the two parts together. If the tool is for lifting, as when the shaft forms a hook, the cross handle should be rivetted or welded on.

RING HANDLES

Another type of handle is a swinging ring that can be used as a drawer pull or a heavier version could be a door knocker. An oval version could be used as a lifting handle on the end of a chest. There are many ways of decorating the handle and its backplate and only a few are suggested here. Similar things can become hitching rings, mooring points or lashing anchorages.

For basic handle or ring bolt, without decoration, a length of rod can be made into a circle and provided with a pivot. One way of making a true circle is to have a rod of the internal size ready, then heat a long piece of rod for the ring and grip its end and the pattern rod in a vise. The hot steel can be pulled around to more than a complete circle (Fig. 7-14A).

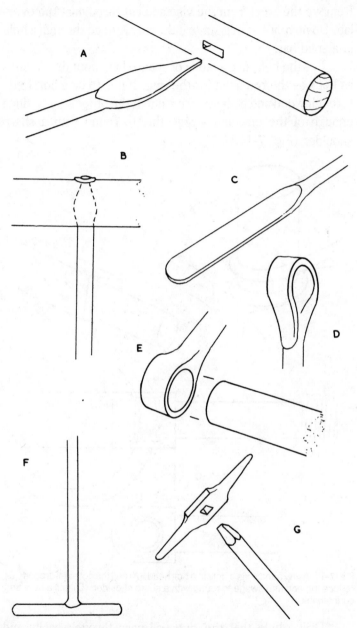

Fig. 7-13. If a tool has to be turned, the attachment to the handle must resist torque: (A) a long flattened point; (B) rivet with a small washer; (C) the eye; (D) weld; (E) forge the eye; (F) weld a T-shaped handle; (G) reduce and swage the ends of the bar.

Remove the steel from the vise and cut through at the overlap. Do no more at this stage if the ring is to go through a hole in a solid bar.

For the bolt, use a piece of square bar about three times as thick as the rod used for the ring. If it is to be a bolt to go through wood and be held with a nut at the other side, reduce enough of the end and swage this to round with a sharp shoulder (Fig. 7-14B).

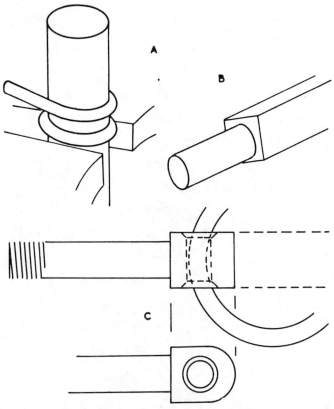

Fig. 7-14. A ring handle fits a hole in a bolt head: (A) pull the hot steel around; (B) reduce the end and swage to round with a sharp shoulder; (C) drill a hole and countersink.

Drill a hole that the ring will pass through easily and countersink both sides (Fig. 7-14C). Cut off the surplus bar and file the end that remains rounded. Pass the ring through

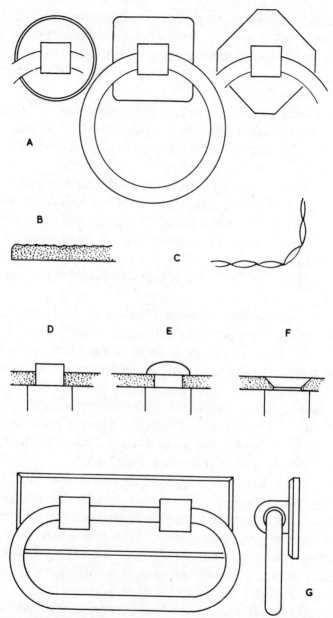

Fig. 7-15. Shaped backplates decorate ring handles: (A) circle, square or diamond flat plate; (B) hammered surface; (C) hammered edges; (D) a tenon; (E) rivet on the surface; (F) a countersunk rivet; (G) two supports for an oval backplate.

153

the hole and prepare its ends for welding in the same way as dealing with chain links. Make the weld and true the joint by hammer if possible, but if necessary, file the weld to the same section as the rest of the ring so that it will move through the hole without catching.

Cut a thread for a sufficient distance on the end of the bolt and provide it with a nut and large washer. There can be another washer under the bolt head to prevent it pulling into wood, or a decorative piece as described below.

If the assembly has to mount on the surface instead of going completely through, there has to be a backplate to take the screws. It could be a plain circle, square or diamond of flat plate, with edges and corners rounded or bevelled (Fig. 7-15A). The surface could be hammered all over with a ball peen hammer (Fig. 7-15B) or edges only could be hammered (Fig. 7-15C).

Make a tenon on the end of the square rod, long enough to go through the backplate and far enough for rivetting (Fig. 7-15D). Keep the tenon as large as can conveniently be ar anged, while leaving enough of the square part for a shoulder. If the wood to which the handle is to be attached can be hollowed, the stronger rivet head is made on the surface (Fig. 7-15E). If it has to be kept flush, the rivet must be countersunk (Fig. 7-15F). For an oval handle, there can be two supports on a longer backplate (Fig. 7-15G).

For a drawer, door, box handle or a door knocker, the ring and the backplate should be decorated. The ring looks better if it is tapered so that the hanging part is thicker than the part entering the support. If the handle is to be used for lifting or dragging a heavy weight, the handle should have its ends welded. For most purposes, it is sufficient for the ring ends to go into the support without meeting.

Even with a tapered and decorated ring, it is easier and with less risk of damage to pull the hot steel around a rod of the correct diameter than to hammer it to shape over the beak of the anvil. Leave some surplus length—maybe a few inches at each end—so one end can be gripped in the vise and the other end pulled around with tongs.

If the ring is made from round rod, draw out both ends (Fig. 7-16A). This need not be much—three-eighths of an inch rod could taper to about one-fourth of an inch. There could be some filed decoration each side of the center (Fig.

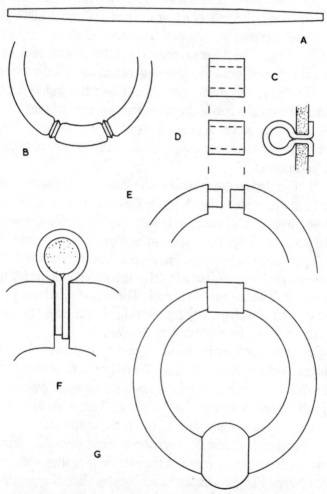

Fig. 7-16. Rings can be decorated in many ways and can be supported by clips: (A) draw out both ends; (B) filed decoration; (C) rivetted support; (D) a clip from sheet metal; (E) cut overlapping ends and file pins; (F) squeeze in a vise; (G) finished door knocker.

7-16B). Heat the rod and pull it to shape in the vise so the ends overlap.

There could be a bolt or rivetted support (Fig. 7-16C) or it might be sufficient to form a clip from sheet metal (Fig. 7-16D). For tapered three-eighth inch rod it should be about one sixteenth of an inch thick.

Cut the overlapping ends of the rings and file pins on the ends to go into the hole of a bolt or small enough to allow the sheet metal clip to be wrapped between the shoulders (Fig. 7-16E). To get the pins into place, heat the central thick part of the ring to redness and squeeze gently at the sides in a vise.

If a clip is used, it will probably not need heating. It can be bent cold around a rod of the same diameter as the pins, then the projecting ends squeezed together in the vise (Fig. 7-16F). Allow sufficient length of the ends to spread behind the backplate.

If the ring is to be used as a door knocker, it is better with a knob at the center (Fig. 7-16G). This is a piece of steel with a hole through it. If the hole is very slightly undersize when both parts are cold, the knob can be shrunk on. Prepare the knob and heat it to redness. Put it over the pritchel hole of the anvil or a partly open vise and drive the straight piece for the ring into it. Then shape the handle. The knob might have to be filed or it can be shaped by hammering after fitting. Hammer marks on it can be regarded as decoration.

Square bar can be used to make rings with twisted centers, either one twist (Fig. 7-17A) or a reversed twist (Fig. 7-17B). There could be a knob with a square punched hole arranged between the twists or just a striker (Fig. 7-17C) welded or held with a pin on the underside.

The twist should be done first, then the ends drawn down so that they are round at the parts where they enter the bolt or clip. File pins in the same way as with the previous rings.

The backplate can be any shape, but it will look best if it is symmetrical about the hanging ring (Fig. 7-18). It could be a

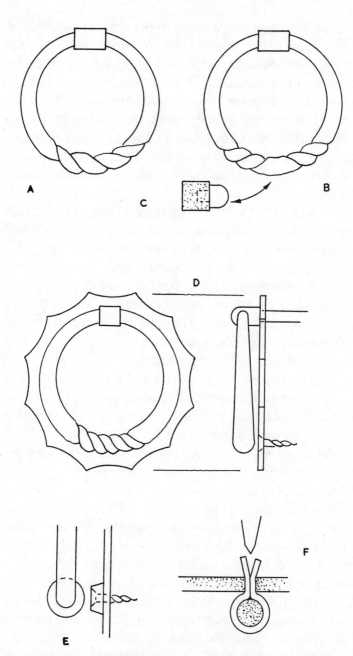

Fig. 7-17. Twists are appropriate decorations for handles and knockers: (A) one twist; (B) reverse twist; (C) a striker; (D) filed edges; (E) strike plate; (F) open the clip with a chisel.

157

circle with hammered treatment on the surface or edges. The edges could be file (Fig. 7-17D). Whatever the shape, the attachment comes near the top and there have to be holes for screws. If the attachment is a bolt going right through the wood, there need only be one wood screw located at the bottom where it will be hidden by the hanging handle. If it is a door knocker, the screw could go through a raised block to serve as a striker plate (Fig. 7-17E). If the wood screws have to hold the handle in place, there should be at least three holes for screws.

A bolt or rivet will go through a round drilled hole, but the clip will need a punched slot. A tool might have to be forged for this. Since the slot is small and the metal thin, the punch can be quite light. Assemble the parts and support the curve of the clip on something softer than the anvil face. A lead block is best, but a piece of hardwood will do. These support without much risk of marking or distorting the clip. Use a cold chisel to open the ends of the clip (Fig. 7-17F), then flatten the opened ends by direct hammering.

An interesting decorative feature for the backplate is to dome its center (Fig. 7-19A). There has to be a flat rim for the bolt and wood screws, but the center is raised to a moderate curve. If the plate is one-sixteenth of an inch or less, doming can be done cold. Use the ball peen hammer to make a slight hollow in a block of lead or in the end grain of a piece of hardwood. Hole the backplate over this, with its front downward and use the hammer on it (Fig. 7-19B). Work from the center, pulling the metal around between blows that are given in increasing circles. Tilt the work as necessary (Fig. 7-19C).

If the backplate is thicker, the work has to be done in a similar way. But the steel must be made red hot. This makes lead or wood unsuitable for supporting. Instead, use a hole in a swage block or one drilled in a piece of scrap iron. It does not have to be very large, but should be bigger than the diameter of the ball peen (Fig. 7-19D). Countersinking the hole helps to soften the edge, but there will be some marking of the hot metal.

Fig. 7-18. A twisted ring handle swings over a hammered backplate.

Hammering the front can remove the marks, but whether thin cold or thicker hot steel has been used, the front can be decorated by planishing. The hollowed part has to be supported on a stake, whicp is a rod with a rounded top of less

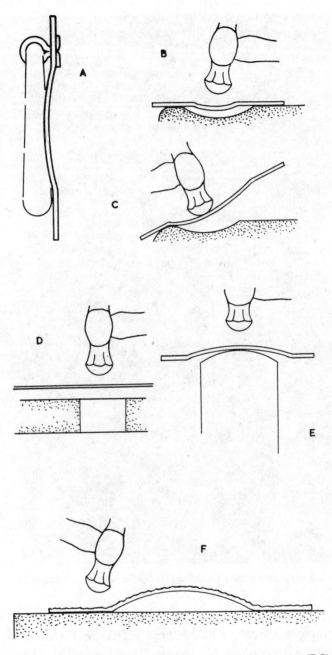

Fig. 17-9. A domed backplate can match a ring handle. (A) domed center; (B,C) hammer over the backplate; (D) use a swage block; (E,F) hammer to shape.

curvature than that of the backplate (Fig. 7-19E). Stakes of this sort are made for sheet metalwork. But there is no need for one of these since the end of a rod ground to an approximate curve will be good enough. Use a ball peen hammer directly over the top of the stake so as to pinch the metal at each blow and move the plate about until the whole front surface is covered with overlapping dents from the hammer (Fig. 7-19F). When the flat rim is reached, the work can continue on the anvil face or any other flat surface.

Easy Tools To Make

It makes a good introduction to toolmaking to form such things as punches, chisels and spikes with steel bar. Success is fairly easy to achieve and the products are useful tools that will serve their purpose at least as good as any bought from a tool store. In the process of learning to forge high carbon steel, a beginner blacksmith can, at the same time, add to his stock of tools for working in wood as well as various metals.

There are minor variations between tool steels and you might have to be some experimenting to get a tool hardened and tempered to you liking. Table 5-1 gives a guide to oxide colors that can be expected to give the correct temper for a particular purpose. Variations would only be slightly up or down in any case. The way you heat the steel is probably more important. It should not remain in the fire any longer than necessary. When it has reached the correct heat, withdraw it and work on it. If the steel is left to "soak" in the fire, the surface becomes decarbonized and a soft skin is formed. This can be quite thin. but it means that after heat treatment the outer surface might not be as hard and tough as the steel below the surface.

There is an old blacksmith's couplet that emphasises the point:

> He that will a good edge win
> Must forge thick and grind thin.

To allow for some softening of the skin, a tool should be forged so that what will eventually be the cutting edge is thicker than eventually needed and some of it has to be ground away to get the size required. In doing this, any decarbonized surface will be removed. What is left will have its full proportion of carbon and should be as hard as required. When working on a tool that will be finished to a point or a thin edge, hammering should not be taken too far. The edge should be left thick, so it has to be finished to size by grinding. About one-eighth of an inch should be enough.

One cause of decarbonizing is exposure to air while heating. Do not put the steel to heat on or near the top of the fire. Let there be fire above and below the steel. Thrust the steel into the heart of fire. Beware of putting it too near the tuyere where the blast might direct air on to the steel. Hardening and tempering are best kept apart from forging. Even if the final work on the steel leaves it with enough heat for hardening, it is unwise to go straight into hardening. There is a risk that the internal stresses set up in forging might cause cracking or distortion when suddenly cooled. It is better to normalize the steel by heating to a cherry red and leave it to cool slowly with the fire or in ashes or sand.

The tool is then as placid as it is likely to be and as soft as it can be. This is the stage where it is better to file, drill or do any other hand work and to grind or polish it. If the operative part is ground, there need not be a cutting edge yet. The taper towards the end should be bright so that the tempering colors will be easy to distinquish later. For an attractive finish, follow grinding with rubbing with abrasive paper and buffing with a rotating mop, if possible. The brightness will disappear with hardening, but it is easy to restore if it was first there.

Trying to brighten unpolished steel after hardening is an almost impossible task. Hardening and tempering have previously been described and for end-cutting tools the process is straightforward.

Steel of almost any section can be made into a tool. For a tool to be held in your hand like a pencil or held to be hit with a hammer, steel can be round, square, rectangular, hexagonal or octagonal. Square or rectangular bar, with small bevels on the corners, is comfortable and a good shape to resist twisting where that may be an advantage (Fig. 8-1).

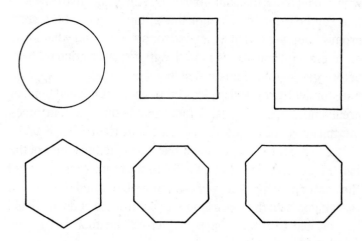

Fig. 8-1. Tools can be made from high carbon steel of several sections.

If the steel to be used has already been made into something and forming a tool from it is a new use, it is always advisable to normalize the steel as the first process. This removes any existing temper and any internal stresses that might have built up during its previous use. This also applies if an old tool has been worn away and there is still enough steel in it to forge a new end. It might be satisfactory to go straight into forging, but to asure quality in the new work, normalize first.

Whenever possible, do the work on the new tool on the end of a bar long enough to hold and do all the work possible before cutting off. Otherwise, make sure you have tongs that will hold and do all the work possible before cutting off. Otherwise, make sure you have tongs that will hold the steel firmly and can be locked on. When you are working on thin tapered sections, if you have not planned ahead it is very easy to lose the heat while trying to get the steel gripped and in position for hammering.

PUNCHES

Center and nail punches can be made in sizes starting with rod no more than one-fourth inch thick and up to any size that can be gripped. The amount of taper has to be a compromise between what is needed for strength and what looks more graceful and allows more length for later grinding back before getting too clumsy. A slender taper might be appropriate for light work and is pleasant to use, but it could bend or break under heavy blows. A taper that is three to four times the thickness of the bar is usually about right (Fig. 8-2A).

Draw out the end to about one-third the thickness of the bar (Fig. 8-2B). There is no need to try to make the point of the center punch by hammering. If possible, grind the taper at this stage. With the extra length to control the ends, it should be possible to rotate the taper across the tool rest of the grinder (Fig. 8-2C).

Cut off the length required. Many punches are too short. Unless it is a very small diameter rod, the length should be 6 inches or more. Cutting can be with a set or hardie, or it might be more convenient to saw through. Bevel the top of the punch all round (Fig. 8-2D) to reduce spreading under hammer blows. Eventually the end will spread and the taper should be ground again. For a small diameter punch, grinding will be all that is needed to shape the top. For thicker rod that is five-eighth of an inch or more, the end can be heated and a bevel hammered all round while the rod is rolled on the anvil face (Fig. 8-2E). There should then be little need for grinding, except to even the shape.

before cutting off. Otherwise, make sure you have tongs that will hold and do all the work possible before cutting off. Otherwise, make sure you have tongs that will hold the steel firmly and can be locked on. When you are working on thin tapered sections, if you have not planned ahead it is very easy to lose the heat while trying to get the steel gripped and in position for hammering.

PUNCHES

Center and nail punches can be made in sizes starting with rod no more than one-fourth inch thick and up to any size that can be gripped. The amount of taper has to be a compromise between what is needed for strength and what looks more graceful and allows more length for later grinding back before getting too clumsy. A slender taper might be appropriate for light work and is pleasant to use, but it could bend or break under heavy blows. A taper that is three to four times the thickness of the bar is usually about right (Fig. 8-2A).

Draw out the end to about one-third the thickness of the bar (Fig. 8-2B). There is no need to try to make the point of the center punch by hammering. If possible, grind the taper at this stage. With the extra length to control the ends, it should be possible to rotate the taper across the tool rest of the grinder (Fig. 8-2C).

Cut off the length required. Many punches are too short. Unless it is a very small diameter rod, the length should be 6 inches or more. Cutting can be with a set or hardie, or it might be more convenient to saw through. Bevel the top of the punch all round (Fig. 8-2D) to reduce spreading under hammer blows. Eventually the end will spread and the taper should be ground again. For a small diameter punch, grinding will be all that is needed to shape the top. For thicker rod that is five-eighth of an inch or more, the end can be heated and a bevel hammered all round while the rod is rolled on the anvil face (Fig. 8-2E). There should then be little need for grinding, except to even the shape.

Easy Tools To Make

8

It makes a good introduction to toolmaking to form such things as punches, chisels and spikes with steel bar. Success is fairly easy to achieve and the products are useful tools that will serve their purpose at least as good as any bought from a tool store. In the process of learning to forge high carbon steel, a beginner blacksmith can, at the same time, add to his stock of tools for working in wood as well as various metals.

There are minor variations between tool steels and you might have to be some experimenting to get a tool hardened and tempered to you liking. Table 5-1 gives a guide to oxide colors that can be expected to give the correct temper for a particular purpose. Variations would only be slightly up or down in any case. The way you heat the steel is probably more important. It should not remain in the fire any longer than necessary. When it has reached the correct heat, withdraw it and work on it. If the steel is left to "soak" in the fire, the surface becomes decarbonized and a soft skin is formed. This can be quite thin. but it means that after heat treatment the outer surface might not be as hard and tough as the steel below the surface.

There is an old blacksmith's couplet that emphasises the point:

He that will a good edge win
Must forge thick and grind thin.

To allow for some softening of the skin, a tool should be forged so that what will eventually be the cutting edge is thicker than eventually needed and some of it has to be ground away to get the size required. In doing this, any decarbonized surface will be removed. What is left will have its full proportion of carbon and should be as hard as required. When working on a tool that will be finished to a point or a thin edge, hammering should not be taken too far. The edge should be left thick, so it has to be finished to size by grinding. About one-eighth of an inch should be enough.

One cause of decarbonizing is exposure to air while heating. Do not put the steel to heat on or near the top of the fire. Let there be fire above and below the steel. Thrust the steel into the heart of fire. Beware of putting it too near the tuyere where the blast might direct air on to the steel. Hardening and tempering are best kept apart from forging. Even if the final work on the steel leaves it with enough heat for hardening, it is unwise to go straight into hardening. There is a risk that the internal stresses set up in forging might cause cracking or distortion when suddenly cooled. It is better to normalize the steel by heating to a cherry red and leave it to cool slowly with the fire or in ashes or sand.

The tool is then as placid as it is likely to be and as soft as it can be. This is the stage where it is better to file, drill or do any other hand work and to grind or polish it. If the operative part is ground, there need not be a cutting edge yet. The taper towards the end should be bright so that the tempering colors will be easy to distinquish later. For an attractive finish, follow grinding with rubbing with abrasive paper and buffing with a rotating mop, if possible. The brightness will disappear with hardening, but it is easy to restore if it was first there.

Trying to brighten unpolished steel after hardening almost impossible task. Hardening and tempering have p ously been described and for end-cutting tools the proce straightforward.

Steel of almost any section can be made into a tool. F tool to be held in your hand like a pencil or held to be hit w hammer, steel can be round, square, rectangular, hexag or octagonal. Square or rectangular bar, with small bevel the corners, is comfortable and a good shape to resist twist where that may be an advantage (Fig. 8-1).

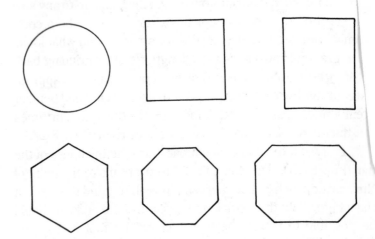

Fig. 8-1. Tools can be made from high carbon steel of several sections.

If the steel to be used has already been made into something and forming a tool from it is a new use, it is always advisable to normalize the steel as the first process. This removes any existing temper and any internal stresses that might have built up during its previous use. This also applies if an old tool has been worn away and there is still enough steel in it to forge a new end. It might be satisfactory to go straight into forging, but to asure quality in the new work, normalize first.

Whenever possible, do the work on the new tool on the end of a bar long enough to hold and do all the work possible

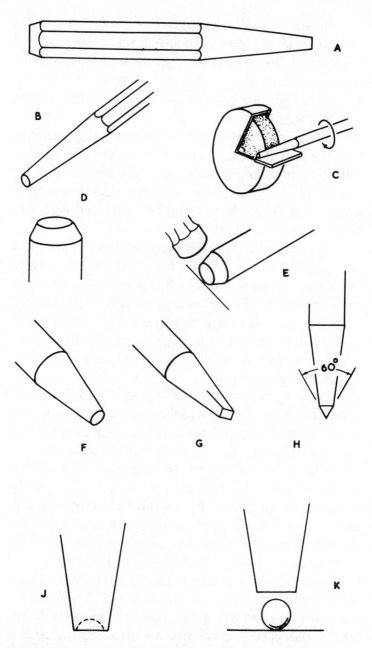

Fig. 8-2. A drawn out rod makes a punch or it can be formed into other tools: (A,B) center punches; (C) grind the taper; (D,E) bevel; (F,G,H) nail punches; (J) hollowed end punch; (K) hot punch driven onto a steel ball bearing.

The top that will be hit should be left soft. Any tool that has to be hit should be soft. Hammer heads are hardened and tempered. If the hammer comes against something else that is hardened and tempered, there is a risk of one or both being damaged. Also, tiny splinters of steel could break off and endanger your eyes.

The working end should be hardened and tempered. Heat the body of the tool for tempering so as to get a slow spread of oxide colors and wide bands of each color. When the correct color is reached at the end, there will be a reasonable length of similar color behind it to allow for sharpening before retempering will be needed.

Nail punches usually have round ends that are ground flat (Fig. 8-2F). For some nails, it is better to forge and grind the end square or rectangular (Fig. 8-2G). Several sizes can be made and similar punches can be used for driving out rivets, hinge pins and other parts through holes. A useful range is from just under one-eighth inch up to one-half inch across the ends by one-sixteenth of an inch steps. Ends can be made to match the sizes of nail heads in regular use.

Center punches are usually ground with 60 degree points (Fig. 8-2H). That angle suits most punches, but it could be slightly more obtuse for regular use on hard materials. A center punch regularly used for copper, aluminum or brass might be more acute. A similar punch used to mark hole centers in wood could be even more acute. It might be necessary to have the end of a center punch for hard materials fairly wide to provide strength, but it is difficult to see the location of the actual point. For general use, the top of the cone should not be more than one-eighth of an inch across.

Some nail punches have a hollow end (Fig. 8-2J). This is supposed to prevent the punch slipping off the nail. It has some advantage when punching pins or headless nails. The end of a red hot punch could be driven on to a steel ball bearing (Fig. 8-2K). It would be easier to control if the end of a round rod was ground to half a sphere and held in the vise for the punch to be hammered on. This will have to be done during forging since there will have to be some truing of the shape around the end.

A longer punch with a slight taper is a drift for pulling holes into line (Fig. 8-3A). When assembling sheet metal parts, the drift goes through holes that should match and is either levered or hit to bring them into line. The tool is made like a nail punch, but care is needed to get the taper gradual. A useful size is made from one-half inch rod with a finished length of 10 inches to 12 inches.

Since the small end has to go into the holes, a set of drifts can be made with ends ranging from one-eighth of an inch to three-eighths of an inch. The handle should only be about one-third of the total length (Fig. 8-3B). As the end does not have to withstand heavy hitting, it is better rounded for comfort in handling.

A pin punch differs from a nail punch in having a parallel part behind the end (Fig. 8-3C). A pin punch can be used for punching nails. However, it is mainly intended for driving out pins, such as are used through hinges, so that the parallel part can follow at least part way through the hole.

Ideally, the parallel part is finished with swages. In the smallest sizes, it might be necessary to forge by eye and get the end to a reasonable cross-section during grinding. Some very fine pin punches, such as those used by watchmakers, are made entirely by grinding. Diameters from one-eighth of an inch and more can be forged and then ground. Do not make the parallel part any longer than necessary. A long slender parallel end could bend and buckle. Let the taper be fairly long and blend into the parallel part with a curve so that there is no sudden change.

Blacksmith's punches are similar to pin punches, only heavier. They can be forged in the same way. Smaller sizes can be hand-held (Fig. 8-3D). Allow enough length of grip for your fist to go around and still leave enough projecting above for hitting without risk of your hand being hit or having to go so low as to be dangerously near the hot steel being punched. For strength, keep the parallel part and the taper short.

For heavier punching, either small holes through thick steel or larger holes through any thickness, it is better for the smith's punch to have a handle. Wrapping a thin rod around is easier to arrange than making a hole for a wooden handle. There is no need for deep grooves. With square bar, the grooves can be across the corners (Fig. 8-3E). With other shapes, there can be a groove all round. This is done with a fuller, either a single over the punch resting on anvil face, or with a pair of fullers if a helper is available as a striker. Have the groove wide enough for the one-fourth inch rod to make a complete round turn (Fig. 8-3F). Above this part, the punch can remain parallel and be tapered only at the top (Fig. 8-3G) or it can be drawn out slightly before making the bevel (Fig. 8-3H).

With punches for many other purposes, the black-smithing part is generally as previously described. The smith who is interested in other crafts can make a stock of punches with blank ends ready to prepare as needed. Many special ends start by being made like nail punches.

Punches to make decorative background patterns are used for leatherwork and repousse work (decorative raised sheet metalwork). The punch can be used in a haphazard pattern all over the background to make an irregular pattern of dots, lines or other shapes. One simple and effective end is made by filing grooves across a round or square end to leave raised points (Fig. 8-4A). Close dots made in the end with a center punch will produce a different pattern (Fig. 8-4B). Alternatively, the end of the punch can be shaped to make a pattern such as a leave or a heart (Fig. 8-4C).

The end can be made broader. Rounding it while keeping it straight across (Fig. 8-4D) allows it to be used to punch a straight border. A variation has a groove filed across it, so that it produces a double straight line (Fig. 8-4E).

The end could be shaped in an arc. For a large sweep, forge the curve first and true it to shape by filing and grinding.

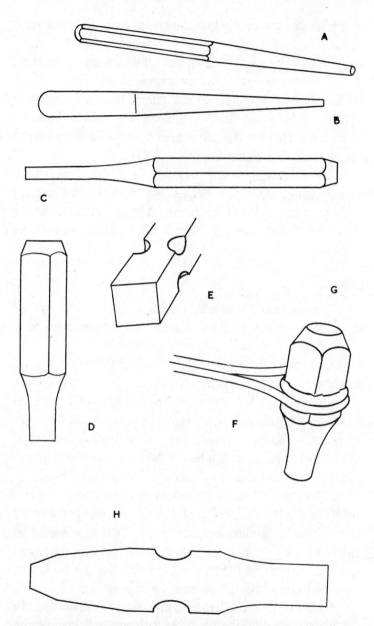

Fig. 8-3. Punches can be held in the hand or arranged to take handles: (A) longer punch with a slight taper; (B) the handle is one-third the length; (C) a pin punch; (D) a hand held punch (E) square bar with grooves; (F) the rod should go completely around; (G) the punch is tapered at the top; (H) draw out slightly before making the bevel.

A smaller arc can be filed on the end of a punch first forged round (Fig. 8-4F). The curved punch can be used to make corners by linking it with lines from the straight punch (Fig. 8-4G) or it can make its own decorative border (Fig. 8-4H) on leather or sheet metal. For a punch to mark complete circles—not just part circles—the end of the punch blank can be drilled. Then the outside is filed to make an even border around the edge of the hole (Fig. 8-4J).

Possible designs are only limited by the maker's ingenuity with a file. S or Z shapes (Fig. 8-4K) can make wavy lines or be intertwined for patterns. A broad punch can have a series of similar hollows (Fig. 8-4L) to make a scalloped border.

SPIKES

Pointed tools are needed for many purposes. In almost all practical activities, there is a use for a plain spike as a simple piece of metal or in a wooden handle.

A marline spike is an example of a plain spike (Fig. 8-5A). It is used for opening rope strands for splicing as well as releasing stubborn knots or arranging the parts of decorative knotting or braiding. For general purposes, it can be made from three-eighths inch diameter rod and finished about 6 inches long. The taper can be the full length or about three-quarters of it and the remainder left parallel (Fig. 8-5B). A full-length taper is usually straight, so it is a simple cone. For the three-quarters taper, the sides of the cone are given a slight curve for a more bulbous shape. That type would be thrust between rope strands until the parallel part was reached, minimizing the risk of the spike slipping back. For more delicate work, the straight taper is better.

Forge the general shape of a marline spike on the end of a rod. Then cut if off (Fig. 8-5C). As with punches, leave some thickness for grinding to a point. A marline spike should finish bright all over, so it should be ground and polished completely before hardening and tempering.

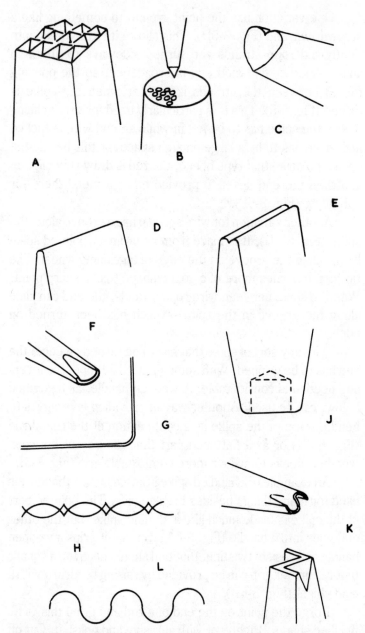

Fig. 8-4. Patterned punches are used for decorative work on many materials: (A) raised points; (B) close dots; (C) heart shaped; (D) rounded; (E) grooved; (F) a small arc; (G) corners; (H) a decorative border; (J) an even border; (K) Z shape; (L) a series of hollows.

One variation has the point ground to something like a screwdriver end (Fig. 8-5D). This allows it to be forced into tightly-laid rope strands and turned sideways to lift them apart. Another flattened end is broadened, so the opening forced between the strands is greater when the spike is turned (Fig. 8-5). This is is particularly used for wire splicing where the spike has to be left in while an end wire is tucked and there has to be a large enough space for this beside the spike. To make that type of end, the rod is drawn out slightly and then the end upset to provide enough metal there for spreading (Fig. 8-5F).

Another variation for wire splicing has a groove along the spike (Fig. 8-5G). It is made from an ordinary pointed spike by grinding the groove on the edge of a grinding wheel. The tip then becomes more of a gouge shape than a sharp point. With the spike between wire rope strands, the end can slide along the groove in the spike—which has been turned on edge.

With any sort of spike that has to be turned on edge, the end has to be gripped. With some tightly-laid rope, the leverage needed is considerable. A wooden handle, as described below, can be used. Another way of providing leverage is to bend the top of the spike as a continuation of the round rod (Fig. 8-5H) or as a flattened part that can be put between wooden cheeks to make a more comfortable grip (Fig. 8-5J).

An example of a handled spike is an ice pick, although it is used for many things besides breaking ice. The pointed part of the spike is made much like a marline spike, but the other end goes into a handle (Fig. 8-6A). So that it grips a wooden handle and resists twisting, that end should be given a square taper. Further grip can be provided by raising teeth in it with a cold chisel (Fig. 8-6B).

Forge the point on the end of a rod and grind this to its finished shape. Brighten it with abrasive and polish it. Cut off with sufficient length to forge the other end to a square point. It need not go to a needle point and the taper need not be very

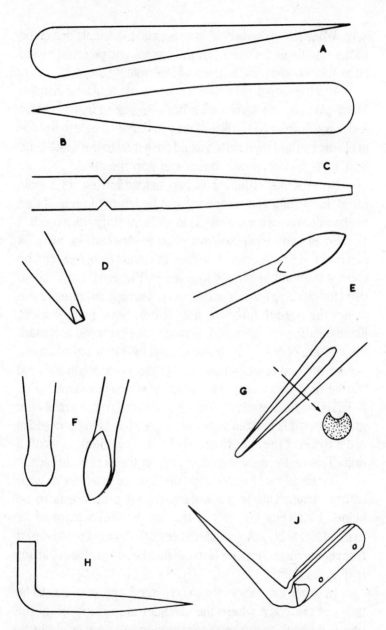

Fig. 8-5. A spike is used for rope splicing and other purposes: (A) marlin spike; (B) taper can be full-length or three-fourths; (C) forge the marlin spike; (D) grind to a screwdriver end; (E) flatten and broaden the other end; (F) draw out and upset; (G) groove the spike; (H) bend the top of the spike; (J) place between wooden cheeks.

long. When the spike is held in a vise and the handle driven on with a slightly undersize hole, the square end pepetrates and grips the wood at the bottom of the hole.

An alternative to a wooden handle is a plastic handle. Many plastics will soften with heat—some in boiling water and some in an oven. Drill a slightly undersized hole in a piece of plastic rod and then soften it and push it on to the spike (Fig. 8-6C). As it cools it will shrink and grip the steel.

If the spike is fully polished before having its handle fitted, hardening and tempering can be left until then so that the handle gives a convenient grip while heating with a torch.

Small handled spikes are used as prickers or awls. A piece of rod one-fourth of an inch in diameter of less can be given a diamond-sectioned long taper (Fig. 8-6D) this can be used for piercing leather and canvas. Turning after pushing in allows the edge to force the hole larger. Small pointed awls, like miniature ice picks, will scratch lines on wood and mark the centers of holes. To make a small hole in wood to start a screw, the end of a tapered piece of three-sixteenth inch rod can be filed to an edge like a sharpened screwdriver (Fig. 8-6E) to make a bradawl. First it is pushed to cut across the grain. Then it is twisted alternate ways while being pressed in order to sever the fibers instead of removing them, as would a drill. This will ensure a better grip on the screw threads.

If a small tool has to be pushed, there is a limit to what can be done. This is particularly true if pressure is to be helped by hitting the end of the handle with a hammer or mallet (Fig. 8-6G). A shoulder is needed to stop the steel part from being forced further into the handle and probaly splitting it (Fig. 8-6F).

In order for a shoulder to be forged, the steel has to be upset at the place where the shoulder is to come. Heat the end as far back as the shoulder position to a very bright heat, then grip in a vise as far back as the shoulder is to come and hammer the end to spread the hot part. More than one heating might be needed to get a sufficient spread.

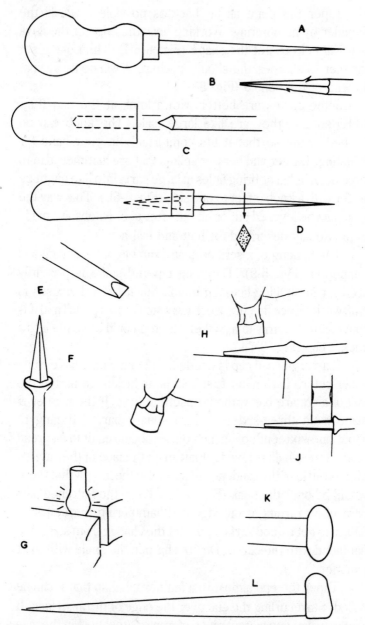

Fig. 8-6. A spike can be a pick or an awl, but if it is to be pushed it needs a shoulder: (A,B,C) one end goes into a handle; (D) diamond-sectioned long taper; (E) bradawl; (F,G) shoulder; (H) work near the anvil face; (J) use a set hammer; (K) spike with a knob; (L) spike with offset knob.

Taper the point as far back as possible towards the shoulder by hammering. Working near the edge of the anvil face will help to get the shape (Fig. 8-6H). Then use a set hammer to sharpen the shoulder where it will come against the end of the handle (Fig. 8-6J).

Some spikes are better with a knob at the end (Fig. 8-6K) so that they are like large nails. The knob can be finished round so that it fits comfortably in your hand for thrusting. Larger and heavier spikes that are hammered in to force open holes or bring holes in large parts into line might be better with a knob offset to one side (Fig. 8-6L). This way the spike can be levered out or hit out after use. Knobs are made as previously described for bolt and nail heads.

The making of a scriber is an example of hardening and tempering (Fig. 5-9). This long tapered spike is primarily used for scratching lines on metal, but it has other uses in craftwork. Since its purpose is very similar to a pencil and it is convenient to carry in a pocket, the top could be made into a pocket clip (Fig. 8-7A).

If a very broad clip is needed, the end would have to be upset before flattening. It should be sufficient to flatten the end of a square bar without upsetting first. If the scriber is made from three-sixteenth inch square bar, fl ttening to about one-sixteenth of an inch thick should result in a spread to about one-half inch wide. Flatten on the face of the anvil so there is little of the tendency to spread in the length that there would be over the beak (Fig. 8-7B). Keep the flattened part parallel by turning it on edge and hammering there. Use a flatter to get a good surface, but let the change from square to flat blend with the curve. Do not sharpen the angle with a set hammer.

Taper the end almost to a feather edge so that it can be rolled. Start curling the end over the edge of the anvil face. If that is worn, use a stout piece of iron or steel held in the vise (Fig. 8-7C). Make about a semicircle in this way, then turn the curl upwards on the anvil and hammer it closed (Fig.

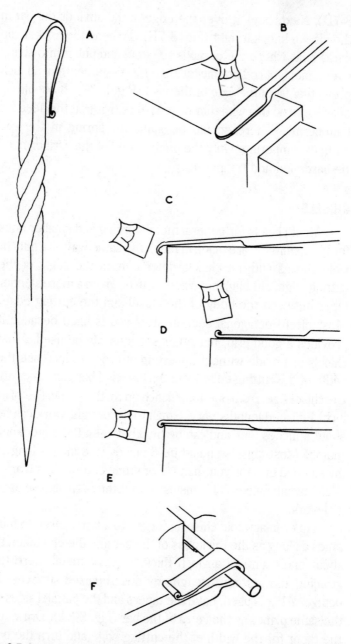

Fig. 8-7. A scriber has its end shaped to make a pocket clip: (A) a finished scriber; (B) flatten on the anvil; (C) curl the end; (D) turn the curl up and close; (E) tighten the curl; (F) bend the pocket clip.

8-7D). Next, hook it over the edge of the anvil or the bar in the vise to knock it tight (Fig. 8-7E). To bend the pocket clip back, heat where the curve is to come and pull it into shape over a piece of rod no thicker than three-sixteenth of an inch projecting from the side of the vise (Fig. 8-7F). It should be possible to do this with thin-nosed pliers, without the need for hammering. There should be sufficient spring in the clip without tempering. Only the pointed end of the scriber need be hardened and tempered.

CHISELS

Most chisels for general metalworking and smaller ones for blacksmithing are made in much the same way as a punch. Cold chisels and hot chisels differ only in the angle of the cutting edge, although hot chisels can be given a more slender taper between the body of the chisel and the cutting edge. Most often, octagonal section steel rod is used because it provides a good grip, but other sections can be used. Most chisels are made without upsetting in order to increase the width of the cutting edge. The thickness of bar can vary with the chisel size, from one-fourth inch up to three-fourths of an inch. Finished lengths vary. Small tools for light work can be about 4 inches long and can be held between the fingers and thumb. Most chisels should be 6 inches to 8 inches long to give a good grip for your hand. For stone cutting, it is worthwhile having longer cold chisels so that they can also be used as levers.

An ordinary cold chisel is forged to a taper three to four times as long as the thickness of the bar and the end taken to about one-eighth of an inch thick to leave metal there for grinding and getting through any decarbonized surfaces. If octagonal bar is used, have the tapers and the parallel sides in the same planes as the faces of the bar (Fig. 8-8A). Draw out the taper for the width of the cutting edge and turn the bar through 90 degrees to hammer the sides parallel. Leave some metal for grinding, smoothing and polishing. Bevel around the

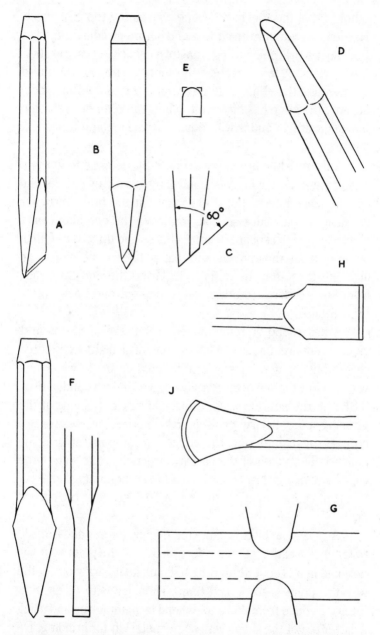

Fig. 8-8. Cold chisels can have their cutting edges shaped in many ways: (A) a standard chisel; (B) a diamond-pointed chisel; (C) a one-point cutter; (D) a round-noised chisel; (E) round one face; (F) a crosscut chisel; (G) draw out and thin a shoulder with fullers.

other end of the tool in the same way as the top of a punch. Harden and temper the cutting end before grinding the edge. For most work, the cutting angle of a cold chisel can be about 60 degrees. A hot chisel can be more acute. Be careful of overheating the edge while grinding. If the tempering oxides appear, the edge has become too hot, the temper of the tool has been drawn and it will require hardening and tempering again.

A diamond-pointed chisel (Fig. 8-8B) is used to get into corners and for making V-shaped grooves. Draw out the end like a square punch, but do not make it too fine. Allow for grinding all four sides so that you leave the end about one-eighth on an inch square in smal chisels and up to one-fourth on an inch for those made with bar between one-half on an inch and three-fourths of an inch. Grind the end diagonally from one corner at 60 degrees to make a one-point cutter (Fig. 8-8C).

A half-round or round-nosed chisel (Fig. 8-8D) is first given a square taper similar to that of a diamond-pointed chisel, but for greater strength it could be made wider one way to allow for one of the narrower faces being rounded (Fig. 8-8E). In the smaller sizes, the rounding can be done at the grinding stage. In larger chisels, take off the sharpness of two corners by hammering to reduce the amount of grinding needed. The width of the narrow direction is the size of the chisel and many chisels can be made for chopping grooves of different widths. Sharpen the end at 60 degrees to the curved face.

A crosscut chisel is expected to chop deeply and is made to taper to a slightly thinner section behind the point so it will not bind in a groove (Fig. 8-8F). To make it, draw out to the size the point is to be and thin a shoulder with ful er (Fig. 8-8G). Reduce from there to the end by hammering and using a flatter to get the shape with some metal left for grinding. Do not thin excessively with the fullers or the chisel will be weak. Grinding the reduction of thickness should only be slight, for the same reason. Providing the cutting edge is a little wider than the steel behind it, that is all the clearance needed. Grind the end from both sides to 60 degrees.

If a chisel is needed with a wide cutting edge, first upset the end of the bar. Then draw down so the width increases and the end can be ground parallel, but wider than the bar (Fig. 8-8H). Cutting edges of special shape might be needed for sheet metalwork. A curved or half-moon end is easily adapted from a wide chisel (Fig. 8-8J).

Woodworking chisels can be made generally similar to cold chisels, for use with a hammer or they can be the more familiar type with wood or plastic handles. The all-metal types are intended for rough work such as chopping through floor boards. The others are more suitable for exact carpentry and cabinetwork. Providing the cutting edge is suitably formed and sharpened, both are capable of good work.

The simplest all-steel woodworking chisel has its cutting edge no wider than the bar it is made from. It can be octagonal, round or square bar. The end is drawn out in much the same way as a cold chisel, but the taper is kept to one side so that a flat back of the cutting edge follows down from one of the faces of the bar (Fig. 8-9A).

So that there is an allowance for grinding, the end should be forged slightly further out and the width should allow for grinding parallel (Fig. 8-9B). The amount of total taper could be rather more than for a cold chisel—about five times the thickness of the bar. Bevel around the other end that will be hammered, in the usual way.

To get a good edge on a woodworking chisel, it is important that the flat side be finished as smooth as possible. Grind it flat and test with a straightedge (Fig. 8-9C). Follow by rubbing on a piece of abrasive paper on a flat surface, then rub flat on an oilstone. For the best edge, start on a coarse oilstone. Then finish on an Arkansas or other fine whetstone.

Keep the tool absolutely flat and use a thin oil while you rub with a circular motion. On the other side of the blade, grind to about 30 degrees and almost to a feather edge. Change to the oilstone and lift the tool slightly (about 35 degrees) to make a sharpening bevel (Fig. 8-9D). When the edge appears sharp, give the back a brief rub on the stone to remove any wire edge (a sliver of steel clinging to a sharp edge). Subsequent sharpening will be on the oilstone until the "sharpening bevel" produced is getting long and regrinding is necessary. Beware of overheating and drawing the temper of the thin edge when grinding. Dip the tool into water frequently.

Letting the end taper back from the edge gives strength, but it is more convenient to use and sharpen a chisel that keeps about the same thickness for a distance from the edge and made so that it steps down from the bar to only a slight taper (Fig. 8-9E). Make this by hollowing with a fuller before drawing out (Fig. 8-9F).

For some work, there is an advantage in cranking the chisel so that your hand can be above a surface while the blade is along it. The amount the tool is cranked need only be enough to give clearance to fingers (Fig. 8-9G). To form the shape, draw out the end as if making a straight chisel, but to a slightly greater length. Make the first bend over the edge of the anvil. Move the chisel to the vise—after another heating if necessary—and put the handle between the jaws with enough projecting to make the second bend. Use a flat piece of steel as a punch to knock over the metal until the end is at the correct angle (Fig. 8-9H). This process is call *joggling*. With this and any other forging of tool steel, never continue to hammer after the steel has become black. Al shaping must be done at a red or greater heat, otherwise damage can be done to the structure of the steel.

Chisel ends can be narrower then the bar, either by tapering to the width or by reducing to a narrow blade. If the edge is to be narrow and is expected to withstand levering to remove wood, it should be finished thicker than it is wide by forging to something like a crosscut cold chisel (Fig. 8-8F) and

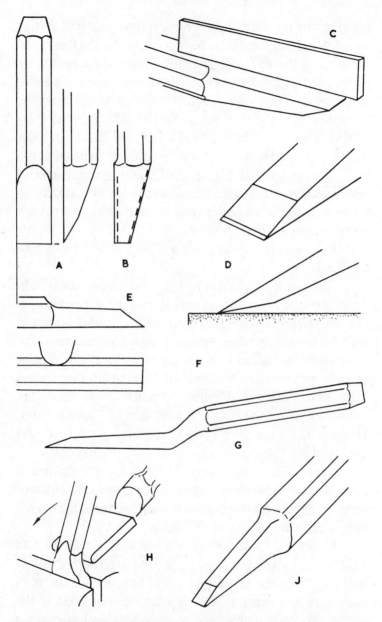

Fig. 8-9. Chisels for wood can be made in much the same way as cold chisels: (A) taper is to one side; (B) make an allowance for grinding; (C) test with a straightedge; (D) make a sharpening bevel; (E) give the bar only a slight taper; (F) hollow with a fuller before drawing out; (G) allow clearance for your fingers; (H) obtain the correct angle; (J) standard cutting edge.

finishing with the usual woodworking cutting edge (Fig. 8-9J).

If the chisel edge is to be wider than the rod it is made from, upset the end with several heatings, if necessary, to give a good bulk to work with. The end can be forged in the same way as a narrower chisel, but with the required width. Some old chisels can be seen with the sides tapered (Fig. 8-10A). This obviously results in a narrower cutting edge as the tool is ground back. It is better to finish with para lel sides, with all faces ground (Fig. 8-10B). Give a slight taper in thickness and let the blade blend into the rod with a curve so that the change of section is gradual and the risk of breakage there is reduced (Fig. 8-10C).

Some woodworking chisels are very wide in relation to the handle.

Although it is possible to forge the blades quite wide after upsetting, there is a limit. If an even wider blade is needed, the process has to be reversed. The work is started with flat steel of the intended width and it is reduced to make the handle. Use fullers to hollow as deeply as can be done at first and then draw out (Fig. 8-10D). Use the fullers again and draw out more (Fig. 8-10E) until the final size is reached. Use the flatter to get the handle to a straight and even section. Hammer and flatten the corners of a square section to make a comfortable grip (Fig. 8-10F).

A very wide chisel is called *bolster*. It could be sharpened in the usual woodworking way or can be given a rather more obtuse angle for cutting bricks. A brick bolster is between 3 inches and 5 inches across the edge.

A mason uses a variety of tools very similar to cold chisels, but for carving stone he prefers to hit with a mallet. The usual thin end of the tool that is intended for the steel surface of a hammer would soon damage the wood of the mallet. To reduce this risk, a mason's chisel is given a rounded knob (Fig. 8-10G). The top should be upset enough to hammer into a suitable shape that is finished on its surface by grinding and polishing.

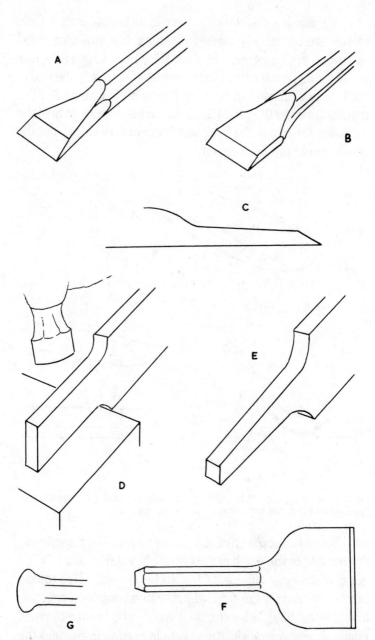

Fig. 8-10. For a wider cutting edge, rod can be widened or wide bar can be reduced: (A) chisel with tapered sides; (B) parallel sides; (C) the blade blends into the rod; (D) draw out; (E) use fullers and draw out more; (F) make a grip; (G) round the grip.

A gouge is a chisel with a curve in its cross-section. Cold chisels are not usually made as gouges, but those for wood and stone can be curved. It is not very easy to get a regular curve for a great length, so it is usual to forge only the end of the tool to a curve (Fig. 8-11A). This is done with a fuller in a matching swage (Fig. 8-11B). It would be possible to hold the tool over the end of the beak and hammer it to shape, but the result would not be as even.

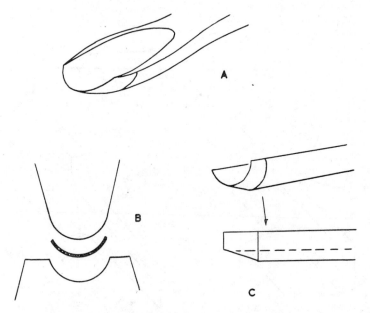

Fig. 8-11. A gouge is made by thinning and hollowing a bar: (A) forge the end; (B) use fuller in a matching swage; (C) the cutting bevel.

There is a problem of grinding a gouge. For most work, the outside of the end has the cutting bevel (Fig. 8-11C). To get a sharp edge the inside has to be smooth. This means careful work on a grinding wheel with a rounded edge, followed by rubbing with a *slip stone* (an oilstone with a rounded edge). For some work, the gouge is ground inside and the outside has to be made smooth. This is easier to do, but a rounded grinding wheel and a slip stone are still needed.

A chisel or gouge that is to fit into a handle is given a tang. For wood turning tools and some light paring chisels, the tang is plain (Fig. 8-12A). For any tool that has to be hit, there must be a bolster or shoulder (Fig. 8-12B) to prevent the tang going further into the handle. This type of chisel can be made from any high carbon steel rod. It is possible to make satisfactory chisels from steel recovered from automobile springs and other sources, but it is also possible to obtain what is described as *ground flat stock*. This is high carbon steel that thas been machined to exact sizes. Since the only forging is at the end remote from the cutting edge, such material can be made into excellent wood chisels that will be true to size and need the minimum work on them.

To form a tang on a length of parallel steel, hollow with fullers and draw out the end (Fig. 8-12C). There is not much need to taper. With thick bar, make the tang square. If it is thin, the section may have to be rectangular. There is no need to taper to a point, but the extreme end can be given a short point like a nail. The handle is drilled almost as far as the tang will go and the tip penetrates the solid wood at the end.

One way of providing some resistance to a plain tang being pushed further in, with a risk of the handle splitting, is to have a piece of tube as a ferrule on the handle and notch this so that the flat part of the tool goes into it (Fig. 8-12D).

If the tang is to be given a bolster, start to draw down the end, but do not make it very thin (Fig. 8-12E). Heat it locally—where the bolster is—to upsetting temperature and grip the end of the tang in a vise so the other part of the tool can be hit (Fig. 8-12F). Upset enough to make the bolster. Hammer this to a reasonable shape on the anvil. Do not try to get a finished shape at this stage.

Draw out the tang beyond the bolster to the usual shape (Fig. 8-12G). Use the flatter or a set hammer close in to the bolster to get it to shape. There must be a flat surface to come against the end of the handle. If necessary, grind or file the bolster and the part of the tool that will be exposed after fitting to a handle.

Tools for woodturning are quite long—the blade length might be 9 inches or more. For general woodworking, the blade should be not more than 6 inches unless it is a slender paring chisel—which could be about 8 inches. Bought woodworking gouges are hollow for most of their length. This can be done with fuller and swage, but it is simpler to only deal with the end—as described for the all-steel gouge. For heavier work on a lathe, this can be an advantage in giving stiffness to the tool.

Handled tools for wood and stone carving can be formed in the way just described for general-purpose chisels and gouges. For delicate work, there is a need for *spade tools*, which have their blades wider than their shafts (Fig. 8-13A). A carver uses a large quantity of these tools, so they can be made in many widths and curves.

To make a carver's spade-ended chisel or gouge, use a piece of round or square steel. Prepare the tang end first. If the bar is thick in relation to the finished tool, it might be sufficient to cut into it to form a shoulder against the tang (Fig. 8-13B). Otherwise it will have to be upset and a bolster made in the usual way.

With thick bar, draw out toward the cutting end, but leave the end thick (Fig. 8-13C). If there is insufficient steel to make a cutting edge as wide as required, upset the end. Otherwise flatten it to a wide fan shape (Fig. 8-13D). It could be ground as a thin flat chisel or it could be rounded to make a gouge (Fig. 8-13E). A carver does not have much use for a straight cutting edge and even flat surfaces are worked with a gouge of shallow curve. The blade could also be curved in its length (Fig. 8-13F). For some work, the shaft is better cranked slightly (Fig. 8-13G).

A carver's *V* or *parting tool* is made like a gouge, except that it has a V-shaped cutting edge (Fig. 8-13H). The usual angles are 60 degrees and 90 degrees. A problem in forging is getting the acute angle. Grind a piece of scrap steel to the angle and have this ready as a stake held in the vise. Hammer

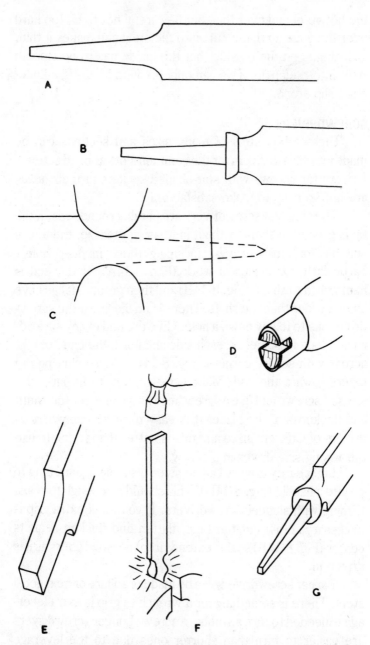

Fig. 8-12. A chisel to be fitted to a handle needs a tang: (A) a plain tang; (B) shoulder; (C) draw out the end; (D) a handle with a ferrule; (E) draw down the end for a bolster; (F) grip in a vise; (G) draw out the tang.

the hot steel end over this, but be careful not to hit too hard over the edge so that it cuts into the steel and makes it thin. Grinding is on the outside, but the inside has to be smooth right into the angle. This can only be done by using a knife-edge slip stone.

SCREWDRIVERS

High-carbon steel of many sizes and sections can be made into screwdrivers for the common slotted-head screws. Drivers for screws with star-shaped sockets in their heads are not so easy to make satisfactorily.

The simplest screwdrivers are parallel round rods. If the tip is ground to shape without increasing the size, the tool is suitable for small screws, including those in deep holes, particularly for electrical work (Fig. 8-14A). If the end is hammered to shape (Fig. 8-14B) and then ground, it can have an end wider than the shaft. There is no binding if the screwdriver has to follow down a hole. Give the end of any screwriver a long flat taper on each side and finish the end straight across with square corners (Fig. 8-14C). Avoid curving the tapers toward the end. Make screwdrivers to fit particular sizes of screws and use a screw head as a gauge for the width and thickness of the blade. It is easy to make many screwdrivers of different sizes and this is better than trying to use the wrong size driver in a screw.

Light screwdrivers can be given a simple square tang to go into a handle (Fig. 8-14D). This should be enough to resist turning with slender screwdrivers. If you think extra grip is necessary, draw out the tang, flatten and thicken near its center (Fig. 8-14E) so this extends into the wood fibers as it is driven in.

Larger screwdrivers can be made of square or hexagonal steel. There is something for a wrench to grip is extra leverage is needed to turn a stubborn screw. Longer screwdrivers are easier to turn than shorter ones due to the leverage gained. If there is not a specific reason for a screwdriver being kept short, make the blades fairly long.

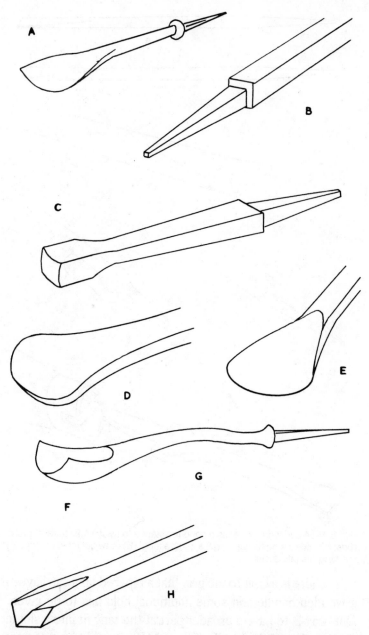

Fig. 8-13. Carving tools for wood are made in many forms: (A) a spade tool; (B) tang; (C) draw out the bar; (D) flatten; (E) grind; (F,G) curve or crank the shaft; (H) a parting tool.

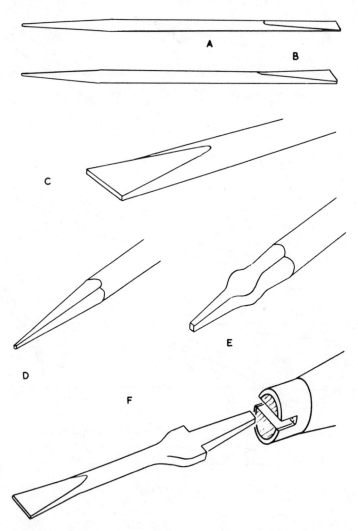

Fig. 8-14. A screwdriver needs a good resistance to twist: (A,B) parallel round rods; (C) give a long flat taper; (D) a square tang; (E) draw out for extra grip; (F) the tang fits into a slot.

There is a limit to the grip that a tapered tang can have in a wooden handle and some additional hold has to be given. One way is to have a broader part at the tang fit into a slot in the ferrule and the handle (Fig. 8-14F). It might be sufficient to flatten the top of the driver, although upsetting could be needed to allow enough metal there. An alternative method is

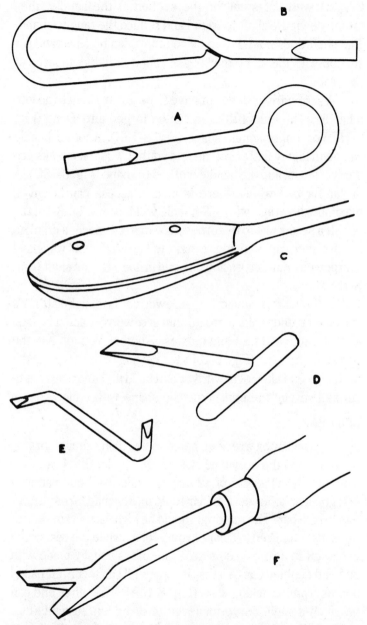

Fig. 8-15. A screwdriver handle must give the hand a good twisting grip. A tool like a split screwdriver is used by an upholsterer for lifting tacks: (A) ring; (B) handle; (C) flattened end; (D) T-handle; (E) a cranked screwdriver; (F) split screwdriver.

to start with flat steel for the section at the handle, then swage down the shaft to round and reduce the tang to shape. The shaft does not have to be round. It can be a rectangular section with the same thickness along it until it is tapered at the blade.

A screwdriver does not have to be given a tang to go into a handle. The end of the rod can be forged into a ring (Fig. 8-15A) or longer handle shape (Fig. 8-15B). Another handle can be made by flattening the end so that wooden cheeks can be rivetted on and the handle worked to shape (Fig. 8-15C). A driver for use where there is limited access can be given maximum leverage with a T-handle welded on (Fig. 8-15D).

If a screw has to be turned in restricted space, a cranked screwdriver can be made. Bend the ends different ways and sharpen one end across and one end in line with the shaft (Fig. 8-15E).

A tool that is similar to a screwdriver is an upholsterer's chisel. The end is like a broad, thin screwdriver and it is used for levering out tacks and staples. Another version has the end split and bent (Fig. 8-15F) for getting under tack heads. Make the end like a screwdriver and bend it. Then use a set to cut and spread the end. True the shape with a file.

CROWBAR

A crowbar or wrecking bar involves doing similar forging operations to the previously mentioned tools. Sizes can vary from an overall length of 12 inches made from one-half inch octagonal or other section bar to 24 inches made from three-fourth inch bar. The material should be high carbon steel, with the ends tempered to a dark brown color, while the rest of the bar is left in an annealed state. The bar is usually made with one end doubled back so that its split end can lever out nailed boards from a packing case (Fig. 8-16A). The other end can be given a slight curve for levering or be left straight (Fig. 8-16B). When kept straight or nearly straight it can be driven like a cold chisel by using a hammer on the other end. If it is curved too much, hammering becomes ineffective.

Forge and grind both ends as if making cold chisels. Split the end that will be bent back and file the slot. Curve the ends over the anvil beak or a stout rod held in the vise. When the shapes are satisfactory, harden and temper the ends. Crowbars can be made with other ends. One end can be pointed instead of having a chisel edge (Fig. 8-16C). The length can be given a dog-leg double curve instead of being left straight. One end can be cranked (Fig. 8-16D) so that the double bend allows the chisel end to be used close into an angle while the body of the tool is levered like an upholsterers chisel. A straight bar can be made like a very long cold chisel, with a straight tapered end and the other end bevelled all round for hammering.

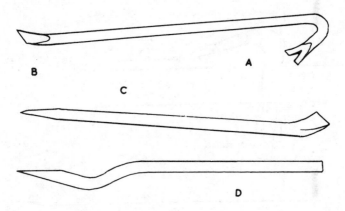

Fig. 8-16. Large tools (A) sharpened like screwdrivers (B) make wrecking bars (C,D).

HOLDFAST

A woodworker can use a holdfast to secure a piece of wood temporarily to the bench (Fig. 8-17A). A blacksmith uses a similar tool to hold a piece of metal on the anvil (Fig. 8-17B). In both cases the holdfast, or hold-down, can be regarded as a third hand when no assistant is available. A woodworking holdfast is usually thicker and larger, but otherwise the two types are made the same.

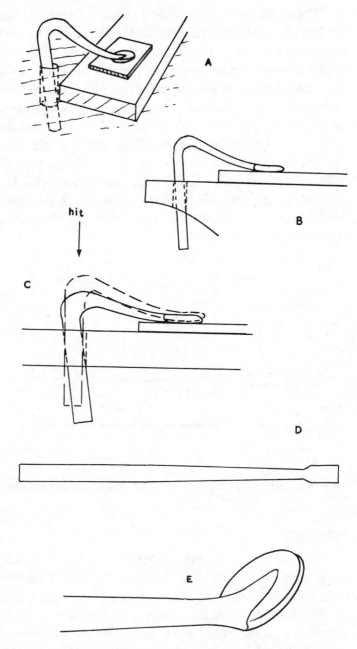

hit

Fig. 8-17. Holdfasts (A,B,C) are used by woodworkers and metalworkers: (D) draw out the end to be shaped; (E) forge the tapered part into a curve.

In principle the holdfast gets its grip by having a loosely-fitting stem through a hole on the bench or the pritchel or hardie hole of the anvil driven down so its angular position grips by friction (Fig. 8-17C). It is released by hitting back from underneath. The thickness that can be held is controlled by the length of the stem. The palm presses down at about the same angle for whatever thickness is being held. The angle the stem takes when hammered tight should be about the same in any position.

Choose a bar of a size that slip easily into the hole. Having it too near the size of the hole prevents it from tilting sideways to get a grip. Usually it is round, even when intended for the square hardie hole, so that it can be swung around to suit the position of the work being held.

Leave the main stem parallel. Draw out the part that will be shaped and leave the end fullsize (Fig. 8-17D). If a very broad palm is wanted, upset this end to increase the amount of metal there. Wood needs a broader pressing surface than can be left for holding steel. Forge the end to a circular or oval shape, but leave final shaping until the holdfast has been curved and tried in position.

Forge the tapered part to a curve and adjust the angle of the palm so that it will press flat when the stem is driven tight (Fig. 8-17E). Grind or file the outline of the palm to an even shape. The face can be flat or given a slight doming to allow for variations in its contact. This should be slight or it will reduce the area of contact too much so that the hold is weakened. For wood, there might be some advantage in filing across the palm to give teeth to bits into the surface. When holding wood is to be worked on, a piece of scrap wood is usually placed between the holdfast and the work so that a finished surface will not be damaged. This can be done with steel on the anvil, with a pad of sheet metal under the palm, but it usually unnecessary.

Hardening and tempering is probably unnecessary since the steel in its annealed state should keep its shape. If it is to be heat treated, temper the curved arm to a spring temper.

Making Blacksmith's Tools

9

A smith has to start with tools bought or made by someone else. With these basic tools you can make others for your use, particularly some of different sizes and patterns. There is always a need for things like swages and fullers in different curves and the variety of tongs possessed might never be enough to satisfy all needs. There are also special tools to suit particular purposes that can not be bought. The basic iron and steel used in tools does not deteriorate to any appreciable extent, so the material in one tool can be used several times to adapt to other tools. Tools that are worn might have sufficient metal left in them to reforge and use again, either as originally intended or for something else that makes use of the available stock. The tools described in this chapter are dealt with as if made from new materials, but many of them could be made from the steel salvaged from something else.

TONGS

Many tongs for general use are by necessity fairly large and heavy. They are about 24 inches long and with jaws of perhaps 1 inch by three-fourths of an inch section. There are uses for lighter tongs. Anyone learning to make tongs will find it easier to start with small ones, about half the size of the normal ones. The method of working is the same, but it is easier to get smaller section steel. Experience gained in this way will be of use when making larger tongs.

Mild steel should be used. High carbon steel might be needed for particular tongs, but for general purposes, mild steel is better. If high carbon steel tongs become red hot and are dipped in water, they will probably become brittle and break.

For small tongs, it is possible to use rod of the size for the handles and upset the part for the jaws. For larger tongs, it is better to start with suitable sectioned steel for the jaws and reduce for the handles. Another way favored by the experienced smith is to make the jaws and short pieces toward the handles from large sectioned steel, then weld on round rod for the handles. The first method is simplest for light duty tongs, but would be unsuitable for tongs with larger sectioned long jaws.

Light Tongs

The two parts of tongs are the same. If there are no tongs to copy, make a fullsize drawing of one part. Trace it and turn the tracing over on the original to see that the parts match and there will be the intended opening. The jaws should finish closed or parallel when the handles are splayed outwards slightly. Suggested sizes for small tongs are shown (Fig. 9-1A). These are made from three-eighth inch round rod.

The hinged part needs to be wider than could be achieved by flattening only. To gain some metal there, upset each rod at the right distance from the end. Grip the rod in the vise and hammer the end (Fig. 9-1B). Upset pieces to match. For pick-up purposes, the jaws can be flattened where they meet and left rounded on their backs (Fig. 9-1D).

Use each meeting face as a guide. Hold the bar so the face is upright and flatten the upset part on the face of the anvil

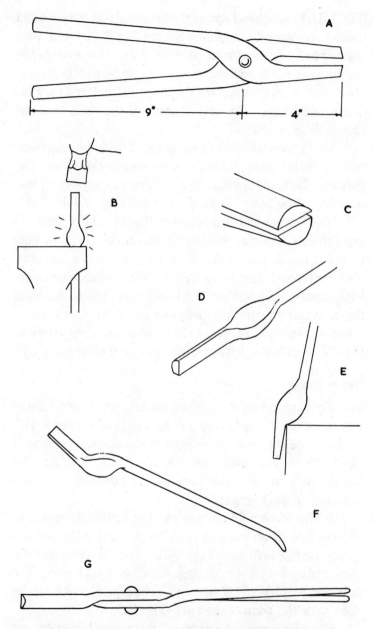

Fig. 9-1. Tongs are made from rod upset to provide enough metal at the pivot: (A) suggested size for small tongs; (B) use a vise; (C) flatten and round the jaws; (D) flatten the upset portion; (E) bend to S-form; (F) turn the end slightly; (G) crank the handles slightly.

(Fig. 9-1D). Now bend across the hinge part so the jaws and handles are opposite ways in an S-form (Fig. 9-1E). Use your drawing as a guide and make sure the two parts match. At the other end of the handles or reins, it might be satisfactory to leave the rods as they are, but the tongs look better if they are drawn out a little. The grip is better if the ends turn out slightly (Fig. 9-1F).

Try the two parts over each other. It might be necessary to use a flatter or set hammer on the meeting surfaces. The jaws and the handles will have to be cranked slightly so that they are in the same plane when closed (Fig. 9-1G).

With a center punch mark where the rivet is to come and drill through both pieces. This will make a better pivot than punching holes. Try the action of the tongs with a bolt temporarily through the holes. There will probably be some adjustment to make to get the jaws or handles as you want them. When you are satisfied, join the parts with a rivet. While it is still hot, open and close the tongs a few times so that the parts bed down and move over each other properly.

Heavy Tongs

For large tongs, it is still advisable to start with a drawing. However, it need not go the full length of the reins (Fig. 9-2A). If you start with three-fourth inch square bar, the jaws can finish about 1 inch wide and one-half inch thick. The handles have to finish about one-half inch diameter throughout most of their length.

It should be possible to make the flattened hinge part without first upsetting. Allow sufficient end for the jaw and spread on the anvil face (Fig . 9-2B). Get the two parts the same and do further work a stage at a time on each piece. The flattened part has to be the center of a joggle, which can be done over the edge of the anvil (Fig. 9-2C).

If the jaws are to be widened, do this next. You can get maximum width without lengthening much by first using a straight-peen hammer or a fuller along the jaw (Fig. 9-2D).

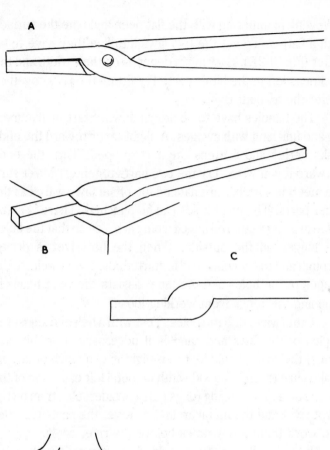

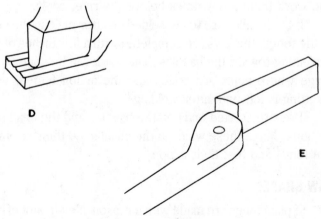

Fig. 9-2. Tong jaws (A) are shaped (B,C,D) and offset to match each other (E).

Follow by hammering with the flat peen and true the surface with a flatter. To get the two jaws into line they have to be offset (Fig. 9-2E). How much depends on their width and the thickness left in the hinge part. Try fitting the jaws together to get the amount right.

The handles have to be drawn down. Start by hammering and finishing with swages. A slight taper toward the ends looks better and lightens the part gripped. Turn the ends outward if you wish. Try the two parts together. Make sure the meeting surfaces are flat and the offset jaws will clear the other parts. The pivot holes can be punched. There is some value in using a tapered punch from each side so that the holes are bigger on the outside. When the hot rivet is driven through and the second head is started, the rivet swells to the shapes of the holes and the taper assists the rivet heads in stopping the tongs from working loose.

Otherwise, drill the holes. Test with a bolt and adjust the angles of the jaws and handles if necessary. For this size tongs, the rivet should be three-eighths of an inch or larger. Make sure there is a good width of metal left each side of the hole. The action of using tongs puts considerable strain on the pivot rivet and the metal around it. Rivet the parts together and work them a few times before the rivet cools.

If the handles are to be welded on after making the head of the tongs, the jaws are completed with a few inches of rod projecting toward the handles. The work can be done to the stage where holes are drilled and the action tested. Only rivetting is left until after welding.

Prepare scarfed ends on the handles and the head projections. Make these welds in the usual way, then assemble the tongs and test their action.

JAW SHAPES

If plain tongs are made with a reasonable amount of bulk in the jaws, it is possible to cut off the rivet and forge the jaws to any special shape needed. Then rivet them together again.

This might be done more than once if there is enough metal in the jaws. However, some other shapes might be forged in the first instance.

Open-mouthed tongs with severa different sizes of gaps are always needed and it is better to make them to suit the common bars than to have to alter tongs. With these and close-mouthed tongs, it is always advisable to actually make them to grip at the tips (Fig. 9-3A). If they start exactly parallel, wear will cause them to open slightly and their grip is affected.

Light tongs can be adapted for pick-up purposes. Allow more length in the jaws and curve them to a bow shape (Fig. 9-3B). They could be given a second curve if they are needed to handle rivets (Fig. 9-3C).

One way that plain jaws can be adapted without spoiling them for normal flat stock is to groove them slightly. Don't make them fully round, but leaving flat surfaces on each side (Fig. 9-3D). This is done with a fuller before assembly. Keep the hollows the same depth throughout their length. If they are deeper at the tips, round stock would only be held tight at the inner end and would not be safe.

Other sections of jaws can be formed by forging the jaws parallel, but not as thick as for plain types. Then for their sections with fullers and swages (Fig. 9-3E). As with the other jaws, be careful to finish so the grip tightens at the tip more than it does further back.

Tongs for bolt and rivet head clearance might look like pick-up tongs, but they should be heavier. The bowed part should be rigid and not springy, as it might for picking up (Fig. 9-3F).

Boxed jaws (Fig. 9-3G) might have to be made separately and welded on. The rod might be upset sufficiently for them to be forged. Another way of getting the thickness for a sufficient length is to make a faggot weld on the bar, then forge that to shape. Boxing one jaw is usually sufficient, then its sides lap over the other plain jaw.

Offset jaws (Fig. 9-3H) are useful for gripping the edge of a tube or cup shape. They are made like long plain jaws and then bent to match each other. Form the inner jaw first, then pivot the parts temporarily on a bolt to get the shape of the outer jaw. Arrange the jaws so that they meet or are at the intended gap before the straight parts of the jaws meet. There is no need for the straight parts from the pivet to meet, as it is the offset jaws that must grip.

HAMMERS

Most hammers in use today are made of high carbon steel. Hammers that you buy can be described as cast steel. The steel is high carbon, but the name describes the method of manufacture. This is not the way an individual smith makes one-off hamers At one time, many hammers made by smiths were of iron or mild steel, with high carbon steel welded on to make a face at one or both sides. A mild steel hammer is easier to make than a tool steel one. Obviously, it would suffer in use without the harder steel face. But for practice, a hammer head can be made from mild steel and it would have limited uses. Some durability could be gained by case hardening the faces, followed by hardening and tempering them.

If high carbon steel is to be welded to a mild steel hammer head, the head is made completely with an allowance for the steel to be welded on. This should be about one-half inch thick and could be the end of a flat bar, with the excess cut off after welding. The end of the hammer head to be welded should be slightly domed, then the two parts brought to welding heat and a butt weld made. If the work is done quickly, the surplus high carbon steel can be cut off with a hot set (Fig. 9-4A) and the part left hammered or ground to shape. That type of weld is not easy to make satisfactorily. It is better, at least for early attempts at hammer making, to make the heads entirely of mild steel or high carbon steel.

Although it is possible to shape hammer heads so that they compare with types you can buy, it is more common to

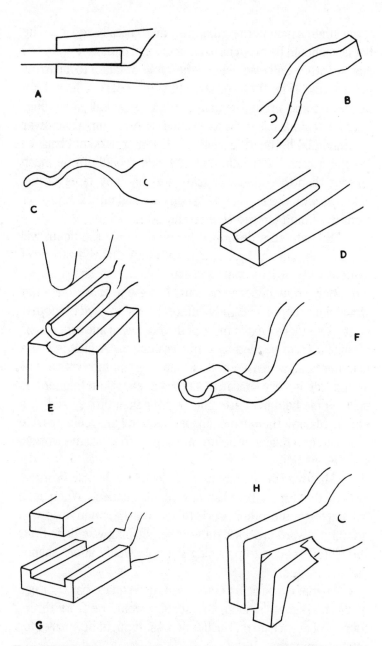

Fig. 9-3. With sufficient metal in the jaws, tongs can be specially shaped: (A) grip at the tips; (B) curve to a bow shape; (C) a second curve can be given; (D) flat surfaces; (E) form with fullers and swages; (F) the bowed portion; (G) boxed jaws; (H) offset jaws.

forge smith's hammers so that they are basically square. The flat face should be brought to an octagonal outline (Fig. 9-4B) and the other end made either the same or taken to a narrow peen across (Fig. 9-4C) or straight (Fig. 9-4D). The end can be forged and ground to make a full—size ball peen (Fig. 9-4E), but since it is most often used for rivetting, a narrower end might be better (Fig. 9-4F). A hammer need not balance exactly across the handle, but one side should not be much heavier than the other. To allow for this, any taper at one side—as with the smaller ball peen—should be taken further from the hole than the face on the other side.

The hammers described here are those the smith will use himself, but any tool catalog will show that the variety of hammers for various crafts and activities is very large. These often only show minor variations, but the user for one craft would not accept the slightly different version used in another craft. A smith can make most of the hammers and other tools of similar form needed by other craftsmen. A pick is just a hammer head with a point. A carpenter's hammer with a claw at one side is very similar to a cross peen, taken thinner and split. Some hammers are much lighter than those used by a smith. Making them from smaller section bar would provide practice for a beginner before moving on to the same work in heavier sections.

Whatever the hammer, the hole for the handle is nearly always the first job. That has to be shaped. When it is satisfactory, the other work to make a hammer head is a straightforward process. If the other shaping was done first, the distortion due to punching the hole would affect shapes already forged.

To make a basic hammer head, use square bar. For use in the blacksmith's shop, the section would be from three-fourths of an inch up to 2 inches across. It might be smaller for other hammers.

The hole through the hammer head has to finish elliptical. How big this is depends on the hammer. It might have to

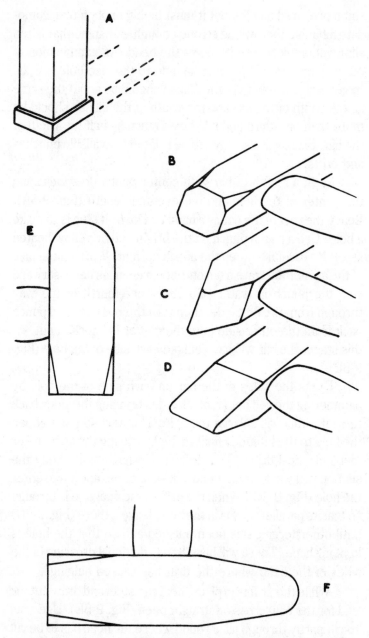

Fig. 9-4. Hammer heads made by a smith start as square bar: (A) hot set; (B) flat face; (C) narrow peen; (D) straight peen; (E) full-size ball peen; (F) narrower end.

suit a prepared handle, but it must be big enough to accomodate a handle that will be strong enough. A handle that is too slim will break where it enters the head. An examination of other hammers will provide a guide to the size hole needed In general, the length of the ellipse should be about the same as the width of the bar and the width of the ellipse should be more than one-third and maybe as much as half the width of the bar. Sizes will also have to be related to available punches and drifts.

Mark a length of bar with center punch dots indicating the center of the hole and the eventual length (Fig. 9-5A). Leave the rest of the bar as a handle. The first step is to make a hole. Use a round punch on the bright red or yellow heated steel. Be careful to keep the punch upright. Work on the face of the anvil. Penetrate from one side, reheat as necessary and cool the punch in water. Go about one-fourth of the way through from the first side, then turn the rod over and punch back from the other side until the center is knocked out. At this stage, the bar will have bulged each side of the hole (Fig. 9-5B).

Dress the sides of the bar on each side of the hole by hammering the red hot steel. Besides bringing the sides back to width, this will enlarge the hole. The next step is to open the hole to the intended final shape by driving through one or more elliptical drifts. The drift should have as its body the section you want, but the end will have to be tapered to enter the hole (Fig. 9-5C). When the drift of the final size is through so that its parallel body is in the hole, leave it there (Fig. 9-5D) until other forging has been finished and so that the hole is kept in shape. There will have to be additional dressing of the sides of the head where the drift has caused bulging.

While the drift is in pl ce, heat the steel and draw out the end for the ball, cross or straight peen (Fig. 9-5E). Use a set to cut partly through all of round where the head has to be cut from the bar. Check the shape of the head before parting off completely. The corners can be hammered or left for grinding

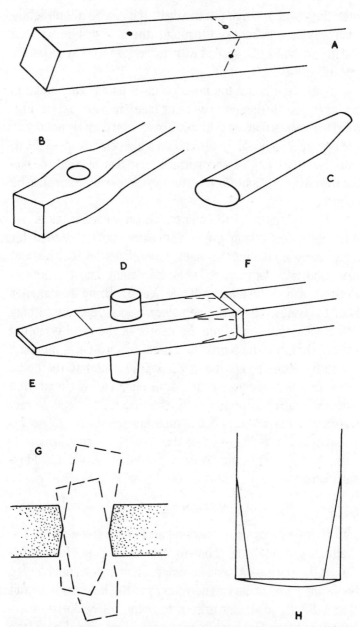

Fig. 9-5. A hammer head is shaped and punched on the end of a bar: (A) center and eventual length; (B) bulge; (C) tapered end; (D) the body is parallel; (E) draw out the end; (F) hammer the corners; (G) tilt slightly; (H) slightly dome the working face.

later (Fig. 9-5F). Drive out the drift. If it can be tilted slightly each way as it is knocked through, the hole will be waisted slightly so the handle spread with its wedges will have a better grip (Fig. 9-5G).

A flat face is not the best for most hammering and it is better to slightly dome the working face when grinding it (Fig. 9-5H). The head can be ground all over. But if this is not done, the two peens should be ground on a high carbon steel head. This removes any of the surface that has become decarbonized. It also brightens the steel so tempering colors can be seen.

The bulkiness of the hammer head means it takes and holds heat for a long time. The slow cooling needed for annealing will take much longer than thinner tools. The heat retention is an advantage when hardening and tempering. Both can usually be done with one heating. Bring the hammer head to redness all over. Then quench each peen, by turning and dipping without letting the center of the head go in the water. Brighten the part of the steel toward each peen and watch the oxide colors moving from the center to the ends. When the color you want reaches the end, quickly quench that side and the head completely when both are done. Exact colors are not critical, but tempering has to be taken far enough to leave the ends of the head as hard as possible without risk of chipping. A deep yellow or brown should be satisfactory.

SETS

If other tools with wooden handles are to be made, the methods are similar to those for hammers. A set hammer is almost the same as a basic hammer. Since it does not have to be swung, the handle can be round and the hole made to suit (Fig. 9-6A). Use a round drift through the hole while hammering out bulges. The bottom part of the tool should be a true square with a flat face. What comes above it should not project (Fig. 9-6B) outside the lines of the square. Otherwise they might foul the edge when being used in a deep recess. Above the handle, the square can be given a slight taper and the top be ground around for hammering (Fig. 9-6C).

Hot and cold set can be forged in a similar way with holes for round handles (Fig. 9-6D). Make the hole first while using

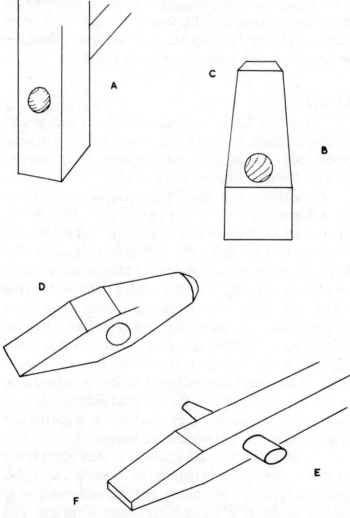

Fig. 9-6. Punches and sets can be made like hammers: (A) round handle; (B,C) slight taper; (D) a set with a round handle; (E) draw down to the cutting edge; (F) allow for grinding.

the bar as a handle, then draw down to the cutting edge (Fig. 9-6E). A cold set needs more strength behind the cutting edge than a hot set so it should be made slightly more obtuse. In any case allow some thickness on the end for grinding (Fig. 9-6F). If the tapered faces are slightly hollow, sharpening during long use can be taken further back before the tool gets so thick that it has to be scrapped or reforged. Make the top similar to the top on a set hammer. Tools that are to be hit should be left soft at the top, but the working ends should be tempered to a dark yellow for most purposes.

FULLERS

Flatters and fullers are better made with wrap-around handles, although they can be made with holes for wooden handles. Sets can also be grooved for wrap-around handles, but a set hammer is better with a hole.

A small fuller can be made by upsetting the end of a bar to get sufficient metal there to forge to shape (Fig. 9-7A). Except for very light work, the tapered part of the finished tool should not be thinner at the top than the rod above it (Fig. 9-7B). The width that can be obtained depends on how much is built up by upsetting (Fig. 9-7C). Work on the end of a rod and forge the end to shape. Be sure to make an allowance for grinding. Above that, use a fuller to make grooves to hole the wrap of the handle. If the basic rod is square, the hollows need only come across the corners (Fig. 9-7D). But with round or octagonal material, hollow all round. Make the hollows wide enough for a double width of the rod. The handle usually has a one-fourth inch diameter. Above the hollows, shape the part to be hit much like you would a set hammer.

The other way to make a fuller is to start with a bar of about the same section as the finished dimensions are to be. Reduce the end, first with fullers, and then by drawing out to the size needed (Fig. 9-8A). Since weight in the tool is an advantage, the upper part need not be reduced very much. Hammer or swage it to shape. Cut off from the bar and draw

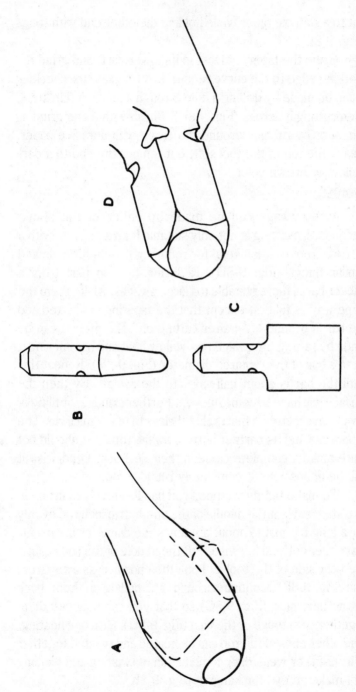

Fig. 9-7. Enough metal to make a fuller is obtained by upsetting. (A) upset the end; (B) taper; (C) width depends on upsetting; (D) hollows.

out to a suitable taper while holding the other end with tongs (Fig. 9-8B).

Grind the taper, at least in its lower part, and grind the working edge to the curve required. A template for checking it can be made by drilling a hole through a piece of thin steel, then cutting it across (Fig. 9-8C). Finish with a fine grinding wheel or by rubbing around the curve with abrasive paper. Leave the top of the tool soft, but temper the end to a dark yellow or brown color.

SWAGES

A top swage can be made by either of the above methods. Upsetting is not only suitable for a small tool with a narrow groove, it is useful for rounding drawn-out nails and similar things (Fig. 9-8D). Reducing the top part from a thicker bar is more suitable for large swages. Make them the same way as fullers, except that the tapering is omitted and the bar is ground level after cutting off. The groove can be made by raising the swage to a yellow heat and hammering it on to a bar of the required diameter (Fig. 9-8E). Repeat this until the bar is about halfway into the swage. By then the surface will have become uneven. Further grinding or filing of it will leave a groove that is slightly less than a semicircle. The top swage and its partner bottom swage together should not quite make a complete circle in their sections. Otherwise it will be impossible to completely round a rod.

To make tightly wrapped rod handles involves fitting in two stages. Heat the middle of the one-fourth inch rod evenly for a length equal to about six times the diameter it is to fit. Have the tool held in a vise. Put the middle of the rod against the near side of the tool and pull the ends across away from you (Fig. 9-8F). Continue around, still pulling on them, back to the near side (Fig. 9-8G) so that you can squeeze them together with tongs or the vise (Fig. 9-8H), all in one heating. The other ends of the rod can be heated and twisted together (Fig. 9-8J) or welded. A combination of twisting and welding will make an eye for hanging (Fig. 9-8K).

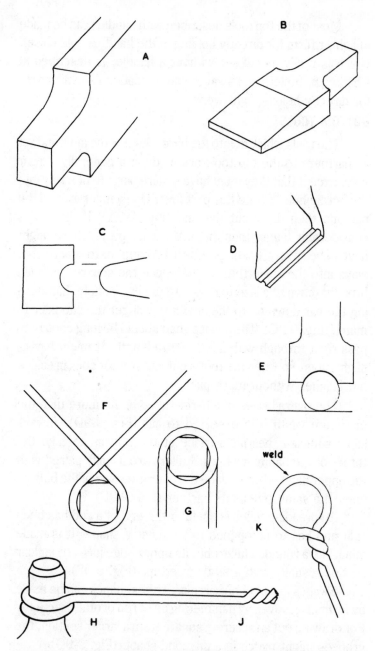

Fig. 9-8. Swages start like fullers. Iron handles are closely twisted: (A) reduce; (B) cut; (C) a template; (D) upset; (E) raise the groove; (F) pull ends; (G) continue around; (H) use a vise; (J) twist.

Most of the top tools described with handles can be made in lighter form for directly holding in the hand. A cold chisel, which is really a cold set without a handle, is described in Chapter 8. Fullers and swages can be made in a similar way for directly holding light work.

BOTTOM TOOLS

The tools which fit into the hardie hole of the anvil and act as partners to the top tools are made in a generally similar way, except that they must have square parts to fit easily into the hardie hole. Forge this part first. Use a fuller around the bar and then draw out the end (Fig. 9-9A). If the bar is considerably bigger than the final square piece, there might have to be several heatings. Use a set hammer to square both ways into the angle (Fig. 9-9B). Once the square has been brought down to a size to pass into the hardie hole, hammering the bar down on to the anvil top will get the shoulder to match (Fig. 9-9C). The square shaft should be long enough to pass right through with a little extra length. It might have a slight taper, so when the tool is put into place it goes in easily, but finishes without much play.

The overall sizes of a hardie need be no more than the mazimum width it is expected to cut (Fig. 9-9D). Always allow sufficient bearing surface at the bottom to take the thrust of the hammer blows. Fullers are usually paired with the upper handled one. Make the operative part of the bottom fuller the same size as its partner (Fig. 9-9E).

A spreading fuller is useful if the end of a rod has been split and has to be opened to an equal V shape. It is made much like a rounded fuller, but its upper edge has a triangluar section, usually with a 90 degree top. (Fig. 9-9F).

Swages are not only circular. Other shapes can be made by forming grooves by hammering on to rod of other sections. For drawing out an accurate square from a larger section, the grooves might match in a diamond shape (Fig. 9-9G).

Although the top swage usually only has one groove, its partner might be given two or three grooves so that one

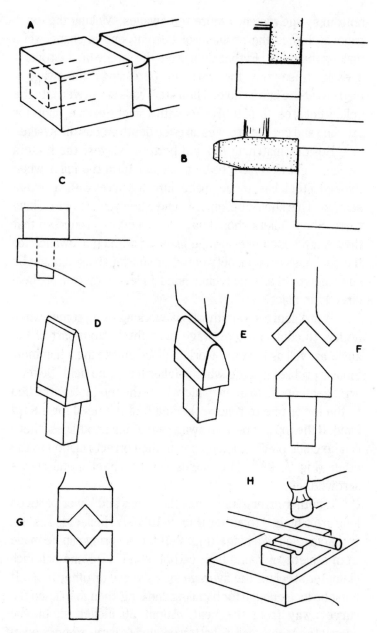

Fig. 9-9. Tools to fit in the hardie hole have the square end made first. Then the top is shaped as required: (A) draw out; (B) use a set hammer; (C) hammer the bar down; (D) overall size; (E) match fuller sizes; (F) triangular edge; (G) diamond shape; (H) drive the steel rod.

bottom swage matches more top swages. Making the extra grooves brings the problem of keeping one in shape while making the other. Rather than drive the swage on the rods, it is easier to see how the work is progressing if the swage is made to fit the hardie hole. Then steel rods are driven into the yellow hot steel (Fig. 9-9H). As with a single groove, allow for grinding and get the grooves an even depth across the swage.

Besides matching top and bottom swages, the bottom swage might also have to be a partner for a top fuller when thinned steel has to be made into a curve with a gouge section. This should be kept in mind when you are are making tools. Some fullers should have their curves ground so that they can be used over swage grooves with an allowance for the thickness of metal between. For smaller sizes, it might be sufficient to make matching hand fullers that can be held directly in place.

A problem for a smith who is working along comes when he has to control a top swage over the bottom part of the anvil, as well as hold the work in place and swing a hammer. Similar problems come when a fuller has to be held. Several arrangements have been made where the top tool is attached to the lower one to relieve the smith of the need for a third hand. If the top and bottom swage have similar outlines, there can be guide pieces to keep one in the correct relation to the other (Fig 9-10A). The guides can be sheet metal pieces screwed on.

Another arrangement has the upper and lower parts on long arms hinged together (Fig. 9-10B). A similar idea uses a spring instead of a hinge (Fig. 9-10C). A spring can be made from a piece of round high carbon steel. Use one-half inch diameter steel for the average size swages or other tools. It must be long enough for handling and long enough to keep the curve away from the heat. About 30 inches should be adequate. At the center, flatten enough to wrap around something about 4 inches in diameter. This is the spring and it should be tempered to a purple color.

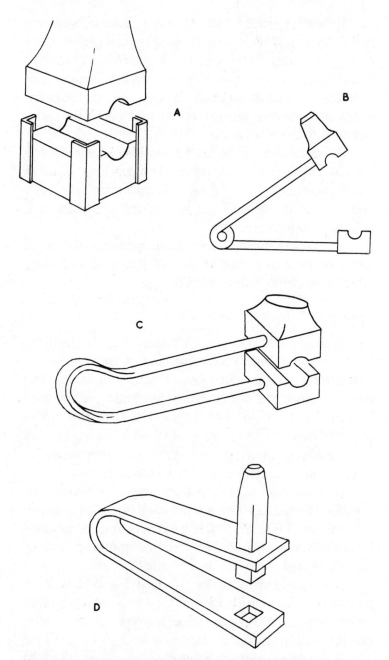

Fig. 9-10. For singlehanded use it helps to make fullers and punches that have the two parts joined: (A) guides; (B) hinged; (C) spring; (D) bolster.

Have the top and bottom tools in an annealed state and drill them slightly undersize. Grind short tapers around the ends of the spring arms. Heat the tools to redness and drive them on to the spring ends. The steel will have expanded on heating and should go on easily. When it cools the joints will shrink and tighten. Alternatively, use flat steel for the spring and weld to the tools.

A similar idea can be used to position a punch over a bolster. This is particularly useful when punching square or other shaped holes. Having a bolster underneath ensures a clean outline to the hole, but when using it freehand it is difficult to locate correctly.

The bolster could be part of the spring and the punch might go through a hole in the other part without being attached rigidly to it (Fig. 9-10D).

STAKES

Most of the heavier work is done directly on the anvil, but for fine and light work there is often an advantage in having something standing above the anvil to hit on. The special needs of nail makers has been mentioned, but when anything has to be shaped with small section steel, a tool generally called a *stake* , can be mounted in the hardie hole. Some stakes are more like slender anvils and they are easier to buy than make. However, many stakes can be made.

An anvil stake is like a bottom swage, but without the grooves. It could be low or it could stand two or three inches above the anvil (Fig. 9-11A). It need not be square, but could be made from round rod or one corner of the square ground off. There could be one of more rounded edges.

A bick iron or horn can be T-shaped (Fig. 9-11B). It can be built up by welding a bar across the end of an upright, then forging and grinding to shape. Another version is made from one bar bent over (Fig. 9-11C).

A saddle is a piece of stout plate, possibly a 3 inch by one-half inch section bent over (Fig. 9-11D). Forge it over the

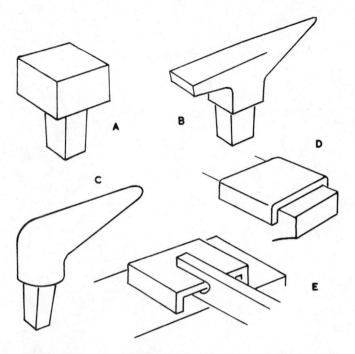

Fig. 9-11. Some small supplementary anvils can be made to fit the hardie hole (A,B,C) or stand on the anvil face (D,E).

anvil face so that it can be put over and used for chopping on when the work is unsuitable for putting across the table of the anvil. The saddle prevents the set or other cutting tool from hitting the hard anvil and damaging itself or the anvil. If the saddle is turned around, it can be placed on the anvil for working on something divided (Fig. 9-11E) that is too narrow to go anywhere else.

Domestic Hardware

10

In modern homes, most of us are surrounded by things that have been mas produced by a manufacturer who turns out many thous nds from the same pattern. We live in an ge where individually-produced items are rare. There is not necessarily any virtue in individual production and in many cases the mass-produced item might be both better and cheaper. In some things there is a definite advantage in mass production, particularly when a replacement part is needed and the spare obtained can be certain of fitting. There is an advantage in standardized screw threads, where nuts made to a standard will be certain to fit any bolt made to the same standard. Not so long ago a nut might fit its own bolt, but would not suit any other. Its head was forged to a size decided by the smith, who also made a wrench to suit.

Although mass production has given us things that we could not otherwise have had if each example was different and individually made, there is still an attraction in having one of a kind items. There is often a beauty and attractiveness in something that has been made by hand as a one-off project. It is enjoyable to be able to say that there is nothing else quite like it. This applies to woodwork furnishings and many other products such as hardware and fittings or equipment for the home which can be produced by a smith.

The parts are not always large or separate items. There was a time when all the more utilitarian items, such as hinges, handles and catches had to be made by the blacksmith. There were no quantity items in plastic or metal and no hardware store where they could be bought. If a house builder needed brackets to support shelving or gutters, the blacksmith cooperated and made each item to suit the intended purpose. There also was close cooperation between woodworkers and smiths in building such things as carts and wagons.

Most smiths had an appreciation of design considerations and were not content to turn out something that was merely functional. Fortunately, iron has a long life and it is possible to see examples of individual smithing in old European houses or those of early American settlers. Nearly all of these things have a beauty due to their proportions or because of decorative touches added by the smith that are not necessarily a functional part of the item. These old examples are useful guides to modern blacksmiths who might have become accustomed to mass production output.

There might be an occasion when a blacksmith can make a purely functional article that is comparable with a mass produced one, but it may have to be a special size. In general, the attraction of blacksmithing is being able to make something that is definitely different and that is an expression of artistic ideas. In some items, artistry might be of primary importance (see Chapter 11). Even when the item must serve a practical purpose, there is scope for giving it those touches that mark it as an individual product worth having for its own character.

CATCHES

Doors and gates can be held closed or open with many sorts of devices. One such device is a hook and eye. In its basic form, a piece of rod is made into a hook to swing on one eye and engage with another (Fig. 10-1A). The eyes are U-shaped pieces like staples that are shouldered to go through backplates and rivetted at the back (Fig. 10-1B). In small sizes, the ends are most easily formed by filing. One-quarter inch or five-sixteenth inch rod can be reduced to about a three-sixteenth inch diameter. Have the ends projecting above the vise jaws. Put a washer over each end and use the file around the rod while resting on the washer (Fig. 10-1C). If possible, use a file with a safe edge (one with no teeth on it). For larger rods the round ends can be accurately forged to shape with swages. The backplates can be simple circles or rectangles, but there is scope for decorating the outlines. Even in the small sizes, the plate can be one-eighth of an inch thick. This is enough to make scalloped edges (Fig. 10-1D) by hitting with a ball peen hammer while the edge is red hot. Drill for two screws as well as for the ends of the U-shaped staple pieces. Countersink for the screws on the front and for the rivetted ends on the back (Fig. 10-1E).

Make the ring end of the hook resemble a small eye by bending back enough rod and hammering it to shape (Fig. 10-1F). The finished ring should be an easy fit on its staple. In the smallest sizes, this will have to be quite a tight curve and the end of the beak might not be small enough to shape it. In that case, curve as far as possible on the end of the beak. Then close the ring around a tapered punch held in the vise.

Put a point on the other end and bend that back before curving to make the hook (Fig. 10-1G). Notice that the point curves outward slightly. Fit the hook on to its staple and rivet that to its plate. Rivet the other in the same way. Fill the countersinks to make secure rivet heads. It will probably not matter if the rivet heads stand slightly above the surface for greater strength since they will press into the wood the plates are screwed to.

A hook that is better looking and obviously appears to have been made by a blacksmith is made from square rod which is given rounded ends (Fig. 10-2A). Allow some extra length at what will be the hook end. This will give you something to hold, without using tongs. Allow enough length for making the ring and make a twist in the part that will remain square. Round the part for the ring by hammering the corners of the square (Fig. 10-2B). It will probably be sufficient to get an approximately circular section by hammering. For a large hook (over seven-sixteenth inch bar) swages can be used to finish the end. Forge that part into the ring to fit the staple.

Cut off the other end and draw it out to a round taper. Do not make it too thin. The main taper should be to about half the thickness of the bar. Then the end is taken down to a rounded finish (Fig. 10-2C). Shape that into the hook. The hook looks best if the shaping of both ends is done in line with a pair of sides of the square section.

For most purposes, the hooks need not have much reach, but a long arm might be needed to hold a door back to a post. It is possible to decorate the rod with more than one twist or it could be given a dog-leg shape instead of being left straight. When a hook is out of use, it hangs down. A long one might swing and mark the door. To prevent this, make a second staple for the hook end to go in across the door. The hook might also function as a door handle (Fig. 10-2D).

In some places, it is better if the hook pivots without swinging. To allow for this, flatten the end instead of forming a ring and drill for a rivet. Put a thin washer between the parts to provide some clearance (Fig. 10-2E).

If attaching the parts with wood screws would not be strong enough, use bolts. Instead of staples, make eye bolts. Forge a ring on the end of a rod to go through the ring on the hook. Cut this off at a sufficient length to go through the woodwork and make a thread on its end for a nut. Make a back plate to go under the nut at the other side. When making the eye bolt into where the point of the hook has to go give it enough clearance for the point to drop in easily. It should not be necessary to force it in.

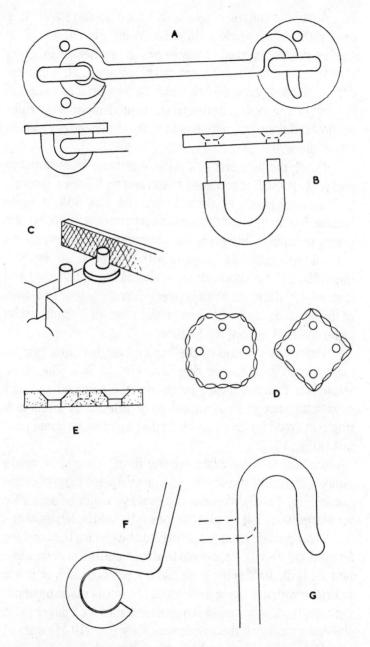

Fig. 10-1. A hook and staple can be made plain or decorated: (A) the basic form; (B) U-shaped piece; (C) use a file; (D) scalloped edges; (E) countersink; (F) bend and hammer to shape; (G) curve to hook.

A variation on the hook and eye is a hasp and staple. It is used with a lock to hold a chest lid closed (Fig. 10-3A). The staples can be rivetted to plates which are held with wood screws or one or both of them can be eye bolts. It would be difficult to upset enough of the end of a round rod to make the flat part of a hasp. It is better to start with flat bar of the right section and draw down its end to make the round part which forms the eye.

Punch the hole first at a suitable distance back from the end (Fig. 10-3B). It can start round and be followed through with an oval punch or drift. Leave the final drift in while hammering the sides of the bar straight after they have bulged during punching. However, the comparatively thin metal will not hold its shape, as happens with hammers, so the drift might have to be knocked out while the bar is flattened and then replaced if more work is needed on the sides. The sides of the bar need not be finished straight and the bulging can be regarded as a decorative feature.

Draw out the end of the bar and forge it to a ring to engage with its staple or ring bolt (Fig. 10-3C). The other staple has to be of a size to go into the punched slot and project far enough for a padlock to be fitted (Fig. 10-3D). A ring bolt could be given an elongated eye for the same purpose (Fig. 10-3E).

Instead of a flat plate for the hasp, it could be made entirely of parallel round rod, with an oval piece to go over the staple (Fig. 10-3F). Welding the oval eye might be advisable for a large hasp, but for most purposes it could be left as bent.

A hasp made from flat plate could be given a bent end for lifting (Fig. 10-3G). This could be developed into a decorative feature (Fig. 10-3H) but it should not project much or it will interfere with a hanging padlock. If the eye is made by bending round rod, it is possible to give clearance for a finger to lift the end by curving the eye in side view (Fig. 10-3J) without interfering with passing the padlock through.

If a lock is unnecessary and the hasp and staple are only there to keep a lid closed, a tapered peg can be positioned

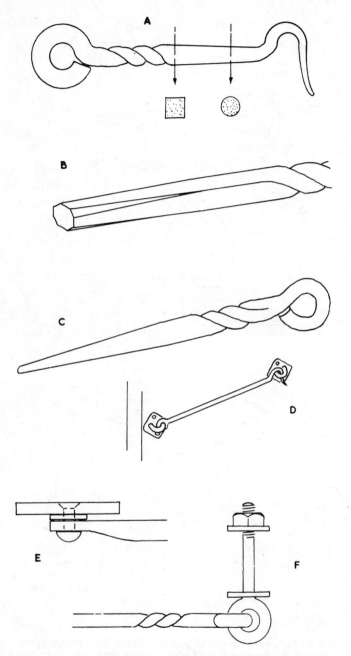

Fig. 10-2. Hooks can be twisted (A, B), tapered (C) and pivoted (D, E, F) in several ways.

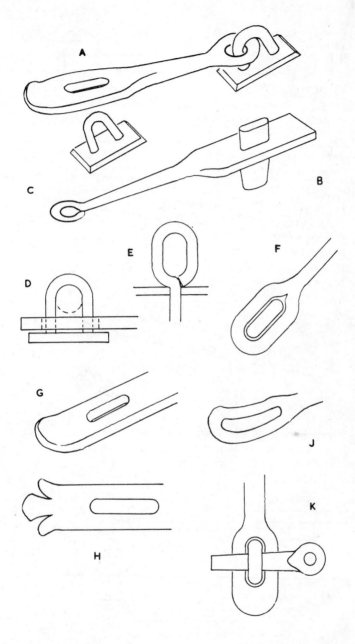

Fig. 10-3. A hasp and staple can be used with a lock: (A) hook and eye; (B) punch the hole; (C) draw out the end; (D) project the staple; (E) an elongated eye; (F) and oval piece; (G) a hasp; (H) decorative feature; (J) curve the eye; (K) flattened end.

through the staple, made by drawing out a piece of rod so it fits tightly. The end can be flattened and drilled to take a cord or chain (Fig. 10-3K).

LATCHES

A hook fastener allows a certain amount of play. If a door or gate has to close and be held reasonably tight the traditional form of fastener made by a blacksmith is a latch (Fig. 10-4). In its simplest form, a latch is operated from one side of the door only—the side from which the door can be pushed closed. If the latch is to be worked from the other side of the door, there has to be a lever through the door. This is usually incorporated into a plate with a handle for pulling the door closed. The sizes shown in Fig. 10-5 are for a typical latch. They might have to be modified to suit a thicker door or the need for a longer reach.

A latch that is a piece of flat bar seven-eighths of an inch by one-eighth of an inch by three-sixteenths of an inch will do for a small door. Nick the sides with a hardie or set and round

Fig. 10-4. An old door latch with a shaped backplate on a door made with handmade nails.

the end (Fig. 10-6A). Much of this could be filed, but for a forged look it is better when hammered. Drill for a rivet. There has to be a handle for lifting the latch. It could be made from the head of a coach bolt, shouldered and rivetted (Fig. 10-6B). If a lathe is available, it could be turned. However, it is more in keeping with the design to forge a knob on the upset end of a rod and rivet this on (Fig. 10-6C). There is no need for a knob on the latch if there is to be a lever through the door from the other side. Some old latches are decorated with crossed lines. These lines can be cut on lightly with a set (Fig. 10-6D).

The plate on which the latch pivots need only be big enough to take two screw holes or it could be made larger and decorated much like the backplates for hooks. The latch must swing up and down easily so that it drops into the catch plate by gravity. Using a plain rivet might result in the pivot being too tight. It is better to use a round-headed rivet, which keeps its full diameter through the latch, and a washer. Then it is shouldered to a smaller size for rivetting through the plate (Fig. 10-6E). In the suggested size bar, this could be a five-sixteenth inch rivet with its end filed to fit a one-fourth inch hole.

The guide is made of two parts. The back is flat and a joggled front piece is held to it by the wood screws driven into the door (Fig. 10-6F). The amount of the opening should be sufficient for the latch to lift clear of the catch plate and wide enough for unrestricted movement. To ensure matching, make both parts too long at first and then cut and file them to agree as a final step. The front part can be hammered to shape, one bend at a time, by using a flat bar as a punch (Fig. 10-6G). Another way is to start the bends, but have a bar of the correct section to fit inside and another of the same thickness to use outside. With the bar red hot, hammer the shape on the face of the anvil (Fig. 10-6H).

The important part of the catch plate is the projection. This has to be shaped so that if the door is slammed the latch

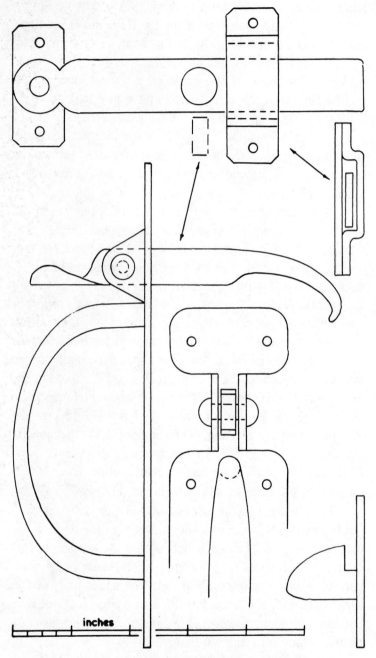

inches

Fig. 10-5. A traditional door latch can be worked from either side.

hits the slope and rides up it to drop into the recess. Forge and file this shape on the end of the bar (Fig. 10-6J) and then cut down the recess. It can be chopped out, but it will have to be filed. Therefore, it might be simpler to do this work with a hacksaw. The back of the catch plate should have a slot punched in it and the end of the other piece filed to go through it for rivetting (Fig. 10-6K). Drill for wood screws.

In some door jambs, it might be better for the catch plate to go into the edge of the door post instead of on its surface. In that case, it can be one piece of flat plate with screw holes (Fig. 10-6L).

That completes the parts for a latch intended to be operated from one side of the door. Screw the parts to the door so that the latch projects enough and the guide has the lower part of the opening level with the lowest position the latch has to go. Try the catch plate temporarily in place to find the best height to mount so that the latch will close properly.

The important part of the equipment for the other side of the door is the lever. To match the sizes suggested for other parts, this could be made from bar about five-eighths of an inch by three-sixteenths of an inch. One end has to be made into a palm to be pressed by the thumb while the fingers are holding the handle. Upset the end of the bar to provide enough metal for shaping. Then spread a flat palm with rounded edges (Fig. 10-7A). Hammer this to a curve, over the beak of the anvil, in a swage or over a bottom fuller. Get a shape that will be comfortable to press (Fig. 10-7B).

The other part of the lever has to be tapered and curved, but before doing this, check the thickness of the door. Your palm should project about 2 inches from the surface of the door and the bar should go through the thickness of the door parallel before starting to draw out. The upper edge of the lever has to lift the latch and the lower edge rests on the bottom of the slot in the door. Further out, it is curled down to provide a grip for lifting on that side.

Cut off the bar and draw out the end to a tail finishing

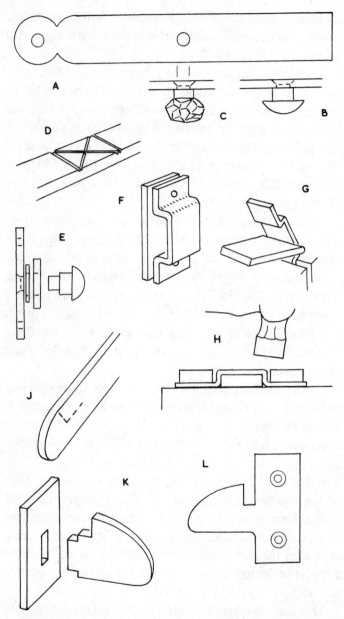

Fig. 10-6. A latch can be plain or decorated and it is controlled by parts made from flat bar: (A) round the end; (B) shoulder and rivet; (C) forge and rivet a knob; (D) cut lines; (E) rivet; (F) joggled front piece; (G) hammer to shape; (H) use the face of an anvil; (J) forge and file; (K) back of the catch plate; (L) flat plate with screw holes.

about three-sixteenths of an inch square. Form an attractive downward curve with enough curl in the end for a finger grip to lift the latch (Fig. 10-7C).

The lever is supported by two cheeks on a plate that also has the loop handle. It would be possible to rivet, weld or braze the cheeks to the plate, but they are shown made from the plate by cutting and bending. The back plate shown is 8 inches by 2 inches by one-eighth of an inch. Mark the position of the slot for the lever and punch this (Fig. 10-7D). Make it undersize at this stage and leave working it to size with files until after raising the cheeks.

Mark the shapes of the cheeks and saw their edges (Fig. 10-7E). Position horizontally a bar with a square edge and a thickness the same as the gap between the cheeks is to be. With open-mouth tongs, hammer and squeeze the cheeks into shape (Fig. 10-7F). File them to shape and mark and drill through for a one-fourth inch rivet that will form the pivot. File out the slot to give an easy clearance for the lever and sufficient room for it to move up and down. Drill the lever and try its action.

The handle for pulling the door is a loop. In its simplest form it could be a piece of three-eighth inch or one-half inch rod bent to shape. However it looks better and is more comfortable to hold if it is worked to an elliptical cross-section at the center, while remaining round at the ends (Fig. 10-7G). Shape this section in the straight bar by hammering, then form the handle shape and cut off. File down the ends for rivetting. Leave marking the rivet holes in the backplate until after shaping the handle. It is easier to modify their spacing than to alter the handle to suit holes already there. Have the upper part of the handle close to the lever so that it is easy to reach with the thumb (Fig. 10-7H).

The basic backplate is shown as straight-edged with rounded corners. It can be modified to a more ornamental outline and it can be hammered all over to avoid the plain look of the surface. It the door is being equipped with forged

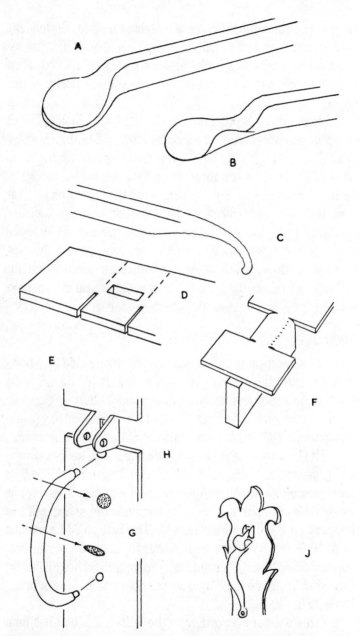

Fig. 10-7. The handle and latch fit through a backplate which can be decorated: (A) flat palm; (B) shape; (C) curve; (D) punch a slot; (E) saw edges; (F) shape the cheeks; (G) round the ends; (H) the handle is close to the lever; (J) a leaf outline.

hinges, the plate can be given a matching outline. Styled leaf outlines are found on medieval doors (Fig. 10-7J). The same motif can be carried on to the smaller plates, guide and catch plate to give them a function as part of the overall design of the door.

Lightly rivet through the cheeks and lever. Make sure all sharp edges are taken off all parts that will be touched by hand. The part with the handle has to be located on the door so that the lever goes through and comes under the latch fairly close to the guide. Fit the latch and the parts that go with it on the door and jamb first. Drill a small hole through the door below the latch at the place where the top of the lever has to come. Use this as a guide for marking out the slot through the door, which is best cut from both sides. When the slot has been shaped satisfactorily, it will give you the position for screwing on the assembly on the other side of the door.

DOOR BOLT

Doors and gates can be secured from one side by a bolt, either as the only fastening or as an addition to it. A horizontal bolt can be short, but for large doors with bolts going up and down extension handles can be used for convenience. These also provide the smith with a chance to decorate the work.

The basic door bolt has a bolt sliding in two keepers, with a stop piece projecting to limit movement each way. The bolt then goes into a similar keeper on the door post. The amount the bolt has to open and close determines the spacing of the keepers on the door (Fig. 10-8A). The bolt could be square (Fig. 10-9) or round. Square is better for bolts with extension handles (Fig. 10-8B). If round is used for a short bolt, it can be turned to bring the knob against the door when it is not being move (Fig. 10-8C).

Sizes will vary according to the bolt. If it is one-half inch across, keepers can be made from three-fourth inch bar and the backplates can be one-eigth of an inch thick. These sections might do for a thicker bolt. For a large and heavy door a

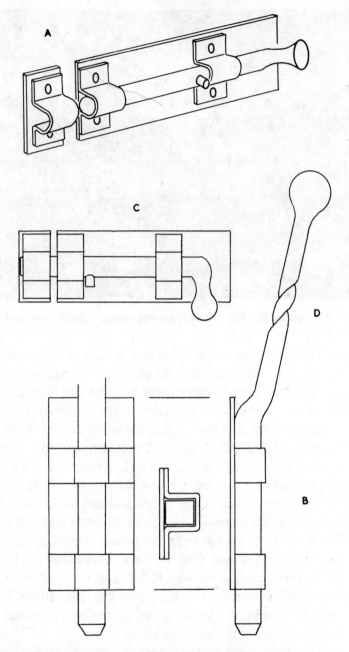

Fig. 10-8. A door bolt can be made of round or square rod: (A) space the keepers; (B) extension handle; (C) short bolt; (D) true the keeper.

Fig. 10-9. A square door bolt on a backplate that has been split at the end and shaped.

more massive constrcution would look better, as well as be stronger. With a three-fourth inch bolt the bar for the keepers could be nearer 1 inch by three-sixteenth of an inch. There is scope for decoration, but a plain short bolt is described first.

Choose the rod for the bolt first and use this or a piece off the same rod to make the keepers. A plain keeper need not be cut to length first. The end of a rod can be heated and shaped before cutting off. Open the vise jaws to a little more than the thickness of the bolt and twice the thickness of the keepers. Put the heated bar across the vise and hammer the rod over it (Fig. 10-10A). Knock the rod down until it is level and the ends can be turned back (Fig. 10-10B). Thicker bar can be difficult to bend easily in this way. In that case, use a bar with a rounded end as a punch to start the hollowing (Fig. 10-10C). When a sufficient depth has been made, lever open the ends and finish to size with the rod in place.

If square bar is used, the keepers for a small bolt can be made over the vise in this way. For heavier sections, you

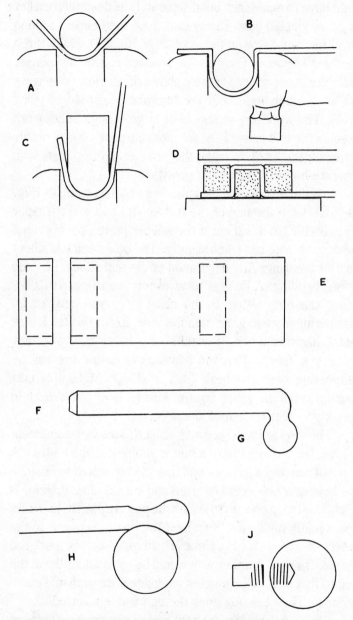

Fig. 10-10. Bolt retainers are shaped from flat strip. The knob is forged over the beak of the anvil and a stop is screwed in : (A) hammer the rod over the bar; (B) knock the rod until level; (C) hollow; (D) true the keepers; (E) backplates; (F) taper; (G) use a knob; (H) thin the bar; (J) drive in a bolt.

might have to make each bend separately as described earlier for other joggled bars. In any cast, true the keepers around bar of the same size on the anvil (Fig. 10-10D). Make three matching keepers. They can be rivetted to the backplates, which are then screwed to the woodwork, or the woodscrews can go through them and the backplates instead of using rivets. The woodscrews should be large enough to not work loose as the bolt is used and for most purposes it is probably better for the smith to make the parts as rivetted units with separate holes for mounting screws.

In a simple bolt, the backplates are plain rectangles (Fig. 10-10E). Give the end of the rod for the bolt a slight taper (Fig. 10-10F)so it will enter the keeper on the post, even if the door or gate has fallen slightly. The other end has a bent part for handling. Any decoration of the end should be done before bending. A knob is most of ten used (Fig. 10-10G). Upset the end, either by bouncing it on the anvil or by hammering it while gripped in the vise. From this thickened metal, hammer a ball, It could be a sphere, an oval or any shape you fancy. Thin the bar slightly below the ball by hammering over the beak (Fig. 10-10H). Make this part round, even if the volt is square. Finally, bend out enough to give a grip that is clear of the door.

The stop is a small peg in the bolt. If screwing equipment is available, driving in like a bolt is simplest (Fig. 10-10J). A piece of rod might have its end threaded to match a thread in the hole or a bolt could be used and cut off after driving. It might be strong enough to shrink the peg in a plain hole. Drill a hole slightly undersize, then heat the bolt to redness so the steel expands. Drive in a piece of cold rod. Cool the work and cut excess peg. Another way would be to shoulder down the peg to fit a smaller hole taken completely through and countersunk. Then the peg goes through and is rivetted.

Check the action of the bolt. See that the movement is as required. Adjust this by positioning the keepers on the backplate to suit. Then drill and rivet them in place.

For a long bolt with an extended handle, sometimes called *tower bolt*, check the length needed to suit a person standing by the particular door. The assembly is the same as for a short bolt, except for the handle (Fig. 10-8D). Crank the rod just outside where it comes in the closed position. It could remain parallel, but it looks better if drawn out slightly to finish with a knob. It need not be straight (Fig. 10-11A). If it is drawn out square, there can be a twist in it (Fig. 10-11B).

The end of this or a short bolt does not have to be a round knob. The end can be flattened and given a roll for a different effect, (Fig. 10-11C). This would be particularly appropriate on a wrought iron gate (see Chapter 11).

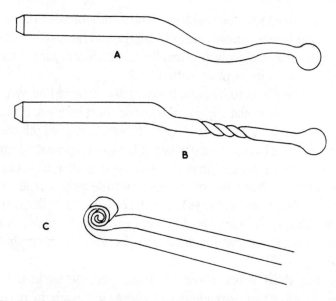

Fig. 10-11. A tower bolt (A) can be given a decorated handle (B,C).

The bolts as described are plain. But if examples are examined on old doors, most will be found to have shaped outlines and they might be hammered all over. Even if the backplates start as straight-edged, working over them with a large ball peen hammer will give an attractive surface. Heavier blows toward the edges will provide a scalloped effect (Fig. 10-12A). This can be done on the ends of the keepers as well (Fig. 10-12B). However, leave the edges straight that face each other between the door and post.

The outlines can be chopped to curves with hot or cold chisels, either as wavy edges or in leaf patterns. Keepers can be made with spread shaped ends (Fig. 10-12C). Parallel bar can be split and opened (Fig. 10-12D), but if you want larger ends the keepers would have to be cut from wider plate (Fig. 10-12E). Split ends can be dealt with after the keepers have been shaped around the bolt, but wider pieces will have to be made first and the bending around the bolt carefully centered afterwards.

DOOR HANDLES

A door handle does not have to be incorporated in a latch. The loop handle shown with the latch could be made separately or a more complicated handle intended for separate use could be used in its place with a latch.

If a handle is to be used horizontally, it should be symmetrical. This would apply to drawer or chest handles. If the handle is to be vertical on a door, it looks better if both the handle and its backplate are wider or heavier in appearance at the top. Whatever design is chosen, the loop should be long enough for a hand to enter easily and the grip should be comfortable. Curves always look better than straight lines, so either the whole thing should be in curves or the important parts should be curved to draw attention away from straight lines.

For most doors a suitable handle can be made from one-eighth or three-sixteenth inch sheet steel, with the parts rivetted and woodscrews used for mounting.

The first handle has a shaped outline (Fig. 10-13A). Draw half of it full-size on paper and turn it over the centerline to get the plate symmetrical. Cut this to shape with chisels and file the outline true. If the steel is to remain smooth, make the outline accurate. If it is to be heated and hammered all over and the edge thinned by heavier blows, there is no need to start with quite as accurate an edge.

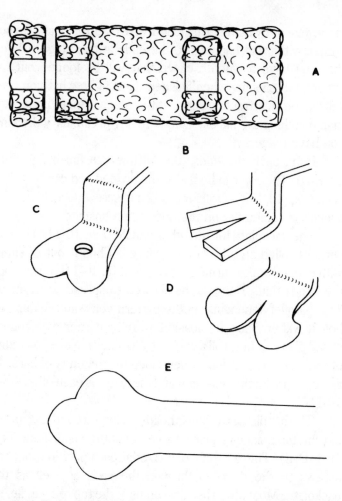

Fig. 10-12. To decorate a door bolt, part can be hammered and shaped: (A) a scalloped effect; (B) scalloped ends; (C) spread shaped ends; (D) split and opened bar; (E) a wider designed end.

The handle is made of the same thickness sheet. Draw its outline before shaping (Fig. 10-13B) and cut this out. Do not drill rivet holes yet. Heat the steel and hollow the part that will be the grip in a suitable swage (Fig. 10-13C). With a further heating, pull the grip to shape over the beak while using two pairs of tongs. Keep the heat adequate since there has to be some stretching of the edges. The hollow made by the swage will probably flatten in parts. True this again, either in a swage or by hammering lengthwise over the beak. Do not bother with what happens to the ends at this stage. Check that you have a smooth curve that will be looped out far enough for gripping when finished. Getting to what you consider to be an attractive curve at this stage is more important than matching the handle exactly to any preliminary drawing you have made.

Bend back the ends, the bottom can finish flat (Fig. 10-13D). The top can be flat or the divided end can be rolled back (Fig. 10-13E). Drill for rivets and screw. Check that the backplate comes flat on the door when finsihed.

The backplate for the other handle (Fig. 10-14A) has its corners rolled and the outline curved. Chop it out of sheet with enough at the corners for rolling (Fig. 10-14B). Hammer the edges thin. They can be allowed to spread or might be kept parallel depending on the pattern you want. When red hot, it will probably be possible to roll a corner with round-nosed pliers. If not, roll a corner by hammering over the edge of the anvil, as previously described for the ends of bars. In any case, make the rolls tight and the same as each other (Fig. 10-14C).

The handle has a similar hollowed loop around the curve, but the top finishes square, while the bottom is divided (Fig. 10-14D, E). There is only one rivet at each position, but the screws to the door go through the ends as well as the backplate. Most strain usually comes at the top of a handle, so more screws go through there.

HINGES

Hinges with catches, latches, bolts and handles form part of what are sometimes collectively known as *door furniture*. There are several ways of providing a pivot on which a door can swing. Pegs can go parallel to the framing, but it is more common to have some form of hings. Hinges can be produced in many ways. Modern doors swing on quantity-produced hinges, but in earlier days individual smiths had

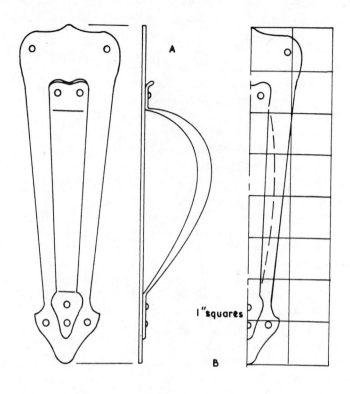

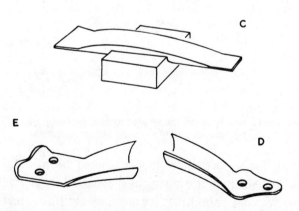

Fig. 10-13. A door handle can be given a comfortable grip by hollowing it: (A) shaped outline; (B) draw to size; (C) heat and hollow the grip; (D) bend the ends; (E) roll back.

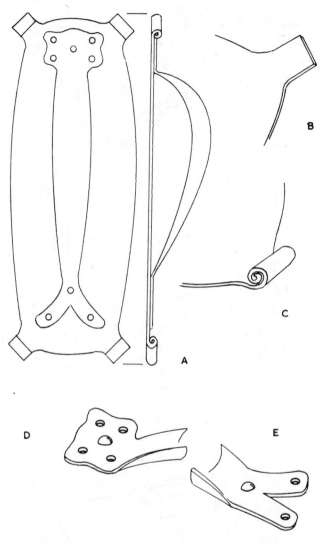

Fig. 10-14. A handle backplate can have rolled corners: (A) backplate; (B,C) roll corners; (D,E) the top finishes square while the bottom is divided.

their own ideas about how hinges should be made (Fig. 10-15). Some of these are ingenious, but a majority depend on a pin on which one or both parts of the hinge are free to pivot.

Some hinges produced by early smiths have lengthy straps across the door. These give scope for decoration, ranging from basic cuts and shapes to elaborate representations of leaves and flowers. The knuckle of the hinge about the pin might not need to be very big, but the parts of the hinge on both door and post can be quite large. In some cases, this large part also served to hold the boards of the door together. In some instances, the hinges went around the frame to brace joints.

Most hinges are made so that the two leaves encircle the pin with alternate pieces forming the knuckle. The methods used in modern manufacture follow those devised by blacksmiths many centuries ago. The parts of a modern hinge knuckle are divided into an uneven arrangement of equal parts (Fig. 10-16A). The number of parts depend on the length of the knuckle. It is more logical to use the same amount on each flap. This shares the load more equally and is seen on some older hinges. With three parts, the central one would be wider than those on each side of it (Fig. 10-16B). A modern smith can still use this improvement over machine made hinges.

Fig. 10-15. An old door hinge with welded scrolls, split end and punched line decoration.

A cast hinge will have the knuckle formed in the metal (Fig. 10-16C). Simpler hinges are made from sheet metal wrapped around the pin (Fig. 10-16D). A better sheet metal hinge has the wrap attached to the flap (Fig. 10-16E). This is obviously stronger for the same thickness metal, but a single wrap is satisfactory if the steel is thick enough. Another construction seen in some medieval hinges has the metal thinned and carried behind the visible part of the hinge far enough for screws or nails to go through it (Fig. 10-16F). The pin through a hinge knuckle is often machined level in a manufactured hinge. But in an individually made hinge, it is stronger to leave a little extra on each end for lightly rivetting (Fig. 10-16G). It is not always easy to decide how thick to make the pin. In modern hinges, it is often no thicker than the metal used for the flaps. It has to share the load without

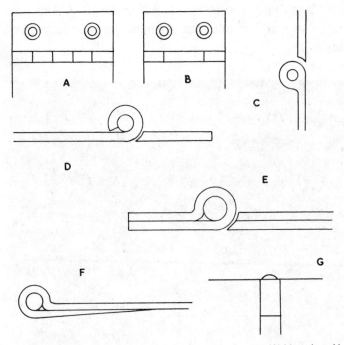

Fig. 10-16. Hinges are made from flat plate in several ways: (A) hinge knuckle; (B) the central part is wider; (C) cast hinge; (D) simple hinge; (E) more complex hinge; (F) the metal is thinned; (G) extra on each end for rivetting.

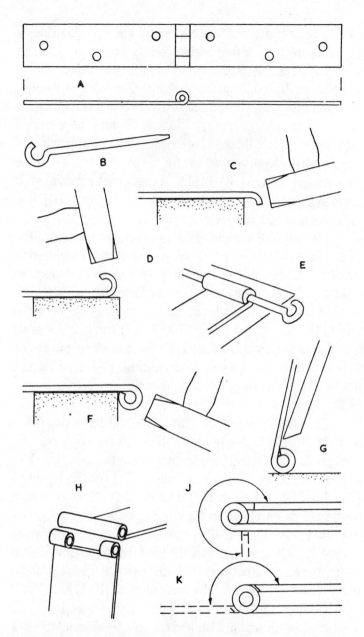

Fig. 10-17. The knuckle of a hinge is rolled around a pin and cutouts are arranged according to the amount of swing the hinge is to have: (A) strap hinge; (B) mandrel with eye; (C) bend; (D) curve; (E) close the bar; (F) hit against the edge of the anvil; (G) final closing; (H) cut to shape; (J) back flap hinge swings 90 degrees; (K) follow the curve of the knuckle.

bending or breaking and it is easier to forge good knuckles if the pin is thicker. A reasonable choice for the pin is about twice the thickness of the metal used for the flaps.

For ease in handling, a strap hinge (Fig. 10-17A and Fig. 10-18) is a good choice for a first hinge. Use a bar about 1½ inches by one-eighth inch. Do not cut off until the knuckles have been formed. Make hinge knuckles over a mandrel of the same size rod as you will use for the pin. It is unwise to use the pin itself, because it will almost certainly be damaged. If the mandrel has an eye forged on its end (Fig. 10-17B), it is easier to grip and pull out.

Start bending the end of the hot bar over the end of the anvil (Fig. 10-17C). The pin will be one-fourth of an inch in diameter. Estimate that you are leaving about this much as you make the curve and work on the face (Fig. 10-17D). As more of the curve is made, insert the mandrel and continue closing the bar around it (Fig. 10-17E). It can be hit against the edge of the anvil (Fig. 10-17F) but final closing is better done with the edge of a piece of steel (Fig. 10-17G) used as a punch. Pull the mandre out and make the knuckle on the end of the other bar.

Mark the cuts on the parts that will have the outer sections of knuckle. Saw down these lines, chop out the waste with a cold chisel and file the opening to shape. Use this as a pattern to mark the other knuckle and cut this to shape (Fig. 10-17H). Try the parts together. If the hinge is to be a *back flap* that swings from the closed position to 90 degrees the other way (Fig. 10-17J), the slots have to be cut away deeply. If, as is more common the hinge has to go from closed to flat, the bottoms of the cutouts are neater if filed at an angle that follows the curve of the knuckle (Fig. 10-17K).

If a hinge is to be made with a double thickness, it can still be formed on the end of a bar and cut off after shaping. If it is a broader one, sheet steel must be folded around. Have the mandrel ready and heat the steel to redness. Bend back enough for a flap over the mandrel (Fig. 10-19A). If it is a

Fig. 10-18. A gate hinge with the strap forked on both sides and a pintle in the post.

suitable size to go in the vise, squeeze the flat parts together there (Fig. 10-19B). If not, use a flatter or set hammer to do the same on the anvil. In any case, flatten so that the knuckle is to one side (Fig. 10-19C).

Do the same with the other part. Cut the spaces in the knuckles. It is always better to start with the half that has outside parts. If there is any error in cutting, it will be less obvious. If there are to be five or seven parts, work progressively with a fine file. The parts should go together tightly at first since they will soon wear against each other.

To follow the method used in medieval hinges, with a part tapered in thickness behind the main part, the end is first thinned for a length sufficient to make a feather edge (Fig. 10-19D). It would be possible to fold around the pin mandrel, but because of thinner steel tends to bend more easily, it might be difficult to get a satisfactory result. Another method uses a stake or grooved tool like a small swage, but with the curve at one side coming to the edge (Fig. 10-19E). The curve in it should match what is to be the outside curve of the hinge knuckle. This can be used with a cross peen hammer or there could be a matching punch to suit the curve inside the hinge material.

Bend down the tapered part and enough of the parallel part to go around the pin, so that it is at right angles to the rest of the hinge (Fig. 10-19F). Have the grooved tool standing as high as possible in the vise. Hook the hinge steel over the tool with the tapered part across it. Use the cross peen hammer or the punch to drive the steel into the groove (Fig. 10-19G). Except for the thinnest steel, this must be done hot. Get as much curve as you can by lifting the long part as you hit. Finish with rather more than a semicircle (Fig. 10-19H). Put the mandrel in and close the hinge over it (Fig. 10-19J). Make sure that screw holes will be placed to go through the tapered part. If any help is needed in keeping the parts tight, put a rivet through centrally.

Once the methods of making knuckles have been mas-

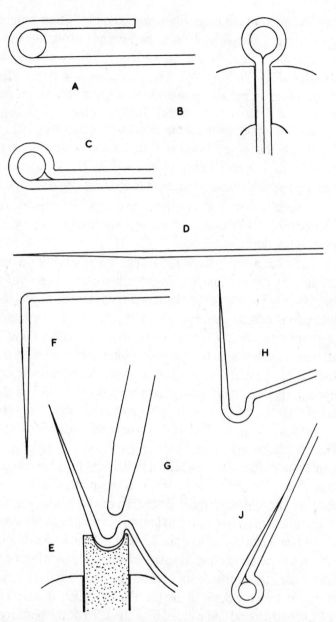

Fig. 10-19. The metal of a hinge can be a double thickness and the back can be tapered: (A) bend to make a flap; (B) squeeze in a vise; (C) flatten; (D) thin to a feather edge; (E) use a stake to make a curve; (F) bend to a right angle; (G) drive the steel into the groove; (H) finish to more than a semicircle: (J) close the hinge over the mandrel.

tered, many kinds of hinges become possible. Strap hinges can be straight and parallel, as in the example used, but they are more often tapered and can be hammered or otherwise decorated (Fig. 10-20A). A T-hinge is the same on one side, but the other is across to provide enough screw holes for fastening to a narrow part (Fig. 10-20B). A hinge with flaps that has the same width as the knuckle is a butt hinge (Fig. 10-20C). If this is extended to provide a greater spread of screw holes, it is an H-hinge (Fig. 10-20D). If it is extended from the knuckle, it is a parliament hinge (Fig. 10-20E) and is used where a door has to swing clear of obstructions. An H-hinge (Fig. 10-2F) has an extra leg to go around the corner of a framed door.

Some hinges only have a stout pin, called a *pintle* on one part and the loop or knuckle on the other part drops over it (Fig. 10-21). The rudder of a boat is hinged in this way and the other part is called a *gudgeon*. However, that name is not used for steelwork ashore. Wrought iron gates are often hung in this way, with loops on the gates dropping over pintles on the posts (Fig. 10-22A). It is then possible to lift a gate off, although this might be prevented with a nut screwed on the end of a pintle. For use with field gates, the pintle might be provided with a spike (Fig. 10-22B) or welded to a backplate (Fig. 10-22C) which is screwed to the gate post. A strap goes at the other side (Fig. 10-22D) and this can also be called a strap hinge. If a gate is to be hung on two pintles, it helps to make the bottom one longer. The strap can be located on that first, instead of having to try to line up at two places at once.

A pintle can be just a parallel rod. But if it is far a gate that will have to be lifted off and replaced frequently, it is better to keep it para lel for the depth of the strap and then draw it out to a slight taper and round the tip (Fig. 10-22E). A strap can be wrapped around and welded (Fig. 10-22F) or the pintle can be shouldered to a smaller diameter and rivetted through the strap (Fig. 10-22G). This can also be brought to welding heat and hammered together. If it is to be a spike, the two sides

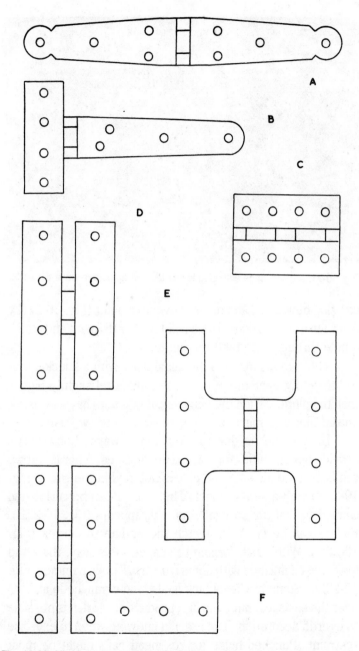

Fig. 10-20. Hinges are arranged with their leaves to suit the arrangment of screw holes: (A) strap hinge; (B) T-hinge; (C) butt hinge; (D) H-hinge; (E) parliament hinge; (F) H-L hinge.

Fig. 10-21. A pintle hinge extended to provide a strap across several boards.

can also be welded and drawn down to a point (Fig. 10-22H). Another way is to start with a solid rod for the point and punch a hole through it to take the pintle.

The strap is made in the usual way, with a knuckle that will fit easily over the pintle. Use a mandrel slightly bigger than the pintle. When the hinge is put into use, have a washer on the pintle to minimize wear between the two parts.

Hinges can be decorated in many ways. Long straps provide opportunities for various decorations. A parallel strap can have its ends split and pieces notched in the sides (Fig. 10-23A) with a set or chisel. These parts can be curled and shaped so that the straight outline disappears (Fig. 10-23B). Fullers can be used to stretch the outline to curves (Fig. 10-23C). With much forging to shape in this way, the strap looks best if finished with dents from a ball peen hammer (Fig. 10-23D). Some medieval hinges also have punched patterns over the surfaces, but even in reproduction work it is possible to overdo decoration. The art is in knowing when to exercise restraint. Punched holes for rosehead nails might be most appropriate for reproduction hinges, otherwise drill and countersink for screws.

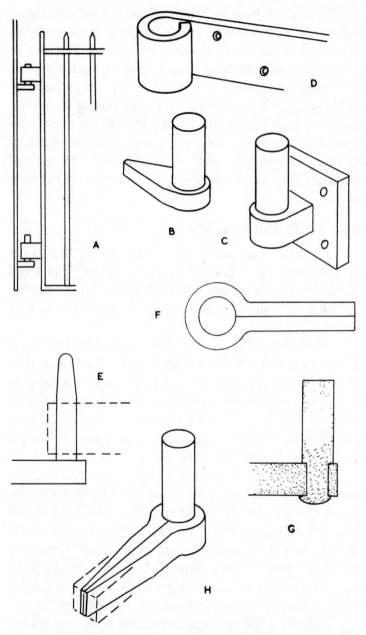

Fig. 10-22. Stout hinges can pivot on pintles: (A) wronght iron gate; (B) field gate; (C) welded to a backplate; (D) strap hinge; (E) taper and round the tip; (F) welded strap; (G) pintle shouldered and rivetted; (H) draw to a point.

Hinges have been both practical and decorative features in furniture and housing for a very long time. It is interesting to examine the work of old smiths and see the difference of fashion and methods. Some examples of wrought iron Jacobean hinges are shown in Fig. 10-24. Notice the unequal widths of knuckle parts so that the same amount of metal is used from each side. In the originals, the outlines would have been obtained partly by forging and partly by sawing and filing to shape. Edges are nearly all bevelled and surfaces are smooth. Countersunk screws came into use during Jacobean times.

WALL HOOKS AND BRACKETS

The need for wall hooks for clothing and other things can be adequately taken care of by mass produced metal and plastic articles, but there is a character about individually produced versions. A smith can easily make a variety of hooks.

A basic hook (Fig. 10-25A) starts as a flat bar. One end is drawn out to make the hook (Fig. 10-25B). The hook is then curved and the top is rounded. An alternative method is to start the other way with round bar, which is flattened (Fig. 10-25C). If all that is required is a functional hook, that is all that need be done. To enhance the appearance, additional work can be done on the ack and the hook.

The rectangular outline of the back can be broken up by hammering over the edge and the surface (Fig. 10-25D). The end can be split and curled outward (Fig. 10-25E). This will have a functional advantage in spreading the points of attachment to the wall. A simple curve to the hook can be improved by giving it a swan's neck shape (Fig. 10-25F). The tip is the most prominent part when the hook has something hanging from it. That is where decoration should be featured.

If the tip is left thick and then upset, before the hook is curved, it can be given a round knob (Fig. 10-25G). Leave hammer marks showing. For ease is slipping a coat loop over

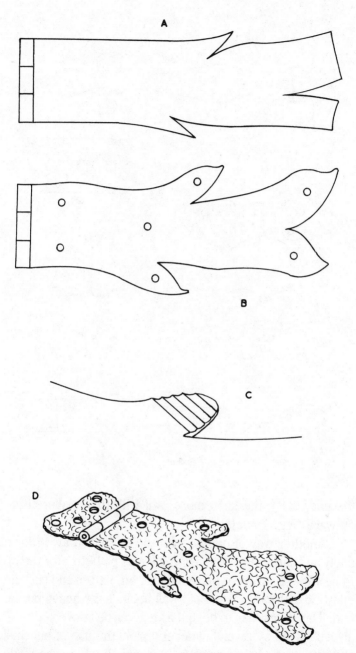

Fig. 10-23. Large hinges can be decorated by splitting (A,B) and spreading edges (C,D).

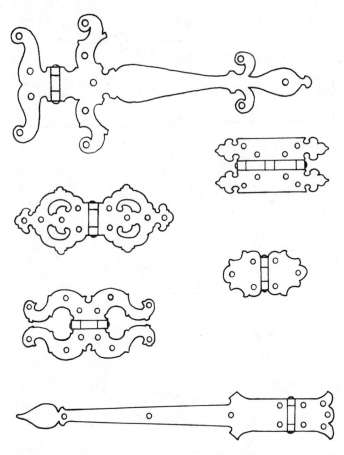

Fig. 10-24. Hinges can be cut to elaborate countlines—as in these Jacobean hinges.

the end, make the knob more oval with the smaller curve outward (Fig. 10-25H).

Another way of dealing with the tip is to draw it down finely and curl it (Fig. 10-25J). If it would be better for the tip to be wider to prevent things coming off, flatten and curl the end (Fig. 10-25K). Some old wall hooks have heads on the end. This is not easy to do, but a knob can be converted to an animal's head by careful hammering and the use of punches and just a little help from files. A double hook can be made with different heads on the ends (Fig. 10-25L).

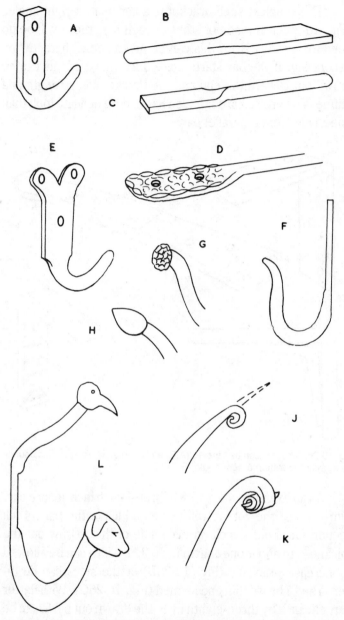

Fig. 10-25. Hooks can range from basic shapes to elaborately decorated ones: (A) basic hook; (B) draw out one end; (C) flatten the other end; (D) hammer the edge; (E) split and curl; (F) swan's neck shape: (G) round knob; (H) oval knob; (J) curl the tip; (K) flatten and curl; (L) double hook.

The simplest shelf bracket is a bar bent at right angles (Fig. 10-26A). If made of stout enough bar, there will be no need for a strut. Even this can be given some character by decorating. If the bar starts quite thick, most of this can be drawn out toward the end and the bracket has strength and stiffness where required. It also has a more delicate look than one made from a parallel bar.

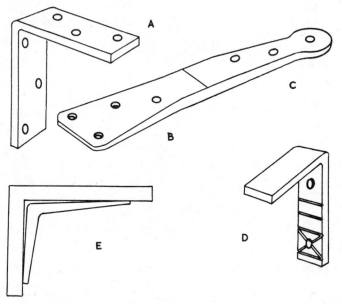

Fig. 10-26. Brackets can be tapered (A,B) and decorated. They should usually be slightly wider than a right angle (E,D).

As an example, start with a three-fourth inch square bar. Mark where the corner will come and leave the bar its full section for about 1 inch on each side of that. Draw out the thickness to about one-fourth inch. The width can be allowed to increase gradually (Fig. 10-26B) or the sides can be ta-pered and a broad thin end formed (Fig. 10-26C). With flatter bar, one inch by three-eighth inch, the drawn out parts can be kept the same width. Decoration can be provided with cuts from a set (Fig. 10-26D). When making any shelf bracket, be careful not to make the angle less than 90 degrees. Even if exactly that, a shelf might look as though it is sagging forward. It is always best to finish a bracket slightly open when tested with a square (Fig. 10-26E).

Making an unbraced bracket means using fairly heavy bar. For many purposes, it might look better and be just as strong to use lighter bar and provide a brace. The basic form is made from strip, with the brace bent and held with rivets (Fig. 10-27A). Appearance is improved if the angle of the brace differs from 45 degrees. Since the upright leg of a shelf bracket is usually longer, the brace or strut will come closer to being upright (Fig. 10-27B).

For decoration, the ends of the struts can be curled by short lifting a drawn out end (Fig. 10-27C) or by making a larger loop (Fig. 10-27D). A matching shaping can be given to one or both ends of the bracket (Fig. 10-27E). The center of the brace should not be thinned in any way, as that would

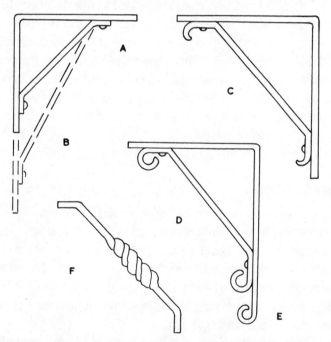

Fig. 10-27. Struts to shelf brackets allow decoration by twisting: (A) basic form; (B) strut; (C) ends can be curled; (D) looped curl; (E) shape one end; (F) twist.

weaken it, but if it is very long it can be made to look better by twisting it (Fig. 10-27F). Do this before shaping the ends since twisting reduces the overall length.

Another bracket can be used for hanging a gong or a flower basket (Fig. 10-28A). Without the need to fit under a shelf, the back can go upward and both the horizontal part and the strut are rivetted to it. The upper part does not have to be horizontal so there is scope for trying the effect of curves (Fig. 10-28B). In Fig. 10-28C, the back strip is drawn out at the end sand split so there can be single curls. The other two parts can be slightly narrower and their riveted ends are neater if reduced slightly in width (Fig. 10-28D). A hook on the horizontal part can be a similar curl to those on the back (Fig. 10-28E) or it can be drawn out round and made into a deeper hook (Fig. 10-28F) with its tip finished in any of the ways suggested for wall hooks.

An interesting exercise is to include a circle between the other parts (Fig. 10-28G). To do this accurately, make a drawing—preferably in chalk on an iron plate—so the parts can be tried on it. So that final adjustments can be made, form the vertical and horizontal parts and make the circle. Bring these parts together. Get the actual length between bends on the strut from this—even if the assembly differs slightly from the original drawing. Otherwise you might find that the circle does not fit at all three points where it should touch.

FOOT SCRAPER

At one time, before the days of paved surfaces, a foot scraper was a common item outside most house doors. The worst of the mud could be scraped off before boots were wiped on a mat. A scraper might still serve a practical purpose when gardening boots have to be wiped. Also, a blacksmith could put a scraper outside the entrance of his home as an indication of his craft and skill.

The important part of a boot scraper is the horizontal bar. The bar should be wide enough for any boot. Its top

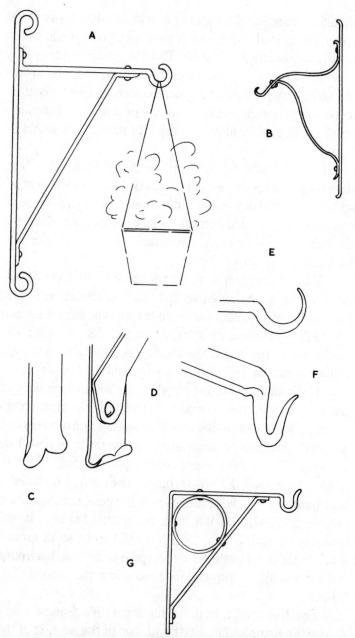

Fig. 10-28. Brackets for other purposes can be made like shelf brackets: (A) bracket for hanging a basket; (B) use curves; (C) the back strip is split; (D) rivet ends; (E) hook; (F) deeper hook; (G) decorative circle.

should be thinned, although not to a knife edge, so as to get under caked mud. What else is incorporated depends on the artistic ideas of the bl cksmith. The design will be affected by how the scraper is to be mounted. There could be spikes placed in a stone wall or a concrete step or there might be wood screws or spikes set in wood. For an authentic appearance, smith made spikes or nails with rose heads would be best.

In Fig. 10-29 the parts can be joined to wood in both directions, but for a stone wall the back strip could be omitted and spikes taken directly into the stone. If the floor is stone or concrete a spike could be forged on the scraper, particularly if the concrete is to be laid at the same time as the scraper is to be fitted.

Make the scraper from a steel bar (Fig. 10-30A). Shoulder the ends to make tenons and taper its center, either by hammering or grinding, but leave the ends at the full section where they will come against the uprights (Fig. 10-30B). Let the tenons be too long at this stage. Their section should suit a stock punch or you might have to make one to suit.

The back is a straight bar (Fig. 10-30C) which goes to just above where the front piece is rivetted. For attaching to wood, split the end so that screw or nail holes are far enough out for the hammer or screwdriver to miss the front part (Fig. 10-30D). Where the scraper comes, punch a hole (Fig. 10-30E). The sides of the bar will bulge. They can be hammered back parallel while the punch is left in the hole, but the curved outline could also be left as a decorative feature. It will probably be satisfactory for the upright to finish at ground level, but it could continue with a spike or be bent horizontal and formed like its top end for spikes into the ground (Fig. 10-30F).

The front piece is the main decorative feature which shows the smith's skill. Start with bar of the section of the largest part. Have a fullsize drawing to compare the work with as it progresses. For the leg that will take the scraper

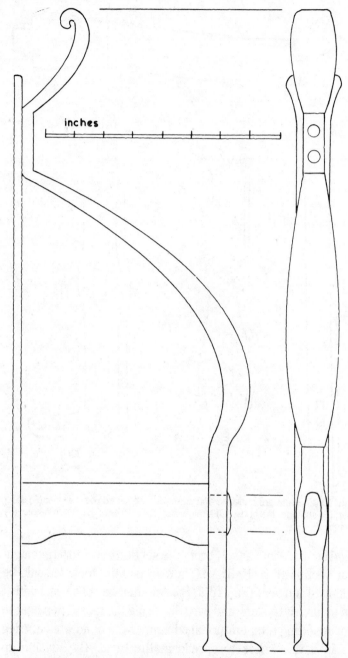

inches

Fig. 10-29. A boot scraper makes a decorative feature near an outside door.

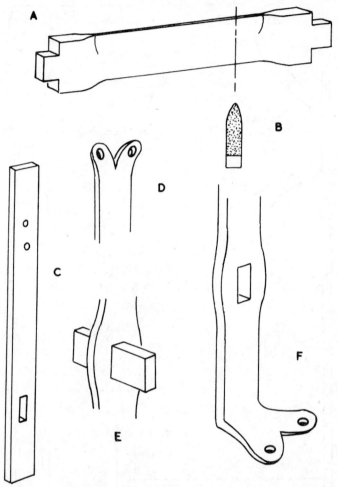

Fig. 10-30. Parts are punched and shaped to be joined with tenons: (A) steel bar; (B) shoulder the ends; (C) straight bar; (D) split end; (E) punch a hole; (F) finish.

and be made into a foot, bring the section down to a rectangular section (Fig. 10-31A). Then spread the foot. It could be thinned and bent (Fig. 10-31B). Another way of dealing with it is to have it too long and partially shape the foot. Then heat to an upsetting temperature and hammer the bend while the leg is in a vise so as to spread at the bend. By building up thickness there, it is possible to forge a foot that is flat

274

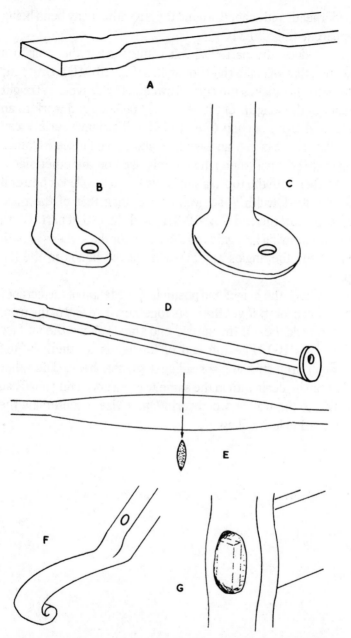

Fig. 10-31. There is scope for decoration on the top and feet of the scraper: (A) the foot is rectangular; (B) thin and bend; (C) forge a foot; (D) reduce; (E) slightly bulbous; (F) curl; (G) front tenon.

underneath and shaped around the leg without any bend being apparent (Fig. 10-31C).

Reduce the part that will come against the wall to a section that will take rivets or spikes (Fig. 10-31D). Draw out the part that makes the curved sweep. Try to avoid a straight taper in the length. Let it be slightly bulbous and work to an elliptical cross section (Fig. 10-31E). The inner surface can be flat, but it is just as easy to make curved since it comes against the anvil when a hammer is used on the other side.

Deal with the top in a similar way, but it will look better if its greatest width is somewhat less than that of the main sweep. Curl the end (Fig. 10-31F) and shape that part. Use a fullsize drawing as a guide to the curve for the sweeps of both parts and the angles and positions of the bends to the flat parts.

Check the height and position of the tenon of the scraper and punch for it. Rivet the parts together. The end of the front tenon looks best if the spread end stands above the surface (Fig. 10-31G). File the end of the tenon so there is just enough projecting for spreading a suitable head. The other end can be dealt with in the same way if a projecting head can sink into the wall or woodwork. Otherwise, countersink the punched hole by filing.

Decorative Ironwork

11

Much of the skilled and artistic work done by blacksmiths in the last few centuries has been seen in the production of gates, railings, grills, church screens and similar objects where the assembly was a mass of individually shaped parts and the whole joined to gether to make a pleasing pattern. In some cases, the blacksmith's work was linked with cast iron. But there are a great many surviving examples that were executed entirely by the smith at his forge with quite simple equipment. His skill and artistic feeling were more important than the equipment. He could not cal on precision machinery and any jigs used were made by him as needed.

The material was iron, but almost all of the designs could be worked in mild steel. However, that might not be so easy to forge into some of the more delicate shapes. The type of work is collectively called *wrought* ironwork. The work wrought in this instance is used in the sense of meaning worked, although the material was also called wrought iron.

Some modern *wrought iron gates* and similar things are very different from the traditional work. If they are examined, they will be seen to be made of bars all of a uniform section. The majority of parts in a traditional piece of wrought ironwork are tapered and twisted and changed section in their length to get the effect the smith wanted. The scrolls are not very thin and are all identical, showing that they were pulled cold around standard shapes, probably in a machine. Although such gates and other assemblies might be attractive, anyone with an appreciation of a blacksmith's craft would not want to own them or be associated with these machine age imitations of the products of real craftsmen.

Like many seemingly complex things, a gate or length of railings is built up from a series of comparatively simple steps. If the steps are understood and each performed properly, the final assembly should be a very satisfying example of your skill. Although the as embled construction might be quite heavy, the individual parts are not. There are some stages where a helper is essential, but much of the work can be done single-handed. The amount of heat required at any time is not great and a small hearth should be adequate. It is always easier to work on a large anvil. But if the work is schemed to suit, much of the shaping can be done on a small anvil. For some of the details, such as twisted leaves, a small anvil might be better than a large one.

Much of the work is the application of techniques already covered in earlier chapters. If you think about what is happening to the steel when you hit or bend it, almost anything is possible as you direct your blows to get the best effect and the maximum result from each action.

Look at examples of blacksmith made wrought iron-work. If you cannot find an actual gate or similar object examine photographs. Obviously, the real thing is best. Old churches might have a gate or screen. After you have enjoyed the object as a whole and noted how the attractive effect has been obtained, look at some of the details. Visualize one length of iron and try to think through how that piece was made. Notice how the parts are joined. See how sections have been changed. There are substantial parts where strength is needed, but the smith has thinned sections down

Fig. 11-1. A candle sconce shows applications of simple scrolls.

to make ornamental twists and twirls. Look at the ends of scrolls (Fig. 11-1) and other parts. There are a large number of ways of shaping the ends before curling them. Think out the shape that was made before the end was rolled tightly. Finishing an end in the form of a leaf is common (Fig. 11-2). Note how the bar is thinned, shaped and twisted or crinkled in leaf form. Look for the leaf veins that have been cut in it (Fig. 11-3).

Fig. 11-2. A pattern in a gate, suing snub-end scrolls and leaves.

SCROLLS

The tip of a scroll (Fig. 11-4, Fig. 11-5 and Fig. 11-6) in blacksmithing is always given some sort of decoration, usually in the form of a tight roll on the end of the drawn-out bar. A machine made modern scroll has the bar of the same thickness throughout and no rolled end. Some ways of dealing with the ends have previously been described, but these and others are summarized in this chapter.

Most decorative work of this sort is done with flat-sectioned bar. Round rods have some uses and there are uses for square sections. But most work is done with a bar that is usually about twice as wide as it is thick. Practice with a bar of this section. First make sure you can draw it down with an even taper almost to a chisel end (Fig. 11-7A). Get as good a shape as you can under the hammer, but use a flatter if necessary. You should be able to get a graceful taper over a long length as well as a short length.

It is possible to curl the end almost entirely by hammering. Have the end at a yellow heat and use a light hammer while the bar is held across the anvil face. Hitting progres-

Fig. 11-3. A combination of flames and leaves provide decoration in this gate detail.

Fig. 11-4. All the scrolls in this fence detail were made around the same scroll tool. The arrow heads are welded. Many other parts are rivetted.

sively with glancing blows on the end should curl the thin metal tightly (Fig. 11-7B). There might have to be occasional moves to the flat of the face to straighten and maintain the thickness, but it should be possible to get a tight curl on a light bar with one or two heatings. The thin end loses its heat quickly, but it also takes up heat quickly. Be careful not to leave it in the fire too long and melt the end off.

A tight curl is not always wanted throughout. It usually looks best if the inner curl is close, but afterwards the small scroll can become more open (Fig. 11-7C). The start is the same, but subsequent hitting comes further back to make the curves longer (Fig. 11-7D).

Some smiths make snub ends with solid centers (Fig. 11-7E). Besides being considered more attractive, the snub

Fig. 11-5. This fine example of a section of railings shows some good twists, uniform scrolls and good angular bends.

Fig. 11-6. The top of this archway uses snub-end scrolls with cast rosette decorations.

helps in the early stages of one method of making a large scroll. To make a snub end, have a length of rod of suitable size and cut it almost through at a length slightly more than needed. Start a curve on the bar, then heat both parts to welding heat and hammer them together (Fig. 11-7F). Snap off the unwanted rod. The welded piece of rod can be hammered on the ends or might have to be filed or ground later.

In much wrought ironwork, the ends of scrolls are not parallel. They can be wider than the bar, whether welded to a snub or the thin end curled alone. If the end is drawn down in the width as well as the thickness, the scroll end gets narrower (Fig. 11-7G). If it is flaired out toward the end, an interesting effect is achieved (Fig. 11-7H). It could be narrowed and then flaired so a narrow neck leads up to the roll (Fig. 11-7J).

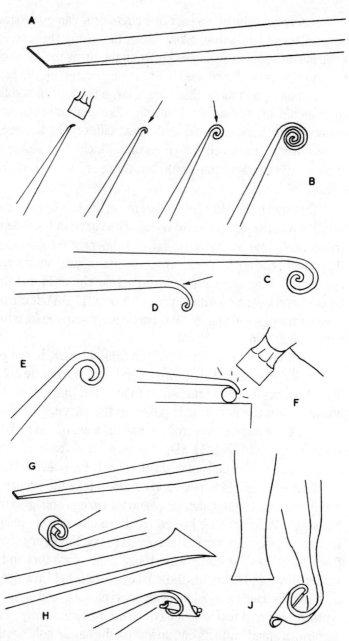

Fig. 11-7. In decorative ironwork, tapered ends are decorated by scrolls: (A) draw down and taper; (B) curl; (C,D) styles of curls; (E) snub end; (F) heat and hammer; (G) the end is drawn down; (H) flair the end; (J) narrow neck and roll.

A scroll can be just a part of a circle or it can go around several turns in a spiral. Skill comes in getting the curves even and in keeping distances between the turns the same or at a regular rate of increase. This is complicated by the fact that in many assemblies there are a large number of scrolls that should be the same. Machine—like perfection is not wanted, but there should not be great differences between scrolls that are designed to be the same. Much of the skill is in the eye and hands of the smith, but there are some tools to help.

One tool is a block of steel that fits in the hardie hole and is called a *halfpenny snub end scroll*. The curve in the side is about the same as an old English halfpenny (pronounced "haypnee") and about 1 inch across. It is used with somewhat heavier bar than can be hammered across the anvil and the tapered end is formed with a curve on it (Fig. 11-8A). It can be used with a tapered end, but it is particularly suitable for a bar with a snub end (Fig. 11-8B).

Another tool is a scroll starter (Fig. 11-8C). It can be held in the vise or provided with an end to fit the hardie hole. The steel has its end curled so as to hold the thin end of the starter, then the hot steel is pulled to the curve.

To get a number of scrolls to match, a smith can make a scroll iron or tool (Fig. 11-8D). This is a scroll made of steel stout enough not to pull out of shape when bar is pulled around it. The center of it is thinned and curled to take the prepared end of the work. But it also stands up for ease in engaging the hot steel, which can be locked on there and quickly pulled around as far as the required scroll has to go. Not every scroll made has to go the whole way. Usually the scroll tool end is turned down and either fits the hardie hole or is held in a vise.

Scrolls can be worked with a scroll fork and a scroll wrench. A scroll tool would have to be made that way. The scroll fork stands with its end upward in the hardie hole or vise and the scroll wrench is used to lever the curves in the hot steel (Fig. 11-8E). With the horizontal action, it is possible to

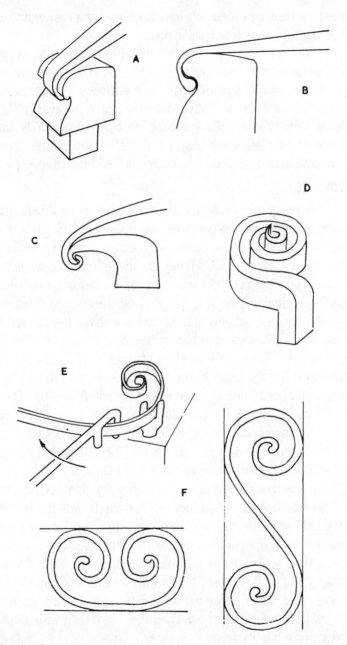

Fig. 11-8. Tools which the smith can make help in shaping scrolls to exact sizes: (A) form a curve; (B) snub end; (C) scroll starter; (D) scroll iron; (E) lever curves while in a vise; (F) matched scrolls.

see how the shape is coming and make adjustments even after you have passed a particular point.

Scrolls are best tackled boldly, with the whole length of the shape heated and pulled or hammered around quickly. In wrought ironwork, many scrolls are enclosed in other parts so they have to be carefully worked to match a drawing. This is particularly so if both ends of the same piece are scrolls, the same or opposite ways (Fig. 11-8F). If the end is free from anything around it, exact sizes are not so important.

COLLARS

Although the main structure will have more substantial joints, the decorative parts between the primary parts are held to them and to each other with straps or collars. Collars are sometimes welded and they are made from bar of lighter section than the parts they are to join. A collar can go around parts of similar size (Fig. 11-9A) or they might have to accomodate a stout part of the framing with the thinner scroll bar. To forge collars, use a bar of the same section that has to be enclosed. Double back a piece of scroll bar (Fig. 11-9B) or hold together thick and thin of other sizes. Usually there are a large number of collars in an assembly and it is simplest to make them all at the same time.

A collar could have the ends meeting in a butt joint (Fig. 11-9C), but it is more usual to cut them diagonally (Fig. 11-9D) or to overlap the ends (Fig. 11-9E).

Cut across the end of the bar diagonally, if that is the type to be made. Roll the former on the bar to get the length needed and partly cut through there with a set. Heat the bar and hammer the end around the former, almost to completion, then snap off the surplus bar. Hammer the collar to shape. But while it is still hot, spring it open to come off the forver (Fig. 11-9F). When it is put in position on the parts it is to hold, hammer it around hot and squeeze it tight with tongs, pliers or a hand vise.

For overlapping ends, draw out the ends to a length that will go around (Figm 11-9G). Since it is difficult to hold a short

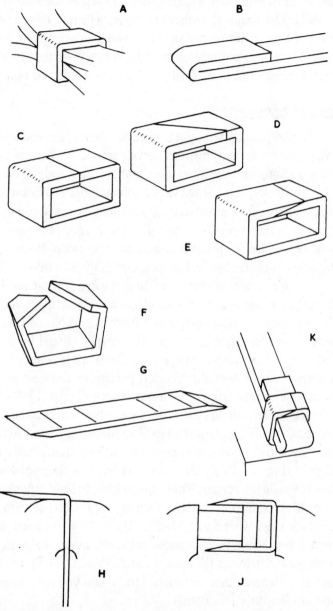

Fig. 11-9. Decorative parts are usually clipped together: (A) collar; (B) boubled bar; (C) butt joint; (D) diagonal cut; (E) overlap the ends; (F) open collar; (G) draw out ends; (H) hammer one leg; (J) position the other leg; (K) close the ends.

piece, form it in the vise. Hammer one leg in the vise (Fig. 11-9H). Then make the other leg around a former (Fig. 11-9J) and put the former on the anvil to close the overlapping ends (Fig. 11-9K). As with the other type, spring open the collar so that it can be put in its final place and be squeezed tight.

SQUARE CORNERS

In good quality wrought ironwork, corners are square or sharp. If a bar is bent, the iron curves around the neutral axis of its section, with the inner edge compressing and the outer edge stretching (Fig. 11-10A). A curve is apparent. For many purposes this does not matter, but in most wrought ironwork structures the corners are sharp. If the corner of a rounded bend is hammered, it can be made sharp outside. However, the section of the bar will be reduced (Fig. 11-10B).

To get a square corner while retaining at least the full thickness on the corner, the steel has to be first upset there. Usually the part has a taper going away to a scroll and care is needed to avoid damaging this. The corner should be dealt with before the scroll is completed. The work is best done in the vise. To protect the tapered part from the vise jaws, make vise clamps from iron wrapped around (Fig. 11-10C).

Have everything ready and heat what will become the corner to welding temperature. Grip the tapered part in the vise jaws and bend the corner into a loop that stands up slightly (Fig. 11-10D). Hammer this hard so the metal will flow towards the corner. There might have to be another heat to build up sufficient thickness there. At this stage, aim to build up steel where you need it. Do not try to square the corner yet. When there is sufficient steel, move the work to the anvil and hammer the corner square (Fig. 11-10E). Do not hammer so much that you spread the metal you have gained and finish with a thin corner.

QUATREFOILS

A grill can be made with flat bars crossing (Fig. 11-11A).

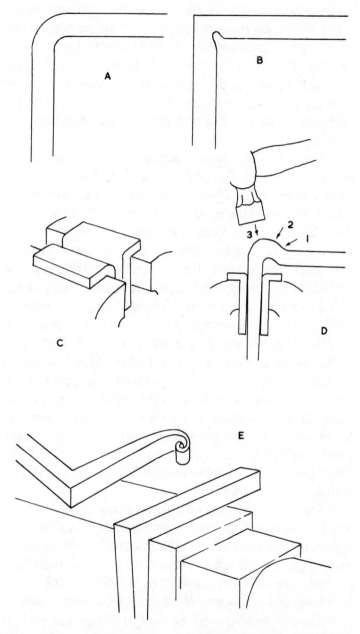

Fig. 11-10. A square angle needs the bend upsetting first: (A) bend the bar; (B) flatten the corner; (C) vise clamps; (D) bend to a loop; (E) hammer the corner square.

291

To bring them into line they have to be offset over each other, either by keeping the bars straight one way and doing all the offsetting the other way (Fig. 11-11B) or by taking half out of each bar (Fig. 11-11C). In many old European churches and castles, the spaces in the squares are decorated by parts cut from the bars to form quatrefoils (Fig. 11-11D). The points might touch, be joined with collars or twisted sideways to overlap.

The process is simple in principle, but is not so easy to get an even result. The pattern should be drawn on a steel sheet and the cuts marked on the steel with center punch dots. Each part of the quatrefoil pattern is cut and bent from the sides of the bars forming the grill.

It is possible to deal with light bar while it is cold, using cold chisels and cold sets. But for stouter steel that has to be heated, do the cutting with hot sets. The end of each slice can be a diagonal cut from a straight-edged tool, but it is better to have a set or chisel sharpened to a curve like a gouge (Fig. 11-11E). Make the curved and straight cuts from both sides, so that the parts curve away (Fig. 11-11F). Shape the pieces over the beak of the anvil or a piece of rod of the diameter you want. At the same time, hammer out any unevenness due to chopping out. There might have to be some slight adjustment to the points when the grill is assembled since the final shape cannot be matched until they are together, but with the thinner sections it should be possible to alter the shapes cold with a wrench or tongs.

That is the basic way of dealing with quatrefoil, but there are a great many variations and some of them are very elaborate. One piece can be cut inside another, the piece cut away might be cut again or the parts that join might have another between them and all could be held with collars. An arrow gripped in this way is common in medieval grills.

A similar technique can be used on a single bar, such as might stand up in an assembly or provide the central decoration at the top of a gate. This starts as a broad bar and parts

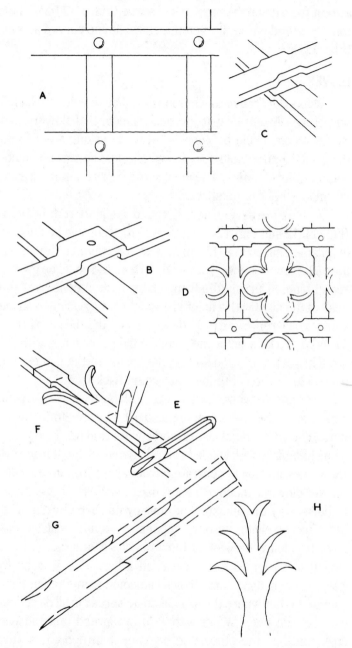

Fig. 11-11. Grill parts are bent over each other (A,B,C) and can be cut to make decorations (D, E, F, G, H).

are cut from it like the branches of a tree (Fig. 11-11G). They can be curved outward, then the end split and curved as well (Fig. 11-11H).

LEAVES

Many decorative touches in wrought ironwork are based on nature. Attempting to produce bunches of flowers and similar things could be considered to be asking steel to do things it is unsuitable for. However, leaf forms are quite common and effective. The most satisfactory ones are in iron, but mild steel can be shaped.

If there are several upright round or square rods in a gate (Fig. 11-12 and Fig. 11-13) or fence, the tops can be finished in a flame shape (Fig. 11-14A). The rod could be drawn out into a flat taper one way only or the whole rod could be given a round taper. Curving the flame shape is then done over the beak of the anvil with a fuller in a swage or by pulling to shape with scroll wrench and fork, depending on the thickness (Fig. 11-14B). To look right, the point should finish in line with the straight part of the rod so that the waves of the flame go to each side of the centerline, but come back to it.

For fine detail work on leaves, a blacksmith uses several stakes and other tools that are also used by sheet metalworkers. The smith might also do some work cold on a lead block, using hammers with shaped ends. In some wrought ironwork the leaves are made separately from sheet iron and welded on. Welding thin metal to thick requires skill, as it is very easy to burn away the thin steel or destroy its shape by hammering. Since welding by oxy-acetylene was not available, we have to admire the skill of those medieval smiths.

It is easier to forge a leaf on a bar. This is done by hammering it thin. Some blows can come from the flat hammer peen, but where the leaf has to be spread in all directions use the ball peen. When it has to be spread more in one direction than the other, the hammer it turned to use the cross or straight peen (Fig. 11-14C). Have the steel red hot.

Fig. 11-12. This gate head combines forged parts with cast iron decoration. Key parts are picked out by gilding.

Fig. 11-13. This elaborate half of an entrance gate shows a combination of fretted sheet iron and cast iron ornaments with blacksmith's wrought ironwork.

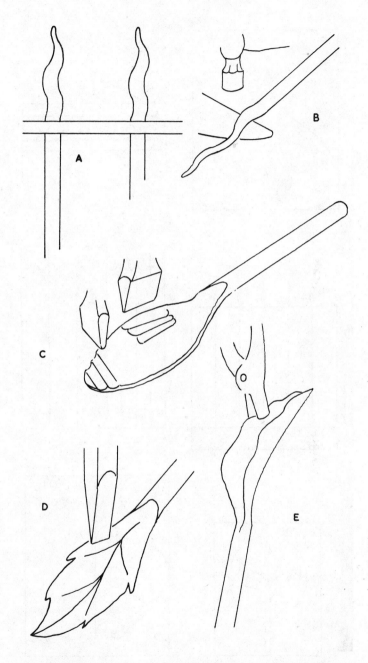

Fig. 11-14. Rail tops can be given a flame shape (A,B). Leaves are made from flattened iron (C,D,E).

Fig. 11-15. Patterns can be sketched and need not be fully detailed.

Be careful not to continue hammering once it has become black. Steel might split or break away at the edges.

Get the shape as near as possible to the shape you want, but there will have to be some filing. Mark the veins in the leaf with a veiner, which is like a blunt chisel (Fig. 11-14D). No leaves in nature are absolutely flat, so the steel ones have to be shaped. If possible, have a few actual leaves available to serve as guides. There should be some hollowing in the length, which can be started with a fuller in a swage, but there should be some curving in the length and the edges made wavy. In many cases the shaping can be done with pliers (Fig. 11-14E).

DESIGNING

There are plenty of examples to use as patterns, but the greatest satisfaction comes in producing your own designs. Work fullsize on paper first. Main outlines and frames will have to be drawn correctly with pencil and straightedge. When you come to draw the scrolls and other decorative features, use a felt-tip pen or something else prominent to make bold lines for your flourishes and curves. Single lines will do. There is no need to try to draw the thickness of the steel in these parts. Stand back and look at what you have drawn. When you have a pattern you like, transfer the drawing to a piece of sheet steel so the hot steel parts can be put on it for testing as the work progresses.

Do not be too ambitious at first. For one thing, anything large will need as assistant almost all the time. A small gate or screen would be a good choice (Fig. 11-15). Make the main structure first. Check it for squareness. This is best done by comparing diagonals. See that the structure is flat when it is put down for the other parts to be made and fitted to it. Make all the decorative parts and their collars and see that they fit in and to each other before finally securing any one part.

Finishing

12

If left unprotected, iron will corrode. Moisture from the atmosphere combines with iron to form iron oxide, which is more familiarly known as rust. As there is moisture in the driest air, rusting will occur anywhere. However, it will be more pronounced in places with high humidity or near water which is evaporating into the atmosphere. Salt accelerates corrosion, so rust is a particularly severe problem near the coast and when in use on boats.

This applies to all alloys containing iron. Although pure iron corrodes, the comparatively slight first rusting might seal the surface and prevent or delay severe deep rusting. This means that untreated iron might last a long time without suffering severely. Mild steel does not have this characteristic and if nothing is done to protect it, rust will affect the surface and eat deeply so that the shape is altered and eventually the material will disintegrate. The effect can be seen in discarded and neglected farm and other machinery which has lain exposed for perhaps only a few years.

There are alloys which various other metals have been combined with iron to minimize corrosion. Some of those form steels with quite small parts of other metals as well as carbon to make the steel something like pure iron in its ability to form a thin layer of rust that prevents further corrosion. Other steels have been alloyed to produce so-called stainless steels, which certainly do not corrode in normal circumstances. However, there are some chemicals that will attack them. Unfortunately, making these alloys from iron also makes most of these materials unsuitable for forging. If they can be forged, the subsequent heat treatment that is required cannot be done without elaborate equipment.

PLATING

Another way to protect an iron surface is to plate it with another metal that has a good resistance to corrosion. Zinc (called galvanizing) or other metal could be used that provides protection without improving appearance much. Nickel or chromium, which produce the bright glossy appearance common on automobile parts, could also be used. However, with some of these, the plating can be porous and rust finds its way through. Plating methods are not common to blacksmithing, except that an appliance might be galvanized by a specialist. It could not be done in the blacksmith's shop.

Any normal product of the blacksmith's shop needs protection. However, some things can be left as they come from forging if they are not expected to have a very long life. Tools and other things in frequent use can be prevented from corroding seriously by handling and using. If they have to be left unused for long, they can be wiped with an oily cloth. Lanolin (the grease from sheep's wool) is a good protector for tools that have to be stored for a long period.

Polished steel will usually resist corrosion better than the black surface, so a scriber, punch or chisel that has been brought to a high finish towards the cutting end might rust on the handle part before the smooth part.

The best long term protection is paint, but if you want a forged article without an applied surface coat of this sort, the simplest treatment is with oil or wax or a combination of the two.

REMOVING SCALE

Scale should be removed. Heating to a high temperature will burn off scale, but that is appropriate to a finished piece of smithing. Knocking the steel against the anvil during the last heating will remove some scale. Any that is left is best removed with a wire brush. This could be a hand brush, which is better for most work, although a powered wire brush can be used on parts where it will reach. Brushing will have a burnishing effect on high parts, but the following treatment with oil or wax will give an even coloring again.

Although scale may be removed mechanically, mainly by wire brushing, there are some things too intricate and scale remains in deeper parts. If a rust preventative treatment is to be effective, that also has to be removed. Quenching hot steel in brine loosens and removes much of the scale. For complete removal the chemical treatment is *picking* in an acid bath. This means soaking in diluted acid.

Of course, all strong acids are dangerous, whether concentrated or diluted. They will attack many things, including their containers. Glazed earthenware makes the best container and it should be given a wooden cover. Have an alkali ready to neutralize any acid that gets on to clothing or skin or anywhere else it should not be . Baking soda or ammonium hydrate are suitable, followed by washing with water.

Make up a pickling bath by pouring acid into water. **Never pour water into acid**, since that would cause it to spurt dangerously. An effective pickle is made by adding one part of sulfuric acid to ten parts of the water. Phosphoric acid can be used in the same proportion. Hydrochloric acid in a rather stronger proportion is most effective. A solution of one part of sulfuric acid, one part of hydrochloric acid to 16 parts water, makes a particularly potent acid bath something like the *aqua regia* of the alchemists that was alleged to dissolve gold.

How long to leave the steel in any of these baths has to be found by experience, but it can be removed and examined until you see that the scale has gone. Keep your hands away and use tongs, which are washed in water after use. Follow descaling by washing off the acid with plenty of water and treating with the alkali to neutralize any remaining acid, before another wash and drying.

In the simplest protective treatment, rub the steel with a cloth soaked in linseed oil, then return the work to the fire to warm it. The oil will carburize. Remove the warm article and rub it with oil again, then leave to cool. Wipe off excess oil, and the surface should remain free of rust for some time, then the treatment can be repeated. You can do the same with beeswax. Have a block big enough to handle, so you can give a first rub, followed by another on the hot steel.

It is better to combine wax and linseed oil. Proportions are not very critical, but about six cubic inches of wax to one quart of linseed oil makes a suitable mixture. Warm the linseed oil and flake the wax with a knife. Stir until all wax has melted. Apply this in the same way as suggested for oil only, in two stages. It is possible to use almost any oil or wax, so you can experiment and make a corrosion preventative to your own formula.

Steel which has been given the oxide colors used as a guide for tempering high carbon steel has a better resistance to corrosion than untreated steel. This applies to mild steel—which cannot be tempered, but will still produce the oxide colors—as well as to tool steel. The oxide colors are only visible on a polished surface so the treatment is only suitable for something that can be made bright and smooth. However, it has possiblities on an uneven surface, such as is produced by hammering all over with a ball peen hammer. The raised parts are wire brushed and made bright with abrasive or by polishing, leaving the hollows black. If a power polisher is used, remove any remaining polishing wax with a solvent and dry the steel.

Hold the article above a flame. It has to heat slightly and slowly where you can see the colors form. A single gas flame is better than a fire. The series of oxide colors will appear and you can stop at the color of your choice. If you wish, a part can be heated differently, so the graduated colors are seen. Remove the steel from the flame when you have the color you want. There is no need to quench the steel in water. Rub it with oil or wax, but do not return it to the fire since that would remove the color. This finish is described as *patination*.

Blueing is a treatment that also provides protection with a colored surface. It is particularly appropriate to firearms. It can only be applied to smooth machined surfaces, so it is not of use to a blacksmith. The treatment is chemical or is a combination of chemicals and heat.

There are rust inhibiting fluids obtainable from automobile sundries suppliers and they can be used on steel with no further treatment or as a preliminary to painting. Follow the instructions on the container. In most cases, the fluid neutralizes any rust that is present and forms a layer of its own corrosion that seals the surface and prevents any further attack by moisture in the air.

PAINTING

For outside work, it is best to finish steelwork with paint. This puts on a protective skin that is not everlasting, but it can be renewed as necessary. If it becomes damaged and moisture gets through to the steel, rust will attack and creep from the opening under surrounding paint—particularly if the steel was not originally cleaned and properly primed. Unfortunately, a coat of paint hides some of the texture of your forgework, but this has to be accepted for the sake of the protection given.

Steelwork that is to be painted should be treated to remove scale and rust as thoroughly as possible, then the first coat of paint applied soon afterward. Rust will attack again if a surface is left unprotected. A small amount of rust, attacking in this way, can be neutralized by the priming treatment or a coating of a rust inhibiting fluid. But if rust is left to continue, it will spread under the paint.

Paint intended for wood and other materials can be used, but it must go over a suitable steel primer. Using paint directly on the steel or over a primer intended for wood, will result in loose paint that soon comes away. The special steel primer has an etching action that eats into and grips the surface. Follow the manufacturer's instructions, but usually a thin coat has to be left to drq for some time before following with other paint. These primers are in colors that bear no relation to the final paint color. This is due to their chemical composition. However, the very different color allows you to see that you have a good coverage when you apply further coats of paint.

In general, steelwork does not lend itself to bright colors. If there is no reason for picking a particular color, black is always a good choice since it is near to the natural look of forged steel. Dark green and red are appropriated, but paler colors do not look right, unless they are needed to match surrounding objects. For the first treatment, use a matte undercoat over the special primer. If that does not obscure the color of the primer, apply another coat of the same paint rather than go on to the top coat. A gloss top coat is the most durable since the constituents that provide the gloss also toughen the skin produced. Be careful not to get an excess of paint anywhere. Pain running into thick blobs in a recess is more likely to come away later than paint applied thinly.

Varnish is not a finish to put on steel. Since it is transparent, the surface cannot be primed first. The color would show through and varnish applied directly to steel would not adhere very well and would soon chip away. With decorative steelwork for use indoors, there could be a black painted surface. If you particularly want the texture of the smithing to show through, treating with clear lacquer is possible. It could be sprayed on or might be a type intended for brushing. There are special lacquers made for treating polished silver and gold. They would be suitable, but a cheaper general-purpose clear lacquer should be satisfactory.

SECTION 2
METALWORKING

General Metalworking

Through most of the history of civilization the blacksmith was the only metalworker in most communities. Specialists in towns might have worked precious metals and there were others, such as locksmiths, who carried the blacksmiths' work to higher standards. But in the rural communities, if anyone needed anything in metal, it was the blacksmith who did the work. This meant that the average blacksmith was an adaptable craftsman who could leave his forge and do work at the bench on things ranging from small locks to large agricultural machinery.

However, as long as horses provided transport and power, the smith was kept almost fully occupied dealing with horse-drawn vehicles and farm equipment. The smith had a never-ending job as a farrier, keeping the horses shod. The coming of the automobile changed that. As the use of horses diminished, the need for the blacksmith's traditional craft became less and the need for general engineers became greater. World War I hastened the process, partly by war needs in weaponry, but also tractors reached a stage of efficiency and reliability so that they were able to do more than horses. Little traditional blacksmithing was needed to accompany these new techniques.

The effect was to put a great many blacksmiths out of business gradually as the need for their services and skills diminished in the years following that war. The need for blacksmith skills was no longer in the small local smith's shop, but many blacksmiths found places in industry where production needs employed equipment too large or complex for the individual smith to have. Many other smiths kept their hearths and anvils, but broadened their scope to include the maintenance of agricultural equipment or the servicing of automobiles. Many modern general engineers, garages and service stations grew from blacksmiths' shops.

It is against that background that anyone with an interest in blacksmithing today should arrange his thinking. While blacksmithing might be the primary craft, a great many projects that involve smithing, either as the larger part of the work or as a base on which other work develops, call for skills in other branches of metalworking to complete the work in hand. Consequently, any modern blacksmith should also be able to augment his forging by the ability to do other work in metal. Something made by using a variety of skills can be a very satisfying project for the maker and an attractive object to the user.

Much of the metalwork associated with blacksmithing is done with hand tools or those portable electric tools that could be regarded as extensions of the hands. If blacksmithing is the main activity, it is unlikely that the use of heavy metalworking equipment as well would be justified. A modern metalworking lathe, for instance, provides enough interest in itself for little other metalworking to be contemplated. Consequently, the following chapters deal with the basics of general metalworking that can be done with simple equipment, in association with blacksmithing or as an extension of it, in much the same way as the traditional blacksmith could deal with work that came outside the normal practice of hammering hot metal on an anvil.

There has to be a slight change of attitude. When working hot steel it is impossible to use close measurements. There has to be some tolerance and much measuring is done by eye. Much of the skill in blacksmithing can be described as art. You can obtain a pleasing and correct shape without the use of many measuring instruments or gauges. The smith sees development of a curve or taper under his hammer and knows that it is right. For many things made by a blacksmith it would not matter if there was an error of one-eighth of an inch or more from the intended size. When you are working on the bench and making assemblies that have several components it is possible to work to very close tolerances, if necessary. A lock will need its parts made as near to size as can be seen on a rule, while a clock will need much closer tolerances if it is to work. These items have to be checked with such measuring instruments as a micrometer and a vernier. Obviously, some things made by benchwork do not have to be any more accurate than those made at the anvil. But when you are cutting shapes by sawing and filing, the craftsman should always be aware of the precision possible.

METALS

Much work on the bench is done with mild steel. It is the basic constructional metal or alloy and information on it is given in Chapter 2. For blacksmithing, it is mostly in bars (rectangular sections) and rods (round sections). Wide lengths up to about one-eighth of an inch thick are called strip, while larger areas are sheet. Smaller rod that is supplied in coils is wire. In addition to these forms there are angles and other preformed sections. It is worthwhile accumlating a stock of mild steel parts from discarded machinery, domestic equipment and similar things. Providing it is not badly rusted, it can be used again successfully.

When buying steel and other metals of easily measured dimensions, there is no difficulty in quoting sizes in feet and inches (or metric measure). For thin sheets and strips or finer wire, the actual measurements have to be checked with a micrometer and might have to be quoted to three places of decimals of an inch. There have been several schemes for quoting thicknesses by a gauge number, to avoid the need to refer to decimal thicknesses. Unfortunately there is no universal standard and you need to know what gauge system is being used to check thickness. Some gauge systems are: American or Browne and Shape, Stub's, Birmingham and British Standard Wire Gauge. Some gauges are used for one metal and a different gauge for another. Because of this, it is always wiser to quote actual measured thickness where possible. In all the gauge systems, the lower number indicates the thicker metal. Most go from a very fine 50 to many zeros representing as thick as about one-half inch. In most systems, 8 gauge is about one-eighth inch while 20 gauge is about 0.035 of an inch and a useful thickness for much light sheet metalwork.

Metals and alloys are often referred to as ferrous or non-ferrous, meaning that they do or do not contain iron. The stainless and high carbon steels are the only ferrous metals, in addition to mild steel, that will normally be used. All the other metals are non-ferrous.

COPPER

Copper is a soft reddish metal, obtainable in sheet, rod and bar form and familiar as drawn wire for electrical work. It can be annealed by heating to redness and left to cool or quenching in water. It is then extremely soft and ductile. It age hardens slightly, but the only way to get it to maximum hardness is to work it, usually by hammering. Copper is mainly used for its decorative qualities and for its good electrical conduction, but it is not strong enough for assemblies that have to take much load.

ZINC

Zinc is unlikely to be used as a metal today. It is grey and can be obtained in sheets. It can be annealed with a little heat.

Too much will melt it. Boiling water is sufficient. Zinc has a good resistance to corrosion and is used to make a protective coating over steel. Galvanized iron is actually mild steel coated with zinc. That method leaves a rather rough surface and a smoother finish is obtained by smooth zinc plating.

BRASS

Brass is one of the most used non-ferrous metals or alloys. It is an alloy of copper and zinc and proportions vary. The type alloyed for good machining qualities cannot satisfactorily be annealed, but the rolled forms of strip, sheet, bar and rod can be heated to redness and left to cool. Quenching quickly can cause cracks. It does not anneal to be as soft as copper, but it can be shaped in a similar way and work hardened by hammering. Brass has a good resistance to corrosion, but in a salty atmosphere the zinc in the alloy could be eaten away and the metal disintegrates. Brass will melt at temperatures obtainable at a smith's hearth, so it is just possible to use it for casting with simple equipment.

Another form of brass is sometimes called spelter and is used in brazing. The alloy is melted with a flame and fused to the surfaces being joined. This process can also be called hard soldering, but hard soldering is really the use of silver solder, which is a copper/zinc alloy with a little silver added. The effect is to lower the melting point. The melting temperature can be varied according to the proportions of the alloy. It is possible to make one joint, using an alloy of a lower temperature near another without fear of the first parting.

TIN

Pure tin is an expensive metal, so it is not used alone. It has been used as a coating for iron and steel sheet to make the tinplate familiar for cans and similar things. Tin is a safe metal to use with food and it has a good resistance to corrosion. Before plastics took over in many domestic applications, tinplate was used for many kitchen items. A tinsmith (a tinner) was a worker in tinplate, not pure tin.

BRONZE

Tin can be alloyed with copper—much like zinc. The result is very similar. But the color is usually a rich golden shade, depending on the proportions. In sheet form, it can be shaped into bowls and similar things like copper, but with greater trength. Like brass, it can be annealed with heat and hardened by hammering. That form of copper/tin alloy is called gilding metal. In rod or bar form it is called gunmetal. The old "brass cannons" were actually copper/tin alloys, usually with small quantities of other metals added. Many modern bronze items are basically copper and tin with small quantities of rarer metals included to give special qualities. While still known as bronze they can be prefixed by the name of an important added metal, such as *phosphor bronze*. Special types of bronze are mostly cast and can be machined, but they are not intended to be bent or otherwise shaped. Most bronze has a very good resistance to corrosion.

LEAD

Lead is the heaviest of the common metals and many of its uses are connected with its weight. It is an unattractive soft grey metal which is not strong enough to retain much detail. Its melting point is low enough for it to flow at temperatures that can be obtained with a gas flame or fire. Consequently, it can be used for casting, particularly for weights to give stability to something made from a lighter material. Lead alloys easily with many other metals and some, such an antimony, can be used with it to lower the melting point and make a stronger casting. Lead is also alloyed with tin to make soft solder, which is the common joining material in electrical work and other assemblies. The melting point is lower than that of either metal independently, with enough heat coming from a copper bit, heated electrically or by a flame.

ALUMINUM

Aluminum is very light in weight and silvery white in color. It is easily melted and can be cast with simple equipment. Pure aluminum is soft, although it is possible to specify the degree of relative hardness required. Resistance to corrosion is good and the metal is safe to use with food, as can be seen in the drink cans made form it. Much aluminum available is actually alloyed with other metals to give special qualities, particularly strength and hardness, which might not be adequate in the pure metal for many purposes.

Aluminum anneals with heat and can be work hardened, but the annealing temperature of 350 degrees is much lower than that of other metals. Too much heat will ruin it. One shop method of getting the right metal annealing temperature is to rub the metal with soap and heat only until the soap turns black. Aluminum is the one common metal that cannot be joined with lead/tin soft solder. There are special aluminum solders, but in general it is better to design aluminum constructions so rivets or other fastenings are used instead of solder.